THE CLEARING TIDE

JOHN CURRY

John Curry (signature)

I believe that an explanation for the title of this book is required. When I first qualified as a pilot of the third class on the 21st August 1968, the Liverpool Pilot's Association had some strange and archaic rules stretching back into antiquity. One of them was the rule of: "The Clearing Tide."

The rule stated that: 'when on the 'sea turns,' (bringing ships in) if you as a pilot were to dock on the flood of a tide, whose flood had started six hours before 1800 Hrs., (1200Hrs.) then you would be clear of duty not only for the rest of that day, but you would also be clear for the whole of the following day, not recommencing duty until the day after that!'

This led to one humourist in our ranks in the days of train travel down to Anglesey and Point Lynas boarding station to come up with the following superstitious (and possibly hopeful?) lines:

"If by Conway a Heron you have espied, You will catch the Clearing Tide!"

In the fullness of time, with the importance of the utilisation of manpower in the modern world, this rule was consigned to history. Now as a memory, it has given me inspiration for the title of this book.

1st Edition

Published 2021 by John Curry
West Kirby, Wirral.

British Library Cataloguing in Publication Data.
A catalogue record for this book is available from the British Library.

ISBN 978-0-9934292-2-3

Book cover and design by Mark Proctor.

Front cover photograph Colin McPherson.

Rear cover photograph Gill Curry.

ACKNOWLEDGEMENTS

I would like to thank Gill, my wife, and Obi, my grand-daughter, for proof reading the manuscript and for making the helpful comments, which have proved invaluable in improving the written text.

My thanks for the photographs not taken by me, but which are accredited to the photographer beneath. Where it has not been possible to trace the photographer: 'Copyright Unknown' is beneath the photograph. My thanks to these unknown photographers and to the poets, writers, and playwrights whose work is quoted from in the text.

Any photographs not credited are my own.

I would also like to thank Gill for the support in writing this sequel to "East a Half South" during the lockdown periods of Covid 19.

Last, but not least, I would like to thank Mark Proctor for the editing of the text of "The Clearing Tide" and that of "East a Half South", which was necessary when Countywise, the original printers, went out of business. My thanks is due both for the invaluable professional help given and for his friendship.

IV

'On first Looking into Chapman's Homer.'

John Keats.

Much have I travell'd in the realms of gold,
And many goodly states and kingdoms seen;
Round many western islands have I been
Which bards in fealty to Apollo hold.
Oft of one wide expanse have I been told
That deep-brow'd Homer ruled as his demesne;
Yet did I never breathe its pure serene
Till I heard Chapman speak out loud and bold:
Then felt I like some watcher of the skies
When some new planet swims into his ken;
Or like stout Cortez when with eagle eyes
He stared at the Pacific-and all his men
Looked at each other with a wild surmise-
Silent, upon a peak in Darien.

CONTENTS

In Place of a Foreword.   VIII

1.   Outward Bound Again.   1

2.   Remembering when… I did go there… India.   17

3   "Be Prepared!"   32

4   "The Wirral Two Man Ship Society."   52

5.   The Port of Liverpool. Part One.   62

6.   The Port of Liverpool. Part Two.   74

7.   "Piloting on the Mersey"   86

8.   Pilotage Reorganisation in the Port of Liverpool.   102

9.   "To whom it may concern…"   124

10.   Trevor's Taxis.   131

11.   "All's well that ends well."   142

12.   Sharing the Piloting Experience.   162

13.   Simulation by Physical Models at Port Revel.   175

14.   A Norwegian Adventure.   180

15.   Wildlife encountered in the Course of Duty.   191

16.   "A Small Corner of Someone Else's Country."   220

17.   "I must go down to the seas again…"   240

18.   Liverpool's "Class of 1960."   250

19.   "Helm Amidships, Finished with Engines."   260

Glossary   270

Bibliography   279

IN PLACE OF A FOREWORD

I was honoured to have my friend Captain Robin Woodall write a forward for my first book "East a Half South." Captain Woodall, best known for his years in command of Cunard's QEII, worked with me with the management group of the Hoylake and West Kirby Lifeboats. I was serving as Operation's Manager of the Hoylake Lifeboat and Robin was the Chairman of the management group. (A position I now hold). I wrote these two poems as a tribute to Robin after he died in 2013.

Ships, which pass in the night.

Robin's,
Another end
Of yet another era.

A last intake of breath
Expired,
Leaving no night orders, in the book
Lying on the chart room table.

Just memories
As elusive as petrels in a wave,
Or the bones
Of long, lost, sunken wrecks
Sheltering
In dark corners on the sea's bed.

"Over and out my friend,
The radio waves from your side
Have sadly fallen silent."

A 'Slack Handful.'

Hoylake Lifeboat rolls
In a low swell,
A 'slack handful' of ashes
Blow low in a breeze,
Mixing forever
With air, sky and sea
Out there in the estuary.

A moment of reflection
Before the unexpected 'flypast'
Of some twenty Manx Shearwaters
On passage
Back out to the Atlantic Ocean
Where you too, once kept watch.

For Captain Robin Woodall. June 2013.

OUTWARD BOUND AGAIN

All my years as a pilot were filled with new and exciting adventures, some more notable than others. Following the success of "East a Half South," many have asked when I was intending to write a sequel. Initially, I was not tempted, but gradually I was drawn to undertake the task. Bearing in mind that the first volume has many stories within its pages and to the present date has sold over one thousand, five hundred copies, but having piloted over six thousand ships there are many more!

Then I recalled a humorous story, which took place up at Seaforth Container Terminal and I was to ask myself: "How on earth did I miss that one out?" That made me think that maybe it was meant to be that I wrote a sequel and that this story was meant to be the one, which would inspire me to begin all over again. The Seaforth 'bus' story, which is a fine example of the quick fire Liverpool sense of humour will come later, as I intend to start "The Clearing Tide" with a tale, which fits into the: 'In my beginning is my end and in my end is my beginning' category, as it were.

So, we go back to Clan Line, or Cayzer Irvine, as the company had come to be called. I had sailed on my first trip to sea on board the T.S.S. *Clan Brodie* in the November of 1960 as a cadet officer bound for India and what was then East Pakistan, now Bangladesh. The years had passed and I had become a First Class Liverpool Pilot, licensed to pilot ships of all sizes in 1973.

This first tale is an elaboration on one, which is in fact in the pages of "East a Half South", but I believe will be a good point of departure for this sequel and one, which will provide continuity as we 'cast off', outward bound again.

The date was March 20th 1975 and I was manned to make up the compliment of pilots on board the Bar Pilot Boat during the afternoon and, once on board, I found myself manned off to pilot the inward bound, first-class vessel M.V. *Clan MacGilivray* from the Bar Station into Vittoria Dock, Birkenhead, to the very berth that the *Clan Brodie* had sailed from just over fourteen years before.

The Service were boarding at the Bar Light Vessel, so the weather cannot have been too bad and I do not recall any difficulties encountered with wind or rough sea conditions. We were to dock on the morning tide of the 21st. The pilot apprentice, or 'boathand' as he was officially called, came into the saloon, where I was waiting bag in hand, to tell me that the punt[1] was in the water and ready for me to join to be taken across to climb aboard the M.V. *Clan MacGilivray*. I knew that the punt was in the water for I had heard that well known scream of the wires in the blocks and I had felt the pilot boat shudder as the davits[2] were lowered.

We made the crossing to the inward bound vessel and as my brief case was being heaved aboard on a heaving line, I made the ascent of the rope ladder to the main deck far above. As I came to the top of the ladder in the darkness and stepped over the bulwarks onto the wooden steps to descend to the main deck, so many memories came flooding back to me. There, as momentarily I stood on the freshly painted bulwark, below me were three Pakistani sailors, the officer of the watch and a cadet officer, the latter who was waiting to lead me up to the bridge.

This would have been the very same job, which I may well have been tasked with almost fourteen years before.

The scents were legion and incredibly nostalgic. Fresh paint, (It was company policy, as with most big shipping companies, that all vessels would be maintained and freshly painted for the arrival back on to the home coast). a mixture of tar, oil, grease, hemp, paint and much more, but above all the smell of mustard seed oil,

---

1 The small motor craft carried by the mother ship, in which pilots were ferried to and from ships.

2 The pairs of small 'cranes' used to lower away and lift the punts, or lifeboats, on ships.

with which the Pakistani crewmen dressed their hair.

I had 'made it,' full circle! I was fortunate to be able to pilot a 'Clan Boat', for Clan Line had 'appropriated pilots' (named company pilots) to pilot their ships, but just occasionally, the younger pilots would be delighted to 'win' one from the appropriated system. I have put 'Boat' in inverted commas, for although these were large vessels, it was customary within the Service to refer to them as 'Boats.' Thus: a 'Clan Boat,' an 'Elder Dempster Boat' or a 'Blue Funnel Boat' for examples. It must be said, however, that the latter were quite often referred to simply as: 'Bluies!'

The docking of the vessel went well and I arrived home feeling delighted to have had the opportunity to 'go back' to where I had started, only this time, I was actually in command.

I piloted only one more 'Clan Boat,' also briefly mentioned in the pages of my first book and that was a sad occasion indeed. Containerisation had revolutionised shipping almost overnight and Liverpool was totally unprepared as a port for the revolution. The ship owners were to take their ships away and invest in containerisation in other ports, whose authorities had been far sighted enough to envisage the change coming and had invested in container cranes and berths to cope. Liverpool was to catch up, but not before the port was to be taken into receivership and all the big companies had left the port to her fate.

So it was that I came to pilot the very last 'Clan Boat,' which was ever to sail from Birkenhead. She was not the last 'Clan Boat' to leave the river, as that was the job of the Clan Line appropriated pilot who sailed the last vessel departing the Manchester Ship Canal from Eastham Locks on the same day tide.

I was manned on the M.V. *Clan Mackintosh* on Christmas Day 1976. I sailed her from Vittoria Dock on Christmas Day morning tide. It was a fine, bright, crisp winter's morning, yet a very sad occasion for me to know that this was indeed the end of an era.

The future looked bleak for the port, as indeed it was to be as has been covered in "East a Half South," but on the day, I held fast to the pleasure of piloting a 'big ship,' as it was in those days, successfully, outward bound from the enclosed space of the Birkenhead Dock System to the freedom of the open sea.

Another early first class ship piloting memory took place two years before on the 21st March 1974. Thinking back, it must have been at the early stages of Ted Heath's government's attempts to convince the country to join the Common Market. It involved me finding myself faced with a serious life and death situation brought about by British fishing boats attempting to stage a protest. We are at present in the process of actually leaving what is now known as the 'European Union.' This story, although history, is indeed topical, as we look again to the still uncertain future of our fishing fleets.

I had travelled down to the Point Lynas Pilot Station the previous evening and had had a good night's sleep in the hostel at Point Lynas. I was boarded by launch in the dawn, as I recall on the M.V. *Sincerity*, a large bulk carrier drawing thirty two feet in the water, (9.8 metres) a deep drafted vessel, equipped with only a single propeller and one rudder. Thus she was heavy and difficult to manoeuvre, requiring lots of time to think ahead in order to be going at speeds to be in control for manoeuvres.

We were the first of three similar vessels, all bound for Liverpool to dock on the flood of the day's tide. My charge was bound for Langton Lock. We were in good time for docking and proceeded with the intent of crossing the sand bar, located just after the entrance to the Queen's Channel, in good time for docking, proceeding at a reasonable speed and with sufficient water under the keel. Sufficient water under the keel was taken to be two feet, yes, only two feet, (Point six of a metre). Although both measurements are exactly the same, the latter never seemed to be as much as the former to me), but with the vessel only going at a slow speed to avoid what is known as 'squat'. That is an increase in the draught of the vessel when going at speed. Small speed boats increase their draught by going down by the stern, as we notice in James Bond films, speed boat chases for example. Large vessels increase their draught by going down 'by the head.' That is by the bow.

The distance between Point Lynas and the Bar Light Vessel was approximately thirty five miles, with a further four point seven miles, (in those days) to the shallow patch, or actual sand bar, at the Formby Light Float. I had noticed quite a large number of small fishing boats up ahead. They were not displaying signals to indicate that they were engaged in fishing, but, having said that, there was no indication from any quarter that there was going to be a problem with their presence.

I had ascertained from my tide tables that I would have sufficient water under keel clearance, when I was to the west of the channel entrance and had increased from a slow speed to a suitable manoeuvring speed. I had indeed passed the point of 'No Return' by actually entering the Queen's Channel on my passage up to Langton Lock, when the fishing boats, which had been funnelling into the channel ahead of me, speeded up and then suddenly stopped, forming a line, indeed a blockade across the channel at Formby Shoal.

I was taken aback, surprised and gravely concerned, but my professional training left me both calm and motivated to immediately take the only course of action open to me. My paraphrasing of my V.H.F. telephone broadcast, which follows, will indicate what that course was.

"Gentlemen aboard the fishing vessels, which have formed a blockade across the Queen's Channel in Liverpool Bay in front of three large bulk carriers, which are inward bound for the port, this is the pilot on the bridge of M.V. *Sincerity*, the first of these vessels speaking. I have no idea for what reason you are trying to do what you appear to be doing in blocking my approach to the port. What I do know is that, for my ship, you have left it far too late. I am less than a quarter of a mile off the blockade line and with the nature of the size and draught of this vessel, with whatever experience I have as a pilot, there is no possibility that I can stop her before she will plough into the blockade. Staying with my present course and speed will mean that I will take out fewer of you than if I were to attempt to go astern and slow down, which would then mean that I would be out of control and swinging to starboard, thus increasing the volume of the ship's side being presented to your blockade.

Please gentlemen, reconsider your present actions and break the blockade allowing me a safe passage through, or, later today this young pilot will be making telephone calls of condolence to your loved ones and families, an act I most certainly do not wish to undertake."

There was no reply from any of the vessels forming the blockade, but thankfully they had been listening out on V.H.F. channel 16 and turned away from the blockade at speed, allowing this much relieved pilot a safe passage to continue onwards up to a safe docking an hour or so later.

That year, 1975, my first year as a First Class Pilot, was an eventful year for I note that later, in the May, I was to be involved with both the grounding and the subsequent re-floating of the *Rhine Ore*, which was fully covered in the Chapter: "A Near Death Experience" in my first book: "East a Half South."

My next ship following *Rhine Ore* was a Danish naval vessel, outward bound from Langton Lock: The F351, H.D.M.S. *Fylla* classified as a Hvidbjornen class frigate. The particular reason that I remember this vessel so vividly is because of the 'welcome,' which I received when I arrived on the bridge. As usual, as with most naval vessels, the bridge was filled with personnel of all ranks, all with 'a specific job to do!' The wheelhouses are generally quite small and therefore with so many bodies, each carrying out their duties, there is very little room for the pilot to move.

I was taken up to the bridge by a young officer and noted that he was unusually quiet after his greeting at the top of the gangway. I entered the wheelhouse where the officer in command was before me and I greeted him with a loud, warm and genuine: "Good Morning Commander." (The time was 0800 Hrs. This was the hour when many warships of all nationalities booked to sail from harbour). The face before me grimaced as the hand was held out for me to shake and his "Good Morning Pilot" was delivered in a hushed voice. This was followed by a request: "Please Pilot, we will all do exactly what you ask for without question, but please, please give your orders quietly. Last night, both my officers and myself were entertained by the Liverpool City Council at the Town Hall and our heads, to say the least, are not too clear as yet. It is a bit too early in the morning after the night before."

The ship was to sail safely outward bound to sea without incident with the pilot whispering my orders, which were followed, as promised, without question. This to my relief and the way the orders were given by me much to the commander's relief.

I have started this book with the 'Clan Boat' story, taking us back in time from the last chapter of "East a Half South," which told of my final act of pilotage in sailing the M.V. *Atlantic Compass* outward bound from Seaforth Container Terminal with Gill, my wife, on board with me, continuing with the *Compass* to actually retire southwest of Ireland on the midnight hour of my birthday, before leaving the vessel some nine days later in New York.

As I have started the present volume with this chapter: "Outward bound Again," my intention is to roam through my tide tables, where I have logged all of the six thousand plus vessels, which

I piloted in my years as a pilot, randomly taking stories, as I have done so far, before settling on more specific themes for subsequent chapters. This is similar to the content of the chapter: "Slop Chest" in the previous book. I also intend to include articles, which I have both been asked to write and, which have been published in nautical magazines.

So, for now, I will stay in the early years of me being a first class pilot. I have told the two Clan Line ship stories and of course in my own sensitivity of my writing, I feel my own excitement of youth in being manned as a pilot of these ships. In the same vein, I believe that we as young pilots, before the advent of containerisation, were always delighted to be manned on ships of the regular visitors of the then 'Big Ship' general-cargo, shipping companies. These vessels were some 400' to 600' long, (121m to 182.9m) 'five hatch jobs', usually requiring three conventional tug boats for manoeuvring in both the river and in the dock systems. They were generally equipped with a single screw, (propeller) and a single rudder. Occasionally, one would come across twin screw (propeller) vessels, as indeed with my ship on my first trip to sea, the: T.S.S. (Twin Screw Steamship) *Clan Brodie*.

The month after the incident with the blockading fishing boats, I was to be manned to pilot the M.V. *Jalamini*, a 'Jala Boat', from the western, Point Lynas, pilot station. She was to dock at Birkenhead on the following early morning's tide. If we were presented with such a vessel, both with the time and with suitable weather conditions, it was customary to bring the vessel up into the river on the ebb of the previous tide to the docking time tide and anchor off the lock.

There were three reasons for this: The first was: 'to Get as Far as you can.' The second was coming up on the ebb of the previous tide it was simple to choose an anchorage near to the docking entrance and thus allow the turn of the tide to swing the ship to the flood tide and put her facing the 'right way', bows north, for the eventual 'flood tide' docking. The third was tied in with the latter, for it stood you in good stead with the agent as the vessel would not need a tug for swinging and thus would save the company the tug's fee for the swing. My apologies to the towage companies would not be relevant for there are none of them left! All towage companies from those days have been taken over in ownership many times since the days, to which I am referring.

I note from my ABC "Foreign Ocean Freighters," from the Ian Allen series of the time (price 2/6) that all of the Scindia vessels were about 450' to 500' (121m-152.4m.) in length. Scindia was an Indian company running much the same routes as both Clan Line and Brocklebank Line. The *Jalamini* is not listed in my book, so she must have been fairly new in 1974 and indeed I remember her being quite 'flash,' as we would have described her at the time.

Another more personal, even selfish reason for anchoring her, early evening on the day before docking, was that I would be able to join the captain at his table in the dining saloon to enjoy a superb, genuine, Indian-curry meal, rather than risking indigestion standing upright on the bridge as so many of my meals aboard vessels as a pilot were to be eaten.

In fact it was the recollection of this particular meal, which brought back the memory of this particular act of pilotage from my tide table page. "Would I like the crew's curry, or the milder one specially prepared for guests?" The answer for me, having sailed with Clan Line, was simple: "The crew's please Captain." The meal was superb and the sole reason that I remember the occasion so it must have gone well.

Another Indian vessel, piloted outward bound in my early years as a first class pilot, was another with that same excitement of anticipation mentioned in the previous story's introduction. This time I had been booked outward bound from Liverpool on the M.V. *Indian Splendour*, a ship of the India Steamship Company.

My memories are a mixture of the pleasure of being manned on the ship, mixed with the frustration of what was to happen that evening and the humour of what occurred in the form of a 'mishap' for the compass adjuster who was to accompany me on the passage.

The M.V. *Indian Splendour* is in my A.B.C. book and I note that: "She was built in 1957, was 9409 gross tons, 508' long (155m.), 66'(20m.) in the beam (wide) and that she was a steam-turbine, engined vessel, which had been capable of seventeen and a half knots." (A 'flash' ship once upon a time). Sadly, when I was on board her, she was old and probably not capable of much more than twelve knots.

I arrived on the bridge, the weather conditions were pleasant with only a light breeze blowing, although strong winds from the west were forecast for later. As it was evening it was already dark.

The compass adjuster joined me on the bridge. He was one of the few, becoming ever fewer in number, whose job it was to adjust the magnetic compass on the bridge of the ship. This adjustment required the pilot to swing the vessel through at least one complete '360 degree' circle, whilst the compass adjuster called out headings to steer as he took bearings on fixed marks. Usually the swing would take place at the Bar Light Vessel, although sometimes, I can recall proceeding westwards and using Point Lynas Lighthouse light as the mark, which is what we were to do on this occasion.

Just about all ships had gyro compasses by this time, but magnetic compasses were still carried as a backup if the gyro failed. Nowadays, satellite navigation systems are more the operational systems to be relied upon, but, even so, compasses are still important today. The magnetic compass in its housing, known as a binnacle, is usually carried on the monkey island[3].

---

3 Monkey Island. The common merchant navy term for the deck on top of the ship's wheelhouse.

"Tugs are arriving Captain. Please tell the crew to standby and make them fast. One forward and one aft, centre leads for the ropes, tug's wires please. The third tug will assist us by pushing. She will not require making fast, but will range free."

The captain relayed my orders without question and made no comment that anything was in the slightest untoward. Then looking down, directly to the main deck, I noticed what turned out to be the first of the foredeck crew emerging from the accommodation housing. I noticed too, that something was not quite right for the individual was hardly moving. Moving he was, but he appeared as if he was part of a very slow motion ballet. I had to observe closely to note if there was any forward motion driven by his limbs at all.

"Have we a problem with the crew Captain?" I asked. "No problem Pilot." Was the reply in that accent, which always reminds me of Peter Sellers! It was about ten minutes later and after more questions about problems and after the second man of the foredeck crew had just about appeared, about three feet (one metre) behind the first, that the captain finally admitted that there was indeed a big problem with the crew.

The crew were literally on 'go slow' in protest about pay and conditions. We had been supposed to sail on the flood of the tide, but at this rate that was never going to happen. I asked if we should cancel the sailing, but the captain protested and insisted that I make every effort to sail the ship, for a cancellation was what the crew wanted. A strike would have cost them dearly, but this 'go slow' was an effort on their part to delay the ship with them 'still working!'

I contacted the lockmaster at Langton Lock and explained the situation to him and he was reassuring in that we were the only ship moving on that tide, which meant that we had plenty of time. I informed both tugs and boatmen in attendance of the situation, assuring them that if we were able to make the tugs fast we could still, bearing in mind our draught, make the tide, even if it was going to be late on the ebb of the tide.

It was indeed flood tide when we were booked to sail from the lock, but with the slow motion pantomime being enacted on the decks, it was late on the ebb of the tide when the ship finally cleared for sea. I do not remember the exact time it all took, but once the tugs were painstakingly made fast and the ship's ropes eventually cast off, we were able to manoeuvre quite swiftly to the lock and the tugs were able to hold me alongside in the lock without ropes. As the outer lock gate was opening, I managed to convince the captain of letting the after tug go swiftly before we left the lock or lives would be in danger.

Fortunately, the crew realised that time and events had beaten their efforts to delay the sailing and the after tug was let go immediately. The forward tug was cast off when we had safely left the lock and made the starboard swing to head out to sea.

Then the wind strengthened to a strong westerly, which meant that the rest of the passage was to be quite a wild one, whereas if we had sailed at our booking time, we would have been clear and away before the wind increased. We proceeded to the west to Point Lynas, off which point we made the compass adjustment swing before disembarking. In those days there was rarely a taxi ride home as in later years, when taxis became the normal form of transport to make the Service more efficient. Instead it was a nightcap and then into bed for a few hours sleep in the hostel before a taxi ride to Bangor Station in time for the first Holyhead to Chester train, changing there for Rockferry Station and home.

I had noticed that the compass adjuster had become increasingly uneasy as the night had progressed. He only revealed to me when I left him, that, believing he would be back ashore in Liverpool in the early hours of the morning, he had left his car parked on a single yellow line at the Liverpool Pier Head. I heard that his fine was eventually paid for by the ship's agent after I had complained about the ridiculous situation, which I had been faced with on what should have been a straightforward: 'outward bound from Liverpool Docks booking.'

Another 'not straight forward booking' is the story of a damaged vessel, which I was manned on to shift from the Manchester Ship Canal to a Cammell Lairds' dry dock in Birkenhead for repairs. She was my first ship in the January of 1973. The ship was the small German container vessel the *Klaus Blok*. She was a regular runner between Ireland and the canal. Her problem was that outward-bound in the canal, she had somehow been forced to go astern to avoid contact with another ship and had backed into the canal wall, damaging her rudder, which had subsequently been jammed 'hard to port.'

I was manned for the afternoon tide, but when I arrived down at the Eastham Locks, I was dismayed to find that the vessel had been berthed in the 'small lock' at Eastham. This lock is only 50 feet (15.24 metres) wide. She had been towed down the canal by two tugboats. The head, or forward tug had 'slipped' as the ship's bow was entering the lock and the 'after,' or stern, tug had 'let go' when the ship was safely in the lock.

I stood on the lock side and was amazed at the decision that had been made to put the crippled vessel in the small lock. My decision was very swiftly made and I informed the dock master that I would not be sailing on that tide. I explained that although a Liverpool tug was waiting to make fast on the bow outside the lock, the Liverpool stern tug would not be able to come in to make fast until we were clear, not only of the layby wall, but also clear of the wooden dolphins, which extend to the north of the lock and were built to help keep deep water in the line of the 'channel' to the locks.

I told the lock master that I thought everybody concerned with the safe departure of the vessel from the canal would have realised an obvious danger before I arrived. With the helm jammed 'hard over to port,' when we moved ahead from the 50 foot lock, on the flood tide (or the ebb tide), there was only one way we could go and that was 'hard over to port,' which would mean that the stern would swing into the dolphins with the inevitable outcome of serious damage.

What did I suggest? I advised that the ship be towed back into the canal and with her canal tugs fast she could be towed into the big, or eighty foot (24.4 metres) lock. My advice was then, that once safely in the wider lock, she could be run down to river level on the flood of the next tide and the Liverpool tugs could then both enter the lock and make fast before we left. We would then be as safe as we could be with the helm jammed 'hard over to port' for the tow north to Cammell Lairds dry docks.

My advice was taken and I sailed the ship on the flood of the next tide. The passage was a struggle from start to finish, but I did get a smile out of the very troubled German captain when we were off the dry dock and I observed that my next order would be: "Hard over to port" with the helm for the ship in order for her to swing across the tide and enter the dry dock.

The 'sense of humour story,' which I referred to at the beginning of this chapter is one, which always for me, illustrates the speed of the Liverpool sense of humour and indeed the depth of the Liverpool wit, is my Seaforth 'bus' story.

This is the story, which, as I mentioned at the beginning of this chapter, has prompted me to write a sequel to "East a Half South" and indeed is the one, which I am amazed was not included in that volume in the first place. Perhaps it was fate, which withheld it from the page.

The weather was fine, the time early afternoon one summer. I had parked my car in the Seaforth carpark, north of the container terminal. I was in good spirits, for I was booked to pilot a

Gracechurch container ship outward bound from Liverpool on the top of high water. I would take her outward bound down to the Western Station at Point Lynas, as I was booked to bring an A.C.L. (Atlantic Container Line) container, ro-ro vessel back in to the Seaforth Container Terminal on the following, early morning tide. This was going to be a most enjoyable day's work for me to be carried out in fine weather. My car would be waiting for me to drive back home.

Having parked the car, I walked past a cheerful 'waving' guard at the perimeter gate and waited at the clearly signposted bus stop for the terminal bus.

Pedestrians are not allowed to walk across container parks for the straddle-carrier drivers, being so high up, have restricted vision and cannot see the figures below. We, as pilots, were warned soon after the terminal opened of this danger. The dark thoughts of early casualties of this possible fatality being scraped up off the tarmac into several black bin liners was sufficient to ensure that the buses were always used!

Through the gates came a white van. I put my arm out and the vehicle stopped. I slid open the door and as I climbed in, shouted: "The *Gracechurch Crown*, please Driver". His reply was not only unexpected, but it took me completely by surprise.

"Its norra bus y'know pilot!"

As he did not tell me to get out and he had stopped, I chose to close the door and sat down facing backwards. The vehicle moved off in a clockwise direction round the working terminal. Opposite me were two men in suits, both with briefcases, who were deeply engaged in conversation.

Minutes later, the vehicle pulled up by the gangway at the after (back) end of the *Gracechurch Crown*. I slid open the door and, as I was descending, shouted my thanks to the driver. I could also

not resist shouting: "It says 'bus' on it driver, in big black letters."
The reply was immediate and totally unexpected.

"Yeah Pilot, it says 'India' on the tyres, bu' we're noh' goin' there
either!"

Surely he could not have known that I was not going to make
that statement, yet his response was so quick. Apparently, I
discovered later, after I had made some inquiries, that the 'bus'
had been commandeered by H.M. Customs and the two be-suited
characters were plain clothes officers taking important papers to
another vessel.

And so we are outward bound and another literary voyage has
begun. We must wait to find out where both the flow of words and
tides will take us. Take us they will, for we are back on the bridges
of ships of memory and on watch for those yarns, which make up
all our histories.

"It's norra bus y'know Pilot."

REMEMBERING WHEN...
I DID GO THERE... INDIA

Ten Year Nirvana.

Mosquito buzzing in the dark of night,
Tiger, prowling round campfire bright,
Dhobi woman
Thigh deep in the Khanapuri River,
Betel juice smile,
Red,
At the Shite Hawk's lust,
Blue-headed, brown
To her sagging breasts
And pubic black.

No children's clothes.
For again, following this deadly cyclone,
There are no children,
Only a wasteland of mud-bodied fever
And a lung, stomach-stench
Over the paddy field remains.

There is no one left to understand
The tongue of yet another
Decomposing corpse.

As there were stories of both trading with India and ships from Indian flagged companies in the opening chapter, I thought that this next chapter would include some further memories of my 'deep sea' exploits, coupled with some experiences, which connect me with those early days at sea.

The poem above is somewhat stark in content, but if we remember the fact that my ship, the *Clan Brodie*, arrived in India and then

East Pakistan only weeks after the horrendous anticyclone of November/December 1960, I witnessed the aftermath of its devastation. A devastation, which killed 20,341 and left 200,000-300,000 people homeless. The storms with winds of over 90 mph. (150 km/h) produced a 20' (6.1m.) storm tide, which swept 10 miles (16km) inland.

I wrote the 'Ten Year Nirvana' poem years after that particular cyclone after the Bhola cyclone, a devastating tropical cyclone, which had struck East Pakistan and India's West Bengal on November 3rd 1970. It is reported still as the deadliest tropical cyclone ever recorded and was one of the world's deadliest natural disasters when at least half a million people died.

On the day, I was involved in sailing a Norwegian coaster of just under 2000 tons gross, M.V. *Basalt*, outward bound from Eastham Locks. She was only 83 metres in length and about 12 metres in the beam (wide). We too had strong winds in the Liverpool Bay, but nothing like those that were part of the Bhola cyclone system. As the winds here were westerly, I was to disembark at Point Lynas, the western station with shelter from the westerly winds in Moelfre Bay.

I listened to the news on the ship's radio as we battered our way down to Anglesey and realised that the cyclone had struck the area north of the Bay of Bengal where I had been aboard the T.S.S. *Clan Brodie* on my first trip to sea. The news brought back memories. The *Clan Brodie* had proceeded from Colombo, the main port of what was then Ceylon, now Sri Lanka, to Chittagong, now Cattogram. We discharged the last of our outward general cargo, along with *Nutty*, the Afghan sheep dog, which we had carried with us from Birkenhead to Chittagong. We also commenced loading cargo, bails of jute, for the homeward bound voyage.

Names have been changed from what was then East Pakistan, now Bangladesh. Chittagong has become Chattogram on the

Karnaphuli River, once the Khanapuri River and Chalna, which I have in my cadet log book as being on the Pussar River, is now apparently on the Rupsha River. Loading at the latter, we were anchored near Chalna, sixty two miles upriver in Karmardanga Reach and we were loading jute from barges.

I note from my cadet log book that as we proceeded up river to both the berth in Chittagong and later to the anchorage on the Pussar River, I have recorded signs of devastation caused by the anti-cyclone, which had wrecked the S.S. *Clan Alpine* in the October of that year. (The officers of the *Clan Alpine* were to join us for Christmas dinner alongside the berth in Chittagong on their way home back to the U.K by plane,) For example I read in my logbook that "I noticed a hangar on an airfield particularly, for it was squashed flat." I remember too, the downed trees and the mudslides along the banks of both rivers as we proceeded both upriver inwards and later downriver on the outward passages.

I also remember the inward bound Chalna pilot telling me that I might hear tigers howling during the night whilst we were anchored. I did hear them in the late eight to twelve watch and the early twelve to four watches when Peter Hardy, my fellow cadet and myself were given 'command of the bridge' for the anchor watches, giving the three ship's officers a rest from their regular 'four on eight off' pattern. The main feature, which I remember of the night anchor watches was that there were no fixed lights never mind any navigation lights to take bearings of and so, as watch keepers, we had to rely on open fires, which naturally burned out and another one had to be found for the cross bearing references required.

"Taken from the pad used for noting anchor bearings:

Tin Shack: 033° T. Tall Tree: 209° T.

Transit bearing: Two small bushes 118° T.

The memories of that voyage in particular, remind me of some of the stories, which unfold in Joseph Conrad's "Lord Jim."

I returned home from Point Lynas by train the morning after the Bhola cyclone and wrote the 'Ten Year Nirvana Poem' on the train in the note book, which I always carried with me as a pilot. I see now that I have 'mixed' the memories of the two ports together for the purpose of the poem, for the 'Dhobi woman' was actually sighted on the Pussar River from the ship's bridge during one evening's eight to twelve anchor watch. The 'Shite Hawk' reference is to the species of raptor, which were often seen circling the ship, along with black kites, but my knowledge of bird recognition was not good at that time.

On one occasion whilst anchored in the Pussar River, a steward taking morning tea and toast across number three hatch to the Chief Officer, Peter Macniven, was dive bombed by one of these huge birds, giving him a terrible fright. The only damage: a steward in shock, a broken plate, a broken mug and the aerial theft of the mate's toast!

After I had left Clan Line, I once visited Peter Macniven, whilst I was in my early days as a Boathand when he was mate on board another Clan Boat, moored alongside the Clan Line berth in the East Float, Birkenhead. A wonderful man, who sadly was to lose his life not long after that visit in a road accident in Bombay. (Mumbai) A lorry braked heavily in front of the taxi Peter and three other officers were travelling in. The lorry was carrying a load of steel pipes, unsecured and the load shot off backwards. One of the pipes pierced the windscreen of the taxi and went through Peter's throat. He was sitting in the front passenger seat.

Whilst Chairman of the Liverpool Pilots, I attended several of the Clan Line Christmas reunion lunches. There I was to meet up with Ivor Hurst, the once young and very efficient Purser/Chief Steward on board the *Clan Brodie*. He was to inform me that of

The Clan Line warehouse in the East Float/Vittoria Dock.

all of the British officers on board the vessel that trip, only Ivor, and myself were still alive. Ivor was still alive at Christmas 2019, from that lunch on, we have sent each other Christmas cards. There was no card from him in 2020 and his phone is now cut off. The lunch was another occasion when, after being welcomed to the lunch as Chairman of the Liverpool Pilots, I was to realise how far I had come.

It was Ivor who suggested that I make the 'tourist trip' from the Seaman's Mission whilst we were in Colombo. There were no other takers from the *Clan Brodie*. ("We will go another time...," I wonder if they ever did?) As a result I went on my own for the day's trip organised by the Seaman's Mission. We visited Kandy and the Temple of the Tooth, The Botanical Gardens near Kandy and a tea 'factory.' (Since the time when I stopped drinking alcohol in 1997, my favourite beverage has turned out to be tea, preferably green or white tea).

Overleaf is a photograph of an elephant on the Katagastota River. The bus made a stop at the river so we could watch the elephants bathing.

Brownie 127 photograph of an elephant by the Katagastota River.

Shortly before we arrived at the river, the bus stopped at a banana plantation, where all the party, two British, three Japanese and eighteen Germans were all persuaded to buy stalks of bananas to 'take back' to our ships. That made twenty three stalks of bananas in all.

The bus had no glass in the windows and whilst we, the passengers, were watching the elephants bathing in the Katagastota River, other elephants in the care of their mahouts, passed close to the parked bus and ate all the bananas, which we had left on our seats!

That elephant story reminds me of a story of an incident, which took place back in our home waters many years later. The story was told by Alan Davis, best known to us as Yak, a colleague and one of my close, game-fishing companions. Yak had been boarded in from Point Lynas on a coaster bound for Mostyn, a small port on the River Dee in Wales. The passage from Point Lynas passes through the Welsh Channel, close inshore off Rhyl, a seaside resort as well as being a small port on the North Wales coast. It was summer and early morning, first light on a beautiful sunny day.

Yak was concentrating on the navigation of the vessel in the narrow channel and was looking east. The German captain was examining the coastal features to the south with his binoculars. Suddenly he was to ask with obvious concern in his voice;

"Mister Pilot, Vot zort of vild animals are zer in Vales?"

"Wild animals Captain? Oh there are rabbits, foxes, badgers and maybe deer I suppose."

"No Mister Pilot, I mean really vild animals,"

"I assure you Captain," Yak replied," There are no wilder animals than those, which I have mentioned."

"But Mister Pilot, I am vorried vor my crew, vor zer are elephants on ze beach!"

Yak took the binoculars and scanned the beach off Rhyl and sure enough there were 'elephants on the beach!' The explanation was simple; a circus was visiting Rhyl and the mahout was exercising the elephants on the beach in the early morning sun!

Two stories, which connect my first trip to sea and my boathand days in the Liverpool Pilot Service may be linked under the title of 'Nautical Peaked Cap stories.' The first is the one, which is of a personal loss, which I 'suffered' on my return to the English Channel on board the T.S.S. *Clan Brodie*. It was at the time when I was experiencing the disease/illness/state of mind (?) brought about in sailors nearing home after a long voyage. The condition is known as: "The Channels." The symptoms are a mixture of excitement and good humour, both accompanied by a sense of wellbeing. A wonderful state to be in!

I was keeping the 2400 hrs.-0400 hrs. watch with the second mate. This watch was customarily known at sea as: 'The Graveyard Watch' for obvious reasons. The most obvious of these being that they were the hours, which are possibly the most unnatural for any human being to be awake. (Although having observed both my children's and my grandchildren's nocturnal habits and timing when 'clubbing,' perhaps this last statement does not hold true in the present day).

The second mate was to send me down for something below, I do not remember what. I exited the wheelhouse on the leeward side. The wind was fairly strong from the north. I was thus sheltered on the starboard side of the bridge deck housing until I had to clear the accommodation for the last flight of steps down to the main deck. Here my light hearted mood was to be dashed when the wind whipped off my officer's cap and blew it over the side. The cap was last seen spinning off into the blustery night air over towards the French coast. I was devastated.

Ironically I noted in my cadet log book that we were then abeam of the rocks known as the 'Casquettes' and, which were marked so on the admiralty chart. (English translation: literally: 'caps'!) Some time was to pass for me to recover the elation of the 'Channels,' which had been lost with the loss of my cap!

After I had been discharged from the *Clan Brodie* and made it to Euston Station on my journey home on the evening of the 24th February 1961, I was amazed, when, upon entering a compartment at random on the train, I was to find another Merchant Navy cadet officer sitting there. He was Ian Findley, a classmate from Wallasey Grammar School who had sat next to me for five years and had never once mentioned that he was at all interested in going to sea! Ian had signed on with Athel Line, a tanker company and he still had his nautical peaked cap!

I had time, even though I was to join my second ship, *Clan Macleod*, which was bound for Australia, just ten days after I had arrived home on leave, to go to a well-known seafarer's outfitters in Liverpool, to buy a new cap and I was given another cap badge by Clan Line. I was to sense, once again: 'Ship shape and Liverpool fashion.'

I am going to allow the 'flow of words and the tides' to take us on to my early days as a boathand in the Liverpool Pilot service before we set sail again for foreign shores. This is to allow the telling of another lost 'cap story.' Again we are in a 'Graveyard Watch' in the early hours of the morning. I was the 'wheel man'.

A four handed watch on a pilot boat consisted of the senior of the four being the 'watch keeper.' The other three were equal, taking it in turns as 'wheel man' to steer the pilot boat an hour about. During the night watches two took turns as 'wheel man.' During the 'other' hour, the boathand, who was not on the wheel, would be 'standby man' in the mess room down aft, whilst the fourth member would be the 'doze,' allowed to sleep through the night watches on top of his bunk, fully clothed, ready to go if there was a 'job.' (Boarding or taking a pilot from a ship). The watch took it in turns for these responsibilities.

When there was a boarding job, or an outward bound pilot to be taken off, (an 'O.B.') the 'wheel' would remain on the bridge with the captain. The senior boathand, (or senior 'lad,' as we were usually called 'lads' by licensed pilots) would be coxswain of the boarding punt, one of the other hands would be 'bowman,' (or 'bow lad') and the remaining hand would be 'lower away' and 'lift up' man, operating the brake and the motor for the davits. He was also responsible for dropping down into the embayment to secure the blocks[4], which had been released when the punt was safely in the water by the coxswain of the punt.

Sometimes, if the senior boathand had been in that position for some time, the captain would permit him to manoeuvre the pilot boat and the next senior hand would become coxswain. This procedure of course allowed 'all hands' to gain more experience.

---

4 Blocks: The pulleys though, which the wires ran from the davits to the forward and aft of the punt.

The captain would generally spend the night watches in his cabin, being called only when his services were required to attend to the inward or outward bound vessels. There were 'two captains' on an operational pilot boat and they would split the 24 hour day between them. During the night watches, if all had been quiet, the captain would often go up to the bridge and relieve the watch keeper for a twenty minute or so brew, which he would take down aft in the boathand's accommodation. This was the case on the night in question.

Relief Captain John Barr, sometimes better known as 'Foggy Barr', came up on to the bridge and sent the watch keeper below. The wind was from the south-south-west, blowing a good force six on the 'Beaufort Scale', so quite a 'strong breeze.' Johnny Barr was a Cornishman and was proud to maintain his Cornish accent, along with an attitude of being very much; an 'Old Man of the Sea.'

The pilot boat was 'lying' all stopped, beam onto the wind and waves, rolling gently in the low swell. Captain Barr opened the windward door and went out onto the wing of the bridge in order to: 'get a better appreciation of the weather.' He leant over the bridge dodger (rail) and gazed out both into the dark and into the strong breeze. A slightly stronger gust blew his cap off and whipped it over the side. I was standing behind him in attendance. Captain Barr remained leaning on the dodger, remarking to me in his Cornish accent: "Arrhh, Curly, (my nickname) I believe that there is going to be a blow from the sou'west. "Aye Sir," I replied, "Permission to lower the boat to retrieve your cap?"

Permission was given and we lowered the boarding punt, even though force six was reaching the limit of doing so safely and we did indeed retrieve the wind-blown headgear. (The doze was not pleased!)

Unfortunately for me with my cap loss, the Clan Boat had been making at least fifteen knots on sea speed homeward bound and the loss of a cadet's cap was no valid reason for making a 'Williamson Turn[5]' in an attempt to retrieve it!

The homeward bound cargo on that first Clan Line trip was a mixture of: tea, jute, sandalwood and rosewood. These cargoes had been loaded in numerous ports. They were Chittagong, Chalna, Madras, Galle, Callicut, Allepey and Cochin, which was the final loading port. When operating as a 'boathand' as crew of the punt taking pilots off Clan Line ships and ships of other lines outward bound for the East, the smells mentioned earlier could be scented when alongside the vessels. Quite often during the long seven year apprenticeship, we would all perhaps wish that we were on board those vessels, outward bound to faraway places with the excitement of visiting foreign parts.

Back now to when I was indeed outward bound with Clan Line on board the M.V. *Clan Macleod* bound for Australia from Alexandra Dock in the North Liverpool dock system. I had collected my seaman's bag with all my gear in it from the *Clan Brodie* a few days before in Liverpool. The Brodie had sailed from Tilbury after only a few days there for Liverpool. After discharging part cargo in Liverpool, she was to sail again and had left the Gladstone Lock outward bound ahead of us bound for Glasgow.

The tide was a high one, about 30 feet at high water. (Ten metres) We were able to pass through the lock into the river with both level, the one with the other. Thus we were not to bring up, (stop in the lock) and were soon on our way, bound for Australia.

I have covered my Australian trip comprehensively in my previous book and in browsing through my cadet log book, I note that with not having to look after livestock, as on my previous voyage, from the beginning the cadets were involved in keeping watches when near the coast and also were involved in a wide variety of

---

5 Williamson Turn: A manoeuvre, which allows a vessel to turn and proceed on the exact opposite course. Used to good effect with a 'man overboard situation.'

'sailorising' jobs from the very beginning of the of the trip.

These, from a wide variety, included painting, splicing both ropes and wires as well as constructing a painting punt with chippy, the carpenter, Chippy Thomas, a fairly rotund individual, who lived in Wallasey near to my family home. Chippy Thomas, not the Pakistani crew, it was who taught me how to make a genuine Indian curry and taught me how to cook perfect rice. "First of all you take a large onion…"

Other jobs included: caulking decks, oiling decks, stencilling names on ship's lifeboats, refilling both foam and acid types of fire extinguishers, overhauling rigging and blocks, holystoning decks, in fact, doing just about every job that you can imagine.

Most of these jobs were to be carried on during the long years of the Liverpool Pilot apprenticeship. Each one of us must have painted the pilot boats, on which we served, apart from the underwater hull, many, many times each! That included all the housing, both masts and the funnel. We did also paint the ship's hull above the waterline and the yellow line, which ran around the hull above the waterline. This yellow line was in memory of the early sailing pilot cutters, which were painted yellow. Tradition has always played a major role in the Service. We would also wire broom the 'grass' growing on the 'boot topping' on the waterline, possibly when all was quiet between tides, whilst at anchor on a calm day.

On board the 'Clan Boat', we were to discharge the majority of our general cargo in Sydney and then proceed north to Brisbane where we completed the discharge of the outward bound cargo. We then returned to Sydney to commence the loading of wool and sheep skins for the homeward voyage. The main cargo of wool and skins was to be loaded in Brisbane, to which port we returned after only a short stay in Sydney.

Because the bales of both wool and skins were only light, we were not only able to fill all five hatches, but also we were to place more of this cargo laid on dunnage (loose laid timber strips), on top of the closed hatches. This cargo was then covered with tarpaulins and lashed down. Leaving Brisbane for the second time, we were to proceed to Freemantle to take on both fuel and water.

On this leg of the voyage I had my 17th birthday. I remember that the day was just another day at sea, but I do also remember that my fellow cadet, Andy Douglas, had managed to save a bar of particularly delicious dark chocolate to give me as a present. I recall that this particular bar had a black and white paper covering with a man sat in an arm chair smoking a pipe!

The journey home was uneventful save for spells of heavy weather in both the Indian Ocean and the Mediterranean. (No lost officer's caps!) We were to discharge part cargo in Genoa, Dunkirk and then in Antwerp before proceeding to Manchester, where the vessel would discharge the majority of her cargo. Looking in my logbook, I note that we were berthed in the three continental ports for only a matter of hours each. It was in Manchester that I was to sign off for good from Clan Line and after just over three weeks at home, I was to join the Liverpool Pilot Service.

One story, which is not in my logbook, but one I remember vividly, is the one when after signing off from the vessel on Monday 10th of July, I was stopped by the policeman on the dock gate. I was searched and the pleasant gentleman confiscated the bottle of gin, which I was taking home for my father, because: I was only seventeen years old. No further comment!

The mention of Dunkirk brings me back to piloting and a story to bring this chapter to a close. It is a story, which was told to me by the captain of a Norwegian vessel, whilst we were waiting in the queue of coasters awaiting their turn to lock in to the Manchester Ship Canal up at Eastham Locks. This was in the days when the canal was busy as it had been on the occasion when I returned from Australia on the *Clan Macleod*. I have never ascertained if there was any truth in the story, but I found it amusing and still do. The French Port was Dunkirk. I turned the story into a poem.

The Clockwork Ship.

Pull up a bollard
And I'll tell you a tale of the sea,
Straight as told to me
By the skipper of a Norwegian packet,
Laced up to the eyeballs in his orange lifejacket
And the wind no more than force three.

A French port and a pilot
Ordered to conduct a vessel by night,
Safely from the harbour to the German Bight.

At the appointed hour,
Monsieur arrived at ze dock
And zer received a terrible shock.
She was light in ze water
And it was clear by ze red of ze rust
Zat ze Greeks had bought her
For she lay like a floating wreck.

"Non Croix de Guerre will I seek,
Zo in performing my duty
I will rid my country's shores of zis pestilent Greek.
But one assurance I demand: Zat 'er engines will answer to my command."

The assurance came from the wheelhouse murk:
"Mister Pilot, ze engines, zey are like clockwork!"
"Encore! Allons!"

So they 'allonsed' together
With tugboats to aid them to back and to fill.
They proceeded with caution and not without care,
Plus a certain artistic skill, with no main engines,
'Til confronted by the lock gate,
Where there befell an unfortunate quirk of fate.

You could tell by the rake of the mast,
She was going too fast
And the order was given: "Go Back."
"Toute en arrière. Full astern.
Toute de suite. But quickly!"

Not a squeak, not a peep, not any sound
And the wreck sped on
Until she ground,
Wood and steel with all her might...

When it was over... what a horrible sight!
Damage excessive and most impressive.
(It would cost more than a few francs to put right!)

The pilot turned on his ethical heel and shrieked:
"My responsibility I vill not shirk,
But what about ze engines zat are like clockwork?"

Now the Greek himself had thrown an 'Homeric' fit,
Yet he managed a questioned reply with such wit,
That it laid our French friend low,
Down on the deck boards:

"Monsieur, 'av you a clock zat goes backvards?"

"BE PREPARED!"

"If you can keep your head when all about you are losing
theirs…"

Rudyard Kipling. 'If.'

The Scout's motto above, along with Rudyard Kipling's poem "If"
became the two simple lessons in life, which my father taught me
from childhood.

My father, Walter 'Curly' Curry, was a Licensed Liverpool pilot
before me and whenever I look back on that childhood there
never seems to me to have been a time throughout my early years,
when my father did not wish me to follow in his footsteps.

My brother Brian, six years older than myself, also became a pilot
before me. Brian, however, was to go back to the sixth form after
what were then G.C.E. exams with a view to going on to study at
university. I remember my brother coming home from school for
the Christmas holidays and making the declaration that he did
not want to go to university, but that he wished instead to apply to
the Liverpool Pilot Service. I admire Brian for this for he had 'lost'
possibly six months seniority by not having been accepted into the
Service until six months after he might have been. Brian was to be
accepted and sailed with Elder Dempster Line for one trip on the
M.V. *Sangara* down the west coast of Africa, before crossing the
Atlantic to St. Johns, New Brunswick. His return home was with
the vessel docking on an afternoon tide into Bromborough Dock,
where he was to be met by both myself and our mother Lillian.
My main news for him after the "Welcome Homes" was that I had
passed the eleven plus examination and that, much to my delight,
I was to go to Wallasey Grammar School and not to Oldershaw
Grammar School, where both he and my sister, Vivienne, had
spent their secondary school years. (The girl's: Oldershaw High
School in Viv's case). I always felt that this stroke of fortune
gave me a chance to make my own path in life at an early stage,

rather than having to follow in the footsteps and always be in the shadows of my siblings. Thus allowing me to break away from the 'baby brother' syndrome.

My Grandfather, Dad's father, John, ('Jack' Curry') had been a seafarer at one stage in his life. He was a wonderful character who lived into his late nineties. Unlike both myself and my father who was shorter than me in stature, he was in excess of six feet tall, an imposing figure of a man. He lived in Granton Road, Anfield, almost under the stands of the Liverpool Football Club. Jack had been born in Clonmel, County Tipperary.

When I was a child, I would sit on his knee and he would tell me the most incredible stories with a delightful Irish accent. I knew that he had not been swallowed by a whale. I believe that he got that one from the Bible! However, I have never been able to prove or disprove the one he would tell me about his service in the Australian Mounted Police.

I do know that Jack went to sea for my nephew Tim's wife, Cheryl, managed to find his marriage certificate, on which he is declared to be a ship's steward. More than that I do not know, but Grandad Curry always maintained that he had jumped ship in Australia and became an Australian Mounted Policeman. His storytelling continued, by telling me that after being allowed home to England on leave, he deserted simply by not returning. In effect then, he was a deserter until the day he died, if the story was true and therefore 'he is still' a wanted man!

Grandad was to marry Elizabeth Lawrenson in Liverpool with her sister as a witness. Elizabeth came from the Shetland Islands. They were to give birth to three children Lily, Eileen and the youngest Walter, my father. Dad was to marry a Liverpool girl Lillian Lear, my mother who gave birth to me in "Rose Cottage" out in LLanarmon-Yn-Ial, North Wales. So, if we put that diversity of countries together, I believe that we will find that it makes me a genuine 'Celtic Mongrel!'

Marriage certificate of John and Elizabeth.

On my mother's side of the family, the members of the families Martin, Davies and Sale were pilots and indeed they owned their own sailing pilot boat. There was also a Martin listed as the Captain of the Number One Liverpool Lifeboat and I often wonder if he was one of my ancestors. There were two lifeboats slung behind the Liverpool landing stages in the days before the R.N.L.I.[6]

My father was dedicated to the life of being a pilot. He was good at it and had many memorable experiences during a long career, retiring at the age of 65, claiming that he had never had a day off sick. I believe that he was very proud that both his sons were to follow in his footsteps.

I was licensed as a third class pilot on the 21st August 1968 and my father was to retire on the 6th November the same year. This meant that I was to serve with him for just over two months. I was in the same group as him, Group One, presumably to 'take his place' when he did retire.

Only once in those months, when I was outward bound in the early hours of the morning did I meet both my father and brother on the same pilot boat. As the punt came alongside the embayment of the pilot boat for me to climb aboard her they were both waiting to welcome me aboard. They had been called specially from sleep to be there. This was a memorable occasion for all three of us.

---

6 The Liverpool Lifeboats. Fitzgerald. P. 2005.

On the morning of the day's tide on his birthday the 6th of November, the day Dad retired, I had been aboard a small coaster, the *Ben Rein* on North Stalbridge dock wall and had shifted her off that berth over to West Stalbridge. Her anchor was jammed and she was unable to sail for sea. After the move I was straight off home. In the days of mobiles, I would have been informed that my father was inward bound for the very berth that I had in fact cleared for him! Dad's first ship as a pilot was the S.S. *Gracehill*, outward bound from Garston, but from the Old Dock, not from the same berth he ended up on then, but close.

Photograph of the Gracehill.

I also know that by an extraordinary coincidence, on the day after my father's funeral on the 9th May, 1985 I was manned on another Gardener's Saint Boat, the M.V. *Saint Oran*, bound from the Bar pilot station for Garston to the very same berth in Stalbridge! What is more, she had missed the day tide and I was able to take her to the old pilot boat anchorage, one and a half miles south-south-west of the old Bar Light vessel's position and there scatter the wreath, which Gill and myself had bought to lay on top of the coffin, on the tide's ebb.

That position has always traditionally been chosen by the Service to scatter the ashes of their former colleagues. It is often called 'Bottle Bank' for some reason or other.

On the day he retired, my father had caught the bus from Garston, but alighted at the Herculaneum Dock and walked north, through the South Dock System to the Pilot Office on Canning Pier Head. This walk I had made with him quite often, when, as a boy, I had accompanied him on a 'shifting job,' which ended up berthing in the South Dock System. He arrived at the office and met, amongst others, my contemporary, newly licensed pilot, as I was, Stuart Wood. Stuart asked him:

"How does it feel Mister Curry, now that you are retiring?"

The reply from my father was quite profound and one, which stayed with me throughout my career:

"Very strange Stuart, for as I have walked north through the South Dock System, I have come to realise that this is the last day that I am going to be learning how to be a pilot."

Dad was often mischievous in his approach to groups of colleagues. Some would say 'silly' even and there are many story examples of this. He would take great delight in coming through the saloon doors at the bottom of the steps leading from the captain's, or boat deck to enter the saloon. (They reminded me of the doors into a saloon in a Wild West movie, for they were varnished, wooden, double doors swinging on hinges on either side). He would approach the group of pilots gathered in the saloon with one aim in mind and that was to cause trouble, which he was able to do with comparative ease.

Dad also had, seemingly a clairvoyant tendency. (Possibly a message 'from beyond the grave' already hinted at in the story of the Saint Boat and the scattering of the flowers!) There are many stories of him thinking about and mentioning someone who was about to or had just died without his knowledge. The awareness of this strange 'sixth sense', which he had prompted many of our colleagues to request that both Brian and myself asked Dad to particularly NOT think about them!

One story, which is about an incident, which took place after Dad's death, was an experience of my own and it connects me to my father through a strange coincidence. We had for some time a survey vessel requiring a pilot, which was engaged in a long term survey of the continental shelf around the United Kingdom. She called into Liverpool numerous times to change crews. Initially she would require berthing at the Liverpool Princes Landing Stage. Later the vessel would proceed into the Langton Dock system and stay overnight for the crew change and to take on stores.

This experience took place on one of those earlier visits to the landing stage. I needed to swing the vessel on the port helm in order to berth starboard side to on the flood of the tide. She was relatively small, no more than 120 metres long, the weather was fine and it was a relatively straightforward manoeuvre. I put the vessel alongside gently and we were exactly in position when she was 'brought up' (stopped) and the ropes were all made fast. The captain thanked me with the following words:

"Thank you pilot, that was a splendid job, you wouldn't have cracked an egg."

My hair stood on end! She was, as I have said, a relatively small vessel, conditions were calm and there had been no real hardship in the relatively straightforward operation, yet the captain had used a phrase, which had sent a shiver down my spine and my hair had stood on end.

"Why did you use that phrase Captain: 'You wouldn't have cracked an egg?'"

"Simply because it was true Pilot, it was a splendid job."

"Well Captain, I realised as you said it, that many years ago, during the Second Wold War. My father was piloting a hospital ship bringing wounded soldiers back from Africa to the landing stage here in Liverpool for hospitalisation. He was standing, possibly in the very same spot as I was standing on the starboard side of the bridge, (only somewhat higher up on the troop ship) when she too was all fast. As they were approaching the berth, however, the captain of the vessel requested that my father put the ship alongside as gently as possible. He explained that if the vessel was to land heavily, with even the slightest of bumps, men would die, for some of them were hanging on to life by a thread."

When the hospital ship was all fast alongside, the captain had turned to my father and shook him by the hand, as my captain had done:

"Thank you Pilot, that was a splendid job, you wouldn't have cracked an egg."

Dad thanked the captain for those words and asked him if he would be kind enough to put them in writing, for the statement under the circumstances, meant so much to him. The captain duly did write, but I am afraid that so far I have been unable to trace the letter, although I believe that it is still in safe keeping, somewhere.

Sadly I cannot ask my father to verify my stories about him, so they must only be taken as anecdotal, rather than as completely factual. Having said that, my memory for stories from the past has always been fairly reliable and therefore I believe that they come to the page much as my father related them to me. Also, very recently, I have been able to sight my father's 'Laver's Tide Tables,' in which he recorded all of his acts of pilotage from the *Gracehill* to the *Saint Bridget* and verify the stories, at least to some extent

With regard to the above story, I did always believe that the hospital ship was bringing troops back from Burma, but on examining the tide tables, I have found that the ship must have been the

U.S.S. *General William Mitchell* (AP-114), inward bound from Casablanca with wounded soldiers from the African campaign on Saturday August 5th 1944. The tide tables show that he anchored the ship at the Bar Light Vessel at 2200 Hrs. on Saturday 5th. He berthed the ship on the ebb of the day tide on Sunday 6th and sailed her on the flood of the day tide on August Bank Holiday Monday the 7th.

U.S.S. General William Mitchell.

She was almost brand new having been built as a troop ship and launched in 1943. Commissioned in the January of 1944, she was 623' long (190 m.) and 76' (23 m.) in the beam, with a displacement of 11,450 tons. The ship is recorded to have had a top sea speed of 21 knots, so a 'flash ship' of the day. Also noted in her record is that she was not scrapped until 1988 in Taiwan, after a long and illustrious career, having served in many theatres of war including the Pacific during the Second World War. In her latter days she was to serve in the Vietnam War.

One other such story is that of the S.S. *Nestos*. This vessel had been built as the S.S. *Arabian Prince*, for Prince Lines, Furness Withy. By the time of her grounding she had had a chequered career and changed both her owners and her name several times.

On the second of April 1941, she had become separated from a convoy, which she had joined after becoming separated from her original convoy earlier on her wartime voyage. She was outbound from New Orleans with a full cargo of sulphur bound for Garston. She had joined her first convoy in Halifax, Nova Scotia. *Nestos* was not a large vessel for the day, but she was a fair sized ship for Garston.

Nestos was 5764 gross tons and she was 405' long (123 m.) and 52' in the beam (16 m.). On the day, the vessel had lagged astern of the main convoy, she was in dense fog and south of her safe course from Point Lynas on the north coast of Anglesey to the Bar Light Vessel. The latter marks the safe entrance to the Port of Liverpool. The vessel did not have radar and we can only speculate that she would have been on reduced speed because of the poor visibility. The flood tide would have carried the slow moving vessel well south of the course line and as a result she grounded on the Hoyle Bank to the west of Hoylake on the Wirral. Her position: 53^0 24.78' N., 03^0 14.35' W.

From the tide tables, the high water on the morning of Wednesday the 2nd of April was at 0256 Hrs. B.S.T. The afternoon tide was at 1536 Hrs. B.S.T. The heights were 25' 7" and 25' 04"respectively. They were neap tides and were 'falling' tides, which means that they had peaked on Friday 28th of March and now they were getting smaller.

Tides are caused by the pull of the sun and the moon on the waters on the Earth's surface. Trying to put it simply, the 'sun stands still,' (As Galileo Galilei proved!) the Earth spins and the moon orbits the Earth. When the moon is in line with the sun on the same side of the Earth, that is in what is known as 'conjunction,' there is a 'new moon' and the combined gravitational pull on the Earth are strongest and the resulting 'heaps' of water are highest bringing the 'spring' tides, (nothing to do with the seasons) for that period, the highest tides.

When the moon moves to a position at right angles to the sun, we have the sun and the moon in 'quadrature,' the gravitational pull of the moon and sun are split and the tides are 'neaps' or small tides.

When the moon moves round to being in 'opposition,' we have the full moon with the smaller but never the less, 'spring tides again, before the moon is on the wane for the monthly cycle when we have the sun and moon in 'quadrature' again. Finally, the moon moves on to 'conjunction' anew and the whole monthly cycle begins afresh.

So, it was vital that the effort to re-float the *Nestos* was completed whilst the tides were of a similar height to the one, on which she ran aground and before the tides fell further causing her to be known as what we call 'neaped.' (Not having enough water to float.)

From the tide table, it is difficult to ascertain the exact time my father boarded the stranded vessel, but it is likely to have been on the flood of the tide after the vessel had grounded, in other words already on a smaller tide in height. There would have had to have been enough deep water from the incoming tide for a small boat to go alongside her in order for my father to be able to climb aboard.

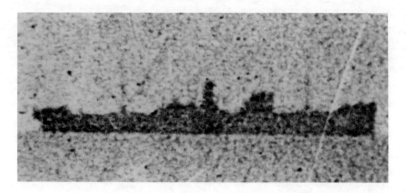

A 'grainy' photograph of Nestos, soon after grounding.

My father's account was that a naval vessel was tasked to ferry the pilot 'manned on' the vessel (my father) south from the pilot station down to the *Nestos*. Another written account states that the pilot was boarded from a pilot boat. I believe my father's account, which includes the reference to a naval lieutenant and five ratings boarding with him to assist the pilot and the crew.

On the bridge, my father acquainted himself with Captain Pandelis and inquired as to her draught in the water. (That is her draught when she had actually been afloat). He checked his tide tables (The very one that I am looking at today). and pronounced the estimated time that he believed that the vessel would re-float on the flood of the next tide.

Unfortunately for them all, the way, in which she had run aground, meant that one end was in deeper water than the other and as the tide rose the force of the water pushed the end in the deeper water upwards. The result was that, with the other end still 'stuck fast' in the sand, she broke in two. Again, referring to the tide tables, it would appear that my father was on board the vessel from the ebb of the morning tide of the 3rd. He notes the time of 7 A.M. -5 P.M, which I believe was the span of time that he was actually on board the *Nestos*.

Whether Dad made this part up or not, I do not know for sure, but he claimed that after the fracture, the captain was on one half and that he was on the other. This was highly likely if the captain had gone to the end of the vessel, which was pointing at the incoming tide and my father had remained on the bridge.

The vessel, now a shipwreck, the admiralty ordered the naval vessel to take off the captain and crew, which she did. Nothing about the lieutenant, the five ratings or the pilot, so they were left on board.

Sometime later, another order came through from the admiralty for the naval vessel to take off the lieutenant and the five ratings. Nothing said about the pilot, so he was left on board on his own.

Following a further passage of time, the order came through to take the pilot off and Dad was 'rescued' bringing with him the ship's cat!

My mother followed this tale up with the fact that Dad had left home with his beautiful head of curly, auburn hair, (Hence my father's nickname of 'Curly') but that he had returned home with a head of white hair. I have read articles that have told me that shock cannot cause this phenomenon, but I believe that this tale proves that it can happen.

At this time, the area around the vessel was believed to be 'mine free' and so the Mersey Docks and Harbour Board sent barges to discharge the cargo from the hatches, which were still intact. However, before the discharge of what was hoped to be salvaged from the cargo could be completed, a coaster, the *Maurita*, carrying coal from the Point of Air to Lancaster, struck a mine in the wreck's vicinity with the loss of all five of her crew. The discharging of the wreck was halted and later on in the war she was to be used as target practice for the R.A.F. parts of the wreck, including her boilers, are visible at low water today.

Present day photograph of the wreck and photograph of her boilers.

On the 13th July 1944, my father was to pilot what had become one of Britain's most famous battle ships, H.M.S *King George V*, which was by then renowned for her part in the sinking of the German Battleship *Bismark* on May 27th 1941.

On May the 1st 1942, *King George V* was to collide with and cleave in two, the destroyer H.M.S. *Punjabi* after the latter made what turned out to be an unnecessary alteration of course under the battleship's bow whilst the vessels were engaged in escorting Russian Convoy PQ 15.

The battleship's bow was severely damaged and she was to proceed to Liverpool to dry dock for repairs in the Gladstone dry docks, docking a week or so after the collision.

KG V in Gladstone Dry Dock.

King George V was to sail from Liverpool on July 1st 1942. She was to return to Liverpool again to dry dock in February 1944 for a major refit before proceeding to the Pacific to join up with the American fleet. She was in dry dock from the 11th February until the 30th of July. On the 30th of July 1944, an entry in my father's tide tables has: "*K.G.V.*" Glad. Dry/Glad N. Above the entry is the note: '6pm. to 8pm.'

The entry would indicate that my father was booked to pilot the vessel from the dry dock itself to a layby-berth on North Gladstone, where she would remain overnight, for the crew to sort themselves out ready for sea after dry dock before sailing for sea with another pilot the following day. Dad was always proud of having this fleeting involvement with the *K.G.V.*

Another of my father's traits, which was to show his love of piloting ships, was that on many occasions, after docking an inward ship, say at Eastham Locks early on a Saturday evening for example, he would sometimes meet a young pilot on his way over from the pilot's rooms to join an outward vessel in the locks. A brief chat with the young pilot about where he would be going for his night out, if he was not piloting the ship, would often result in the young pilot having his night out and Dad sailing as pilot on the outward bound ship!

An extreme example of this was his voluntary assistance given to a then young first class pilot, who had got himself into all kinds of trouble on board the Japanese tanker *Eiho Maru*. The trouble was that in a very short space of time, twenty four hours, from the morning tide of the 21st October 1953, the tanker was to run aground, not once, but three times in various parts of the river.

During the groundings, I am not sure exactly when, but I believe on the morning of the 22nd, my father was on the Canning Pier Head outside the pilot office. I note that on the previous evening he had docked the *Wokingham* having piloted her from the Bar Light Vessel to Gladstone Dock. I can only assume that he commandeered a tug boat, which was lying on the Liverpool Landing Stage to take him to the stricken vessel, for the pilot's river launch only operated until sunset. He boarded her using a pilot ladder and gave assistance to the young pilot.

From the tide tables, I note that my father boarded the tanker at 1 A.M. on the 22nd October at about three hours after the previous high water of a thirty feet, four inches high, spring tide. (9.2m Newlyn. The latter was where the tide gauge for all the British Isles was taken from before the advent of the 'Astronomical Tide Range.' i.e.: 'The level below, which the tide rarely falls in any particular area. This new chart datum came into use in 1984. In Liverpool Bay, this was the low water of a ten metre tide.)

The following day's tide was at 1035 Hrs., with a height of 30 feet, two inches. (9.2m) Dad stayed with the vessel, commanding the re-floating operation at this next high tide. For this procedure he ordered every available tug boat on the river (and there were many more than there are available today) to come alongside and push/pull. Bearing in mind that this was now a salvage operation it would have been costly.

In those days the towage companies published a magazine called 'The Gog'.[7] I remember, as a child, seeing within the pages of this magazine, a photograph, which showed the *Eiho Maru* being re-floated on the flood of a tide. The stricken tanker had no less than eighteen tugs alongside, according to the report within the magazine, all lying one next to the other. The photograph below shows seven of the tugs, a great deal of smoke and the after end of the tanker.

Re-floating the Eiho Maru. Daily Post and Echo.

Following the final successful re-floating operation, my father headed for the nearest open lock, which happened to be Sandon Lock in the North Liverpool Lock System. I seem to remember

---

7 Gog Rope: A short rope used to hold down the towing rope on a tug and tow, thus shortening the scope of that towing rope, making the tug more effective in a confined space.

that Dad said that Lieut. Commander Hill, the Marine Surveyor and Water Bailiff, had also boarded the tanker and was with him on the bridge.

Following the next event in this tale, I have the vision of the vessel, being towed into the Sandon Basin by tug boats passing an irate dock master jumping up and down on the quayside screaming:

"You are not bringing that ship in here pilot."

As the basin was tidal, the gates would have been open on the level, the basin and the river being equal on the high tide, with the lockmaster being helpless to prevent the tanker from docking there.

My father would have been using the maritime law relating to: 'A port of refuge,' believing rightly that the ship had to be taken into the safety of an enclosed port both to assess the damage and to keep her out of the way of other traffic. The tanker was safely moored in Sandon Basin at 1045 A.M.

Later the *Eiho Maru* would be taken across the river to be dry docked in Birkenhead Dry Docks in the West Float. I can remember, as I was ten years old, being taken in his 'plum coloured' Morris Ten saloon car, number plate: DKC 874, to see one of the then 'largest tankers in the world' in Birkenhead West Float Dry Docks! My father's pronunciation of the ship's name was: 'EE Aye Oh Maru,' rather like the children's chant about the farmer who wanted a wife!

The final story, of so many, which I have chosen to end this chapter with is another of my father's 'highlights' of piloting. He was the second Pilot on the launch of H.M.S. *Ark Royal*, she of the: 'We are sailing...' song fame. The date was May 3rd 1950 and I was in my second year at primary school.

My mother, Lillian had been invited to be in the crowd of dignitaries, by the 'launching box' where her Majesty Queen

Elizabeth, wife of King George VI, was to launch the aircraft carrier by breaking the bottle of champagne on her bow on the Cammel Laird's slipway where she had been built.

I had been given into the care of my sister Vivienne and was to join her and her sixth form class on board one of the Mersey ferries. Not sure where Brian was, but suspect possibly with his form on the same ferry. It was a momentous occasion, watching the huge aircraft carrier slide ever so gracefully down the slipway and into the River Mersey, which was crowded with vessels of all shapes and sizes, the air filled with the blaring of ship's whistles, fog horns and the clanging of bells.

Photograph of launch of Ark Royal.

"Much Ado about Nothing."

So, there's much ado about nothing.
Now I am on the mend,
I'm going home,
This is my last sunset.

I've travelled the world all over,
I've sailed the seven seas,
If there's a land that I've not been to,
Then, I can, without a lie,
Tell the folks who are listening,
That I've certainly passed close by.

I've 'Been Prepared' in Java,
Honolulu, Vizagapatam.
I've spoken to many people
And I have never given a damn,
Whether it was royalty or the gentry,
Or the poorest of the poor.
I told them, I would help them,
I'd do what I can,
Whilst reminding them, I only was a man.

Sunrise over the Mersey,
Dawn in the Liverpool sky,
In my memory I see those ghost-ships sailing by.
I was first to say "Good Morrow,"
The last to say "Goodbye."
I'd meet them in the offing
And bring them safely in,
Then leave them, as you leave me now, on the highway,
My distant coasts to win.

I'm going home, this is my last farewell.

For Walter 'Curly' Curry, my father, who died on the 1st May 1985, "Mayday!" (The international distress call, taken from the French: "M'aider", "Help me," whilst I was attending a performance of Shakespeare's play of the same name: 'Much ado about nothing,' by the 'Wool Gatherers' in Heswall Hall on the Wirral).

Walter 'Curly' Curry. Official wartime pilot's pass.

"THE WIRRAL TWO MAN, ANTIQUE SHIP SOCIETY"

Stan Frith, whom I had met through our involvement with the Hoylake and West Kirby Lifeboats, was old enough to be my father. Stan had two daughters Shirley and Hilary. I believe that I was a bit like the son he never had, as I was much younger than him and not much older than his daughters. We both supported and shared an interest in the running of the Hoylake and West Kirby R.N.L.I Lifeboat Stations.

Stan was at one time Treasurer, later becoming Chairman of the Management Group of the two stations. I was initially a crew member at West Kirby Inshore Lifeboat Station, transferring after twenty years of service to become a Deputy Launching Authority at Hoylake. I later became 'Hon.Sec.' and when the name was changed: Lifeboat Operations Manager. In 2016, on my 72nd birthday and my retirement from Lifeboat Operations Manager, I was also to become, as Stan had been before me, Chairman, a position I hold as I write.

Stan was a Master Mariner, once having had an interest in becoming a Liverpool Pilot, but had opted to remain at sea as his father had been, serving with a Liverpool shipping company, Booth Line, running to South America and in particular up the Amazon to Manaus. He sailed with 'Maggie Booths,' as the company was affectionately called.

Stan had been torpedoed twice during the Second World War. The first time was when he was serving as third mate with a second mate's qualification, on July 5th 1941 on board the S.S. *Anselm* in a position south west of Ireland when outward bound on passage from Liverpool to Freetown. After the sinking, which was the cause of a great loss of life, Stan was in the water for over four hours before being picked up by a naval vessel.

The second time, later on in the war, when, after surviving the Straits of Gibraltar, the Mediterranean and the Suez Canal on board the *Fort La Maune*, the ship was torpedoed by U-188 some five hundred miles south east of Aden in the Indian Ocean with no loss of life. Stan was serving as second mate with a first mate's qualification. The second time, after the sinking, he was in command of one of the ship's lifeboats for many days, finally bringing the boat and her crew safely to land, for which he was awarded an M.B.E.

Once when we were walking on the front, outside the Lifeboat Station at Hoylake, Stan told me the stories of the two incidents. Noting his qualifications and the positions, which he was serving in on board the two torpedoed ships, I could not help but ask the question:

"You did not go for your master's did you Stan?"

He did of course, but never served as master in command, choosing to come ashore after the war and becoming involved with the shore side of cargo handling.

Stan's father, Arthur Frith was master of the S.S. *Aguila*, which was a vessel in Convoy OG 71, carrying amongst other personnel, twenty two young wrens outward bound for duties in Malta. Having safely survived earlier attacks on the convoy by U-boats, Arthur allowed the wrens and the other passengers to go below to rest on their bunks providing that they kept wearing their lifejackets. Not long after the *Aguila* was hit by a torpedo from the U-201 and sank very quickly with the loss of all those wrens and all but one of the other passengers and most of the crew.

According to Stan, his father opened his cabin door as the ship was sinking and literally stepped into a life raft, which was floating past. The vessel, which picked him up, H.M.S. *Wallflower*, took some of the rescued seamen to Gibraltar. The vessel, which was then to convey Arthur from Gibraltar back to the United Kingdom was also torpedoed, but Arthur survived that one too!

By coincidence, another of my friends, whom I met at the Master Mariner's club in Liverpool and one who Stan introduced me to, is David Howel, whose father, John was chief officer with Arthur aboard the *Aguilla*. John was rescued by the tug *Empire Oak*. Sadly, the tug was also to be torpedoed soon after the rescue with the loss of all hands including David's father.

Stan and myself would talk about many subjects whilst the lifeboat was out either on an exercise or a 'shout[8].' One of our favourite subjects was, with our backgrounds, naturally the sea and all that went with that interest.

I cannot remember whether Stan had actually visited the *Cuttysark* before our visit, but I had been several times. We decided to take a day out to London by train to visit the famous clipper ship and so the "Two Man, Wirral Antique Ship Society" was founded.

We had much in common in our interest of the famous vessel and there were so many things to talk about, such as the details of shipboard equipment that one of us had noted. We had lunch at the Greenwich Museum and went on to visit the museum. Naturally there is so much there to have interested us both, but the one aspect, which we found ourselves talking about more than any other was Nelson and the Battle of Trafalgar.

On the train home, we planned that our next outing would be to Portsmouth to visit H.M.S. *Victory*. We made this a two day visit, staying the night in the famous old inn, 'The George,' where Nelson was known to stay and where he had had breakfast after his overnight coach journey from Merton, where he had left Lady Hamilton the night before he joined *Victory* to sail to both his most famous battle and of course his death.

---

8 'Shout:' A Lifeboat crew's word for an official callout for the lifeboat.

Stan and H.M.S. Victory at sunset.

On the way home from this outing we made a detour via Bristol to visit Brunel's masterpiece S.S. *Great Britain*. A great two day trip and Stan insisted that we stop at a motorway service station so that he could buy us fish and chips from Harry Ramsdens.

Stan at the wheel of S.S. Great Britain

This visit we had made by car and we determined to return on another occasion to visit H.M.S. *Warrior*. This we did, again by car the following year. *Warrior* was the first steam driven, metal hulled warship of the Royal Navy. I remember many things about the historic warship, including the fact that she was such a menacing presence in the English Channel, that she never actually fired a shot in anger! One of the few successful deterrents ever I believe. *Warrior* was built as a 'metal shoebox' shape with a wooden bow and a wooden stern. Because she was steam driven, there is an elaborate 'bathroom' on board with a number of baths, which could be provided with hot, fresh water from the ship's boilers!

Stan with H.M.S. Warrior.

On the second day of this trip we went back to the dockyard to visit the *Mary Rose*, Henry VIII's 'famous' flagship, which sank in the Solent beneath the monarch's personal gaze whilst helping to fight off a French fleet in 1545. I remember that we talked about separately watching the wreck being raised from the Solent on the morning of the 11th October 1982 on the television.

The journey home, as coming home from Bristol, would not have been the same without a stop at a motorway service station for the now traditional eating of Harry Ramsden's fish and chips.

Our next visit took us out of the country when we flew from Manchester to Stockholm to see the *Wasa*. We made the visit worthwhile by staying in Stockholm for several days. We visited the warship on the second day. I refer to her as a 'warship,' but more accurately I believe that she would be better described as a 'work of art.' As we stood looking at her with our combined sea going experience, the historic vessel is clearly top heavy and her fate on her maiden voyage across Stockholm Harbour proved this fact when she capsized and sank on her first tack! She is, however, a work of art with carvings and many fine artefacts beautifully restored in the most amazing museum.

Wasa.

We stayed at the Hotel Gamla Stan, (Stan liked that name!) situated on Gamla Stan Island, where Stockholm was originally founded in 1252. Whilst we were there, I had arranged to meet a Swedish family, Grosschop, who had stayed near us in West Kirby some years before and, indeed one of their daughters, Maria, had actually stayed with us for a month some years earlier. Anita and Bengt, had an additional surprise for me, for Lena, the eighteen year old girl who had first stayed with us when Gill and myself were in our late twenties, now a fully-fledged architect working with Bengt, miraculously appeared from behind a wall in the gardens of the Royal Palace in Stockholm.

Stan and Lena in the Palace Park, Stockholm.

Our final trip was over to the east coast to visit the warship *Tincomalee* in Hartlepool. This was in many ways a sad occasion. The weather was fine and again we managed the fish and chips on the way home, but after boarding the vessel and walking aft on the main deck, I could sense that Stan was not feeling himself. Stan was obviously tiring and when we reached the ship's wheel, he leant against the bulwarks and insisted that I went below decks on my own. He would wait for me. As I went below decks, I realised that this would be our last visit together and that our next planned trip to Norway and the *Kon Tiki* would sadly never take place. The fish and chips from Harry Ramsdens were as good as ever and we both did enjoy the day.

Me at the wheel of the Trincomalee.

Stan's health deteriorated over the years after this visit, but I was later able to drive both Stan and Brian McShane, (also a launching authority at Hoylake Lifeboat Station) but on this occasion in the capacity of Marine Operation's Manager of the Port of Liverpool, to the opening of the Merchant Navy Arboretum at Alrewas on the 16th May 2001. I was there in my capacity as Chairman of the Liverpool Pilots and it was an honour to be there with Stan, a survivor, who had been torpedoed twice and rescued twice, living to fight on!

The Liverpool Pilots had paid for the planting of two trees in the Arboretum in memory of the two pilot boats, which were lost with great loss of life, one in each of the two World Wars.

Another fascinating visit, which we made together during this time, was to the Admiralty's Western Approaches 'Secret Bunker' in Liverpool. The bunker is situated in the basement cellars of Derby House in Liverpool. I seem to remember that we thought that we would be there for about an hour, but at least three hours sped by.

The most amazing memory I have of the visit is of the table where the convoys were laid out across 'the Atlantic,' and the main positions of the U-Boat packs. The table reminded me of and seemed to be the same as those we see in the ops. rooms in the wartime, R.A.F. films such as "Reach for the Sky." It was as if the last pencil had been thrown down on the table when the news that the 'Battle of the Atlantic' was over and nothing had been touched since then.

Younger than I am now. (V.E. Day, Fifty Years on).

Girls, this may seem like a basement,
Flat, with little interest,
But within these walls,
Girls and Boys,
Not much older than you,
Played, thousands of them,
Played out the lives of others in the daily duties
Of those who worked
And slept
In this secret Atlantic bunker.

Here they monitored the lives
Of other girls and boys,
Not much older than you,
Who battled
With gale-swept seas
And those who wished to send them down.

"Katz und Maus!"
The board before you
Displayed the losses,
Even as one witnesses
Paper money lost
In a game of Monopoly,
Lost as easily
As lives were lost then.
"Do not pass go."
The gains were immeasurable.
Their pencils, pens (and rubbers) are left behind.

For Captain Stan Frith. M.B.E. Torpedoed and sunk twice, but lived to fight on.

Stan spent some time in St. John's Hospice on the Wirral. He was, however, to spend his final days in a nursing home in Hoylake close to the Dee Estuary. On one occasion, after an exercise, we were able to bring the Mersey Class Lifeboat, the *Lady of Hilbre*, back along the beach on her carriage close to Red Rocks, so that Stan could see her from his window.

I was able to fulfil a promise, which I had made to him years before, when he had asked me if I would present the eulogy at his funeral. After I had agreed, he made me swear that I would never speak of it to him again. I never did, but I did consider it a great honour to present his eulogy, many years later.

We had worked well together for both Hoylake and the West Kirby Lifeboat Stations and he was always in support of my efforts in negotiations to have the new Hoylake Lifeboat Station built. I am pleased to be able to report that he was with me when both the R.N.L.I. agreed to build it and he was with me when the Wirral Borough Council gave us the planning permission. Sadly, Stan did not live to see the building constructed, or to witness the arrival of the Shannon Class Lifeboat, which was to be stationed there, but I have always strongly felt that he was there in spirit.

Stan, with medals by the 'Merchant Navy Convoy' Memorial at Alrewas.

THE PORT OF LIVERPOOL

Part I: Early Beginnings to the turn of the 20th Century.

"Centuries long,
The river has flowed
Through an hour glass
Carrying in suspension
The sands of time.
…All our histories…"

The river referred to in the poem is the River Mersey upon whose eastern shore is the site of one of the greatest seaports in Britain, the Port of Liverpool. On the western shore lies the Port of Birkenhead and the Tranmere Oil Terminal, which supplies the huge oil refinery at Stanlow. The distance across the river between New Brighton and Gladstone Lock is one mile. Between the famous 'Old Pier Head,' from whence the trans-Atlantic liners sailed to the New World and Alfred Locks, is a mere half mile before the widening out again to over a mile across to the southward of a line from the Dingle to Bromborough Dock River Wall. Hence the line where the poet likens the shape of the river banks to an hour glass through, which the river flows. At the narrowest part, the flow at half-tide on a spring tide can reach in excess of six knots. At this point the bottom is rock and there is poor holding ground.

Unlike many of the ports in the United Kingdom, which have featured in this spot in "The Pilot," (Magazine of the United Kingdom Maritime Pilots Association) Liverpool was not favoured by the Romans. In Roman sailing directions Liverpool is referred to as "a rocky creek in the vicinity of Deva (Chester)" and they chose instead to navigate the River Dee with their galleys to found and supply their northwest stronghold at Chester. The tides, which flow through that "rocky creek," have a range of from around seven metres, neaps, to in excess of ten metres, springs.

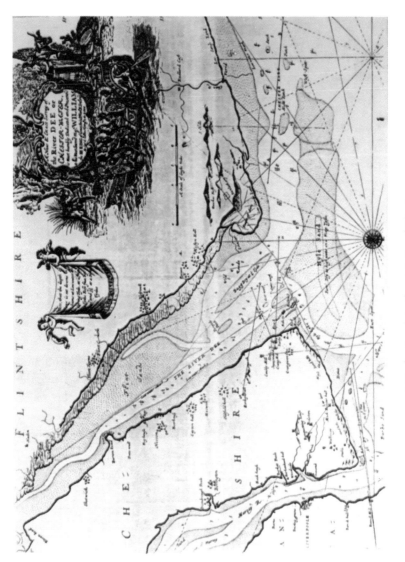

A Rocky Creek in the vicinity of Chester.

As the vessel's drafts increased and the River Dee silted, the main ports on the Dee shifted sites northwards, downriver to various quays and jetties including the Port of Parkgate from where William of Orange set sail for Ireland and where Lord Nelson's dear Lady Hamilton was born. Liverpool is said to have been colonised by Norseman during the eighth century. The name is possibly from the Norse 'Hlilthapollr, meaning Pool of the Slopes.' Another possibility is that it is derived from a combination of terms: 'Liver' from the 'Liver Bird' (almost certainly the cormorant), which frequented the 'Pool.' The pool was at the outlet of a stream, which flowed (and still seeps into the cellars and basements of buildings) on the present line of Paradise street where Maggie May plied her trade with the 'Homeward Bounders.' The 'Liver Bird' has become the emblem of the city and the unique emblem of the Liverpool Pilots.

Since I first wrote this article, which forms the basis of both this and the next chapter, whilst teaching Anglo Norman French at the University of Liverpool, I developed my own theory of the origin of the name of the city, and it is one, which I believe is more plausible than any of the others.

I have referred to this theory in "East a Half South," but I believe that my short note: "Why Liverpool?" first published in 'Precinct', in the January/February 2000 edition, would be of interest. The 'Precinct' used to be the regularly published magazine of the University of Liverpool. At this point I will digress and add the full note as it first appeared:

"Why Liverpool?"

John Curry, Honorary Research Assistant in the Department of French, is also a Mersey River Pilot, so that his interests not only cover the history of the French language, but that of the river and its great city. His research into both had led to an interesting and unique theory of the origin of the city's name. John writes:

The city was granted its first Royal Charter by King John in the year 1207. The charter is written in Latin and is jealously guarded in safe keeping in the vaults of Liverpool Libraries. It is in fact not a charter, but rather a 'Deed,' which is only six lines long. King John and the intelligentsia of the period would have been well schooled in the Latin language, but their everyday tongue was that brought over by William the Conqueror in 1066, Anglo Norman French.

The River Mersey had not been favoured by the Romans because of the strong tides experienced in what the Roman sailing directions described as: "a rocky creek in the vicinity of Deva. (Chester.)" The winter gales of today are not welcomed by navigators of the most powerful of modern ships with engines. For the cockle-shell, hulled galleys of the Romans, the tidal flow in the Mersey, together with strong winds, would have presented nightmare conditions for mariners.

Following the equinox in March, however, the River Mersey can be somewhat more docile (but ever to be respected) and the concept of the Anglo-Norman use of the estuary, with the availability of a safe anchorage in the 'pool' itself would have been attractive. Its situation, that much further to the north, across the Mersey and facing Ireland to the west, with the concept of a safe anchorage in the springtime for the sturdier vessels of the Normans, could well have led to the naming of the small hamlet, which we know existed on the 'pool,' to be preserved in the name that the present city bears. It is the Anglo-Norman translation from the Latin: "Li ver Pul (vinarium)." That is: "The Springtime Anchorage." (li –the, Ver-springtime, Pulvinarium-anchorage.)

The Normans used the written Latin Language for legal purposes, but in examining the 'Deed' of King John, negotiated between the King and a certain William Fitzwarin, the present writer has experienced a visual inconsistency in the language of the 'Deed,' which can be quite simply explained. The name of the small hamlet involved. "Liverpul" is not Latin, but rather is it the language of the day, that is "Old French," which is academically described as "Anglo Norman."

The six Line Deed.

I return to the text, where I digressed to present my published, personal theory of: "Why Liverpool?"'

We could perhaps take the history of Liverpool as a seaport beginning in 1207, when the fishing hamlet on the "Pool" was given a charter (referred to above) from King John, which created the borough and Port of 'Liverpul.' King John and his advisors had obviously recognised the potential of a new free borough on the sea. Situated on the west coast of the realm the position of the port had the advantage of deep water and shelter for vessels from the prevailing westerly winds.

Henry III was to progress the rise of Liverpool's importance in 1229 with a further charter establishing a guild of merchants to trade from the port. On the other bank in 1318, we know that Edward II granted by Royal Charter, the prior and monks of the now abandoned Benedictine Priory, the right to build the priory and the right to sell victuals to travellers about to cross over the 'arm of the sea.'

A second Royal Charter granted by Edward in 1330 gave the prior and his monks (and their successors forever) the right to ferry men and goods and other things safely over the river. The royal crowns still top the gangway posts on both sides of the river to declare this charter. Gerry Marsden's hit of the sixties: 'Ferry cross the Mersey' is testament to this even in modern times, it must be said, however, that with one rail and two road tunnels, plus the effect of the, now, three Runcorn Bridges (one rail and two road bridges) the ferry service has been reduced to a tourist attraction.

The Priory Birkenhead.

A Royal Charter to cross the Mersey

There followed some four centuries of slow growth until the late 17th century when trade with America was intensified and the maritime and commercial possibilities of the port were both recognised and capitalised upon. In 1715 Thomas Seers was to utilise the 'Pool' to create the World's first commercial wet dock and the city spread outwards from this centre of trade and upwards through what is now the shopping centre to the top of the slope, which is at present occupied by the University of Liverpool, Britain's first "Red Brick" university. The latter term was derived from the fine Victoria building and clock tower built in red brick so popular in Victorian times.

Today the university site stretches out on both sides of 'Hope Street,' which has at one end the Roman Catholic Cathedral and at the other the Anglican Cathedral. Liverpool is indeed a city of paradox. Many of the university's faculty buildings, such as those in Abercromby Square, were originally built for the ship owners and traders who operated from and within the port below. The Victorian gentlemen had inherited the prosperity of their predecessors who had profited from the highly successful and lucrative trade in slaves from Africa to the West Indies and the southern states of America. The first Liverpool slaver was a ship of some thirty tons, which sailed from the port on its infamous voyage in 1709. From the records it appears that she was to carry fifteen slaves from Africa to be sold to the plantation owners who had begun to produce the valuable crops of both sugar and cotton.

The Liverpool slave trade fleet grew rapidly and by the end of the century no less than 185 slave ships were operating out of Liverpool and the port had outstripped its rival west coast ports in the trade. Bristol (together with London), along with many other continental and Scandinavian ports, were also heavily involved and committed to this nefarious trade.

The trade could be described as 'triangular', for the slavers carried cargoes of tools and nails to trade with the West Coast slave traders for their captives. The second side of the triangle was the carriage of the slaves themselves. (Very few of the slaves were carried to Europe). The triangle was completed on the homeward leg with the carriage of sugar, rum and cotton.

No visit to Liverpool in the present day would be complete without a visit to the now obsolete South Docks, or Brunswick System. Here in the Albert Dock, the visitor may view the superb architecture of the turn of the eighteenth and nineteenth centuries architect Jessie Hartley. Apart from the shops, and restaurants, art lovers may visit the Tate Gallery of the North West. Maritime historians must visit the Maritime Museum, which includes historic vessels.

One such vessel of particular interest to pilots is the pilot cutter *Edmund Gardner*. The converted warehouse on the north side of the Albert Dock also houses many maritime treasures and the visitor may also view the superb permanent exhibition featuring the 'Slave Trade' and even experience the cramped conditions and scent of the below decks stench of a slaver. Liverpool has faced up to its past.

Jessie Hartley's Albert Dock.

We know that during the Seven Years War (1756-63) and during the American War of Independence (1775-82), Liverpool became an important centre for privateering. The 1778 records show that no fewer than one hundred and twenty privateers were sailing out of the port. In 1766, following an ever increasing loss of vessels on the treacherous sands that surround the approaches to the river, a pilotage commission was established to set up a pilot service, which would choose and train specialists who would become Liverpool pilots.

As trade with America grew, so did Liverpool's importance as Britain's West Coast Gateway. In particular copper was being imported from South America, whilst cotton was the main import from North America feeding the demand of the rapidly expanding Lancashire cotton mills. William Wilberforce succeeded in abolishing the slave trade in 1883, but by this time Liverpool was firmly established as one of Britain's major ports.

Macgregor Laird further increased the importance of the River Mersey in establishing what was to become a giant ship building yard with dry docking facilities on the Cheshire Bank close south of the present position of the Port of Birkenhead. During the early part of the nineteenth century, when the steam engine was being developed and adapted for maritime use, Lairds yard was to build many famous vessels including some of the world's first iron steamships. Together with his brother, the Scottish merchant built the S.S. *Alburkah*, which was a 55 ton paddle steamer. Sailing from Liverpool to the Niger River in 1832, she became the first iron ship to complete an ocean voyage.

In 1862, Laird built the American Confederate cruiser *Alabama*. A three masted schooner with auxiliary steam power, the *Alabama* sailed on 'steaming trials' as the *Eurica*, or job lot No. 290, with ladies and a party of musicians on board. She thus evaded the officers of the British government, which had declared its neutrality in the American Civil War.

The vessel first put into Holyhead and landed the 'revellers' before proceeding and avoiding capture to the Azores. Here she completed her 'fitting out', which included taking on board the armament, which had been forged for her at Lairds. Following renaming, the *Alabama* proceeded to take up her devastating rôle as part of the Confederate fleet.

Lairds were also to build the world's first submarine: the *Resurgam* ('I will rise again'). Unfortunately her fate was to sink in a gale off Rhyl on the north coast of Wales whilst under tow and has not so far 'risen again' at the date of writing. A replica of the vessel has recently been built by apprentices of the (then) Cammel Laird's ship-repairers and may be viewed in a 'dry dock' constructed from the old floating roadway to the north of Woodside ferry terminal. Liverpool pilots pass the replica to and from one of their present launch boarding positions and are only too pleased to know that they shall not be called on to pilot her!

Resurgam Replica.

During the last century, Lairds continued to build notable ships including *Ark Royal* (she of the "We are Sailing" fame, mentioned in chapter 3) and tankers up to the size of the Shell 'S' class.

The Port of Birkenhead to the north of Lairds further enhanced the importance of the River Mersey. This section of the port utilised the mouth of the River Birkett to create the first enclosed docks and became operational in 1847.

The Port of Birkenhead.

The Port of Liverpool had been expanding both south and north of that first enclosed dock and generally speaking, as ships increased in size, the need was to build docks ever larger in dimensions to the north of the Pier Head. All these docks were built on the foreshore and there is in truth only one dock (Stanley Dock) in inland Liverpool itself. With the ever rapid growth of both Liverpool and Birkenhead, these two great ports rose to become what we know as one of the largest seaports in the world.

The River flows through an hour glass.

Both this and the next chapter were first published as consecutive publication articles, which I was commissioned to write for 'The Pilot' magazine in July 1997, immediately after the Liverpool Pilots had won their battle against the Mersey Docks and Harbour Company and had returned to self-employment in June of that year.

THE PORT OF LIVERPOOL

Part II: Onwards towards the Millenium.

The pilot vessel Edmund Gardner with the M.D.H.C. building (the Kremlin) in the background.

Throughout the nineteenth century traffic on the River Mersey was increasing, for the industrial revolution had brought prosperity to the North West. Railways were rapidly covering the area and in particular, cotton mills were drawing the work force from rural activities to those of urban pursuits. One vital aspect of these developments for the River Mersey and its pilot service was the completion of yet another Victorian feat of engineering: The Manchester Ship Canal.

With the opening of the canal in 1898, large ocean liners could proceed with full cargoes to the heart of the cotton industry in particular and with other cargoes in general to this growing centre of commerce after proceeding through the Liverpool Pilotage

District. Indeed, initially Liverpool pilots operated on the canal, until the need for two services was recognised.

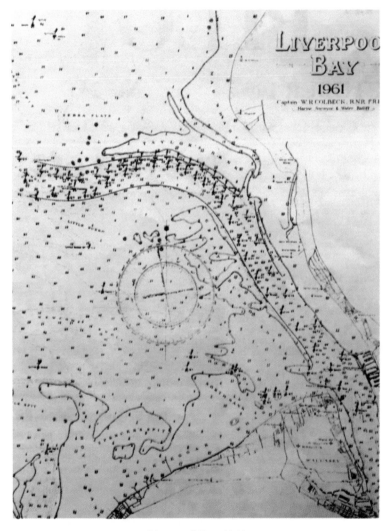

Liverpool Bay 1961.

At one period during the twentieth century, there were so many pilots in both districts that the two services were remote and their members simply 'passed' on the lock gates. Now with greatly reduced numbers on both sides of the gates, the two services have come closer together and although separate districts, work in both friendship and harmony with each other for the common good of pilotage. Following the building of the Shell Refinery at Stanlow in 1921 and the I.C.I. chemical plants, coupled with the importance of the Runcorn salt works in the vicinity of the canal, through trade in the Mersey increased rapidly.

Reports from the early years of the nineteenth century had stressed the extant and important Horse and Formby Channels to the north of the Rock Channel, were swept by tidal action alone. With the line of the Liverpool Docks being built ever northwards, it was decided to try and find a way to both enhance and strengthen the flow of the tide to assist in the self-sweeping of the channel approaches. In 1833, M.M. Denham, the Marine Surveyor to the trustees of the port, discovered and established a buoyed, mid bay channel, which forms the present deep water approach of the Queen's Channel.

Earlier in the century, Captain Robert Fitzroy of H.M.S. *Beagle* and Darwin fame, had been appointed as the First Acting Conservator under the provision of an Act of Parliament and was one of the several hydrographers of the period confronted with the mystery of a 'vanishing and reappearing' channel, which had never been satisfactorily explained. Denholm's survey settled the matter and a 'two course' channel was buoyed and maintained with difficulty. The difficulty arose as a result of the sand bar, which formed when the strength of the ebb tide diminished as it flowed from the narrow confines of the river and thus deposited silt, which formed the actual sand bar. It was G.F. Lyster, Engineer of the Mersey Docks and Harbour Board who pioneered dredging at the bar. The work was necessary due to the demands of the ever increasing size and needs of large trans-Atlantic passenger vessels using the port.

The initial success of the dredging of the 27' (8.2 metres) at low water springs channel was short lived as erosion began to take place on the north side of the bend at Taylor's Bank. The resulting problems of a narrowing and north shifting channel were threatening the advantages achieved by the dredging of the bar. In 1905, A.G. Lyster, son of G.F. Lyster, decided to build a revetment wall at Taylors Bank. Later during the period, which spans the years from 1914 to as late as 1962, training walls were built on both sides of the approach channels.

There are some 15 miles of wall built from stones from Welsh quarries calculated at the rate of some eighteen to eighty tons per foot run. Over the century, many bucket dredgers, including the mighty *Leviathan* with a crew of forty four and later the *Mersey Venture*, a suction dredger, have managed to maintain, with difficulty, a 6.7 metre channel, which at the time this article was originally written (1997) was the least water in the working approaches to the Port of Liverpool at the low water of a 10 metre tide[9].

With the establishment of ports at both Widnes and Garston on the Lancashire bank and Bromborough on the Cheshire bank over the turn of the century, the Liverpool pilots were ever in demand, although it must be said that Widnes had its own 'upriver pilots,' the last of which, Captain Vivian Thomas, following the closure of the port, was still operating on the River Weaver, when I first wrote this article.

During the First World War, many pilots answered the 'Call to Arms' in the service of their country. For those who were left behind, a heavy responsibility rested with the pilots of the port, for Liverpool was of great significance in receiving supplies for the war effort. The enemy concentrated on laying mines in the

---

9 The latest depth, after intensive dredging to attract Post Panamax vessels to Liverpool 2, is in the region of 8 metres. Liverpool 2 is the tidal container terminal to the west of Gladstone Lock, opened in 2016. Therefore not in existence when this article was first written.

Liverpool Bay with devastating effect to shipping in the area. Indeed, the No. 1 Pilot Boat, S.S. *Alfred H Reed* struck a mine at the Queen's Channel entrance early on the morning of December 28th 1917 and sank within minutes with the loss of 'all hands,' save two who were rescued. We know now that the mine was laid the previous evening by UC 75.

In the Second World War, however, there was to be a most important moment of unwanted but necessary glory for the Port of Liverpool. As the folksong: "In my Liverpool Home" tells it: "Hitler threw at us everything that he had." Then in the true Liverpool sense of humour, the following lines relate:

"When the smoke and the bombs
Had all cleared the air
Thank God said the Old Man,
The Pier Head's still there."

The reason for this is twofold, one, the German bombers quite simply 'missed it' and secondly: Western Approaches Command H.Q, operating with few escorts for the Trans-Atlantic convoys, was based here. On a visit to Liverpool it is essential for those interested in the period to visit the command bunker, which was opened to the public, only a few years ago. (This is the bunker referred to in Chapter 4). Within the bunker, it is as if the young people who played out the lives of others in their daily duties have just left: "...their pencils, pens and rubbers are left behind."

Nicholas Monserrat vividly further encapsulates the spirit of defiance of those who sailed from Liverpool under the command of men of the calibre of Captain F.J. 'Johnny' Walker, in his novel "The Cruel Sea."

Many authors and poets apart from Monserrat have been influenced by the relationships with the Port of Liverpool, including Joseph Conrad, and the "Old Conway," John Masefield.

The latter served his time on the famous school ship when she was moored in the River Mersey. Masefield's words taken from the "Conway" magazine, published in 1933, capture the spirit of Merseyside in the heyday of ocean liners and cargo vessels before the advent of the container vessels, V.L.C.C's and U.L.C.Cs[10].

The Tall Ships visit in 1992

10 V.L.C.C: Very Large Crude Carrier. U.L.C.C: Ultra Large Crude Carrier.

"...the flower of all England's shipping belonged in Liverpool: the river and docks were always busy with the best ships of the time. The Cunard moorings were just downstream from us: the White Star and Inman moorings beyond them: with the P.S.N. and Alfred Holt moorings further on still, but still in sight. The Elder Dempter ships were near us on the Sloyne. The steamers from many famous lines were weekly visitors to the river. We knew them by their funnels, house flags and tenders: even the foreign steamers and their cargoes were known to us." Masefield continues to reflect upon the fact that at the time he was a cadet, the bulk of the world's freight was carried in sailing ships, "...which had reached their last, strange, beautiful perfection." Tradition has been kept alive with Liverpool having had the honour of hosting the 'Tall Ships' twice in the last decade[11].

From its inception, the Liverpool Pilot Service operated a fleet of sailing vessels, sloops, cutters and latterly schooners. These craft were privately owned and operated with a full compliment of pilots on board, sailing from Liverpool, often as far south as the Bristol Channel offering their services to vessels inward bound to Liverpool. When all the pilots had been boarded they would return to Liverpool to collect their pilots for another sailing.

With the advent of steam, many of these vessels were lost by being inadvertently rammed by the vessels they were endeavouring to assist. The first steam pilot boat, the S.S. *Francis Henderson* arrived in 1896 much, to many of the older pilot's consternation. In the paintings by marine artist Joseph Witham, it may be observed that this steam driven pilot boat also has sails! It is as if the pilots agreed to their 'sail giving way to steam,' providing that they had sails to fall back on!

---

11 The Tall Ships have returned for a third time in 2008, when I was to pilot the Swedish 'Tall Ship' *Statsraad LehmKhul* outward bound in the parade of sail. (See "East a Half South" Chapter 23)

Oil painting of Francis Henderson. J. Witham.

At this point the Liverpool Pilots 'gave up' what has become known as the "Boat Rate Company," believing that costs involved with owning large steam driven vessels would be prohibitive. This company is now, as it was then, funded by the ship owner when paying the pilotage dues. This is hopefully, simply explained from the days of the presentation of the pilot's 'white card' for the payment of services rendered.

In modern times, approximately 'half' the charges on this card were for the services of the pilot, piloting the ship from A to B and the other 'half' were the charges incurred in getting him (or her, sadly at present, still no female pilots in the Port of Liverpool) both to and from the vessel. These charges now include taxis, rail fares, flights, and of course the cost of both building and running the present pilot launches. (In the present day, no white cards, everything is computerised).

Following the arrival of steam and then motor-driven vessels, the Liverpool Pilot Service had streamlined itself over the course of the century to operate with four pilot boats, each having approximately twenty two in their crews. Half of these men were apprentice pilots, or 'boathands.' One pilot boat was stationed at the Bar Light Vessel for her first week of duty. Her second week was spent 'on the run,' ferrying inward and outward pilots to and from both the Bar and Lynas (The Western Station) stations. The final week of the 'cruise' was spent at Lynas and the fourth (glorious week for the apprentices) was spent in dock. It must be said that the standard of seamanship achieved by these young 'boathands,' as I have said they were officially called, was considered worldwide, to be second to none.

Time and changes in the industry led to the reduction in the number of pilots and hence the reduction in the number of pilot boats, which were rapidly cut from four to three to two and then to none with the establishment of an efficient launch service based at Liverpool and down at the Western Station at Point Lynas. By promoting the launch systems, the Liverpool Pilots were instrumental in shaping both their future and the future of the port.

The Liverpool Pilot Service, prior to the container revolution of the seventies, had peaked with a number of one hundred and eighty six serving pilots. The Mersey Docks and Harbour Board, as it was then in the late sixties, had fallen short in planning for the future and having failed to anticipate the container revolution and were behind in plans to construct the Seaforth Container Base. The Royal Seaforth Container Dock, when eventually constructed and opened in 1972, was advertised as an area, which would engulf the Seven Wonders of the World. The area included berths for container vessels, grain boats, timber carriers and refrigerated cargo vessels.

The A.C.L. 'waltz', Seaforth style.

Latecomers to the "Container Trade," Liverpool was eventually to hold its own despite the fact that the 'Non Profit' making organisation under the auspices of the "Board," had lost the moment and was in the hands of the receivers. The Mersey Docks and Harbour Board had fallen and with the fall had withdrawn its (the ship owner's) vessels from the port. The port suffered immeasurably, but the pilots of the port remained steadfast at the helm and were on watch when the "Mersey Docks and Harbour Company" superseded the "Board" and began to make headway against the industrial tide.

Seaforth was completed and the large 'Box Boat' conglomerates competed for the advantages of a U.K. port with the facilities of a Panamax[12] sized lock and a non-tidal berth to work twenty four hours a day. Liverpool is unique in being able to offer this facility and the Atlantic Container Line, which uses it to the full, has been described as the jewel in Liverpool's crown.

When we look back at Liverpool's history as a port, as we have done in these two articles, (i.e: Chapter 5 and Chapter 6 in this book) we may see that because of the port's physical and geographical position, there is always likely to be another crown. The largest U.L.C.Cs ever built, have visited the SBM (Single Buoy Mooring) off Point Lynas and Liverpool Pilots piloted them and cared for them. With the cost of these U.L.C.Cs and the towage for them to be kept 'in line' with the strong tides for safety, the SBM was closed down in 1990. (At the time of writing this chapter, there are, no longer any U.L.C.Cs left afloat as there were few harbours in the world, which could accommodate them and they soon became obsolete).

V.L.C.Cs, albeit partly laden, (Liverpool, as explained earlier with the reference to the 'sand bar depths,' is restricted on draft). pass,

---

12 Panamax: ships with the maximum length and beam to fit in the locks of the Panama Canal. Now that these locks have been increased in size, vessels are referred to as 'Post Panamax.' Hence the building of Liverpool 2, in the hope of attracting these larger vessels to this river berth.

not offshore, but rather through the 'Centre of the City', guided by Liverpool pilots.

Nisa, 306,000 tons, passing the Pier Head in 1988 bound for the Tranmere Oil Stages.

It is true that there is much that the narrator has omitted through publishing space, but it is hoped that an overall literary picture of the history of the Port of Liverpool has been achieved. The Liverpool pilots who were subjected to employment status after over two hundred years of self- employment, returned to self-employment at 0001 Hrs. on June 1st 1997. In Liverpool, we as pilots, quite simply state that there is always another tide and we wish each other, as we wish you readers (of 'The Pilot' magazine), as colleagues and fellow pilots: "Good ships and Many of Them!"

"PILOTING ON THE MERSEY"

Sometime after I had been a Liverpool pilot for more than thirty seven years, I was asked by Iain Wakefield, then editor of "Ships Monthly," to write an article, with the above title, for the magazine describing the River Mersey from a pilot's perspective. Iain also asked me to describe how a pair of the Atlantic Container Line Ro-Ro. (Roll On Roll Off) G3 vessels regularly performed a well-choreographed manoeuvre in Liverpool's Royal Seaforth Dock, a piece of ship-handling, which came to be known as the "A.C.L. Waltz." I have chosen to reproduce this article, which I wrote for "Ships Monthly," December 2005, in a modified version for this chapter of the book. Thus it is important to note that my description is of the port at that time of writing unless otherwise stated.

The Port of Liverpool, often referred to as England's Gateway to the West, is proud to be called the 'Guardian Port of the Western Approaches.' Today (2021) the port handles record breaking amounts of cargo. We know from earlier remarks that the port had grown from its humble beginnings as a fishing hamlet, which was taken over to trade with Ireland in 1208 by King John when it was known as 'Liverpul.'

The port has passed, along with so many other ports, both in the United Kingdom and in Europe, through the years of both sail and steam as well as through the infamous 'Slave Trade' (so justly topical in world news as I write) up to the present age of large bulk commodities and both Ro-Ro. and container ships.

Shipping both entering and departing Liverpool today is served by pilots of the Liverpool Pilot Service, an organisation, which has been in existence since 1766. At the time of writing this chapter, the Service is a self-employed Cooperative of some fifty pilots. The year 2020, saw a number of retirements as well as an intake of new pilots, so it is difficult to say anything other than an approximation as given.

The famous J. Witham painting "Follow the Leader." Schooner No.2 Leading ships across the bar.

As has always been the case of the established present day Pilot Service, the Service operates from two boarding stations to the seawards of Liverpool. The main station is situated in the vicinity of the Mersey Bar, approximately fifteen miles north of the Liverpool Pier Head. The 'weather' or Western Station is located in the prevailing westerly, wind lee of Point Lynas on the north coast of Anglesey, approximately thirty five miles to the west of the Bar Station.

Douglas, on the Isle of Man, fifty miles to the north of the Mersey Bar, becomes the pilot station when the wind blows strongly into Liverpool Bay from the north. Many 'large ship' companies like A.C.L. are happier to have their pilots on board their vessels earlier than have pilots boarding at the Bar because this enables them to avoid a 'build up' of traffic and possible delay, if they are operating on a busy tide.

For the pilot, boarding a large vessel at a distance from the port, gives him or her time to adjust to so many variables including existing weather conditions and it also gives him or her time to assess whether or not there are any problems on board a vessel, which need to be taken into consideration for the inward passage.

The extra time and distance also allows the pilot to organise a safe passage plan for the inward voyage in good time, rather than being thrown into a swift assessment with only a few miles to go before the vessel must needs be committed to a narrow and 'restricted draft' channel. There are of course many occasions when the latter scenario does take place and then it is of course vital for the pilot to make all necessary decisions wisely in whatever time is available in the interests of safety.

The Port of Liverpool is tidal and with spring tides in excess of ten metres, when the tidal flow can be in excess of five knots, this makes the port one, which experiences some of the highest tides on the Earth's surface. Bristol, as well as St. Malo in Brittany, has very high tides, even higher than Liverpool, but the highest tides in the world are to be found in the Bay of Fundy. The natural phenomenon of differing heights of tides is caused by what are known as 'nordal points' on the Earth's surface and they are points, upon which the concentration of the gravitational pull from the Sun and the Moon are strongest.

When I was an operational pilot, the minimum depth of water at low water of a 10 metre tide in the Queens Channel was always supposed to be kept dredged to a depth of 6.9 metres. Now, with the hopes of attracting post Panamax container vessels to the new river container terminal, Liverpool 2, dredging is taking place in an attempt to keep the minimum depth of water in the main channel at a depth of around 8 metres. If we add a ten metre tide to this minimum depth, then at high water, there will be 18 metres of water over the shallow patch at the actual bar. If the pilot allows point six of a metre under his or her keel, if the vessel is proceeding at a speed slow enough not to incur squat[13], then he or she will be able to cross safely with a draft of 17.4 metres.

Atlantic Companion In Royal Seaforth Dock.

Obviously, the maximum draft, with which a vessel may negotiate the approach channels will depend on the actual height of any particular tide. Thus: if the tide was predicted as only 7.6 metres, (a neap or small tide) then, taking away the safe under keel clearance, .6 of a metre, then the pilot would only have 7 metres to add to the least water, 8 metres, giving 7 plus the 8, equalling a maximum draft of 15 metres at the high water of the tide.

An acceptable under keel clearance may also depend on a particular shipping company. Although I was always personally happy with the .6 of a metre under keel clearance for safety underneath any size vessel, which I piloted, some companies insist on a metre of water under keel clearance. This restriction would naturally further limit the maximum draft that a vessel could be loaded to for entrance into the port.

13 Squat: The term given to the increase in draft experienced by a vessel when travelling at speed.

Shipping movements are at their busiest 'on the tide,' that is the period around two and a half hours before the high water and the high water itself. The deeply-laden, large tanker bound for Tranmere Oil Stages for example, will be planning to pass the Bar Light Float somewhere at around the two and a half hours before high water. The tanker will commence the 'run' from the west of the Bar Light Float with approximately 20 miles to run.

It is a 'timed run' passing 'way points[14], at particular times whilst proceeding at regulated speeds, so that the vessel may arrive at the jetty she is bound for just on, or just after the high water of the tide she is berthing on.

The timing is adjusted so that her moorings may be made safely fast when the tide is slack or indeed, just starting to ebb.

For safety, she will have a tug made fast aft throughout the passage to assist in all necessary slowing down movements and to be there in cases of emergency. This run will have a passage plan agreed to by both the pilot and the master of the vessel, well before the passage is put in to operation.

The passage plan will take into consideration the prevailing conditions as well as the tide times. Conditions such as fog, mist falling snow, heavy rainstorms and any other conditions, might make alterations necessary to the passage plan, or indeed even lead to the cancellation of the berthing on a particular tide in the interests of safety. The Crosby Sands and the twisting track of the tide make the channel approaches and the River Mersey itself, a waterway to be both feared and respected. A pilot is able to use the tide to his or her advantage, but the pilot must never 'play' with the tide.

With so many craft of various sizes and in various trims entering and leaving the river, I am sure that it will be of interest to the

---

14 Way Points: Navigational marks to be passed on a timed run from A-B on a designated passage.

reader to follow a typical inward bound passage as an example. I am choosing one of my favourite inward passages, which I have carried out many times as the example and this is the passage of an Atlantic Container Lines 'G3' Ro-Ro/container vessel from Point Lynas to the Seaforth Container Terminal.

There were five of these magnificent vessels running a transatlantic service from Gothenburg via the continent and Liverpool to New York. (They have now been replaced after many years of service by the next generation of G4s, which are both slightly longer and slightly wider in the beam). The G3s themselves were 292 metres long, with a Panamax beam width of 32.5 metres. They had a maximum draft of around the 11 metres mark. Other ports were included in the run and the five operated a 'conveyor belt' service of both containers and Ro-Ro traffic.

Since my retirement in 2009, the G3s have been replaced by the Chinese built G4s. These vessels are slightly longer and wider, but they still 'just fit' into Gladstone Lock and allow A.C.L. to continue using the tidal Port of Liverpool in their trading programme.

The A.C.L container vessels call at Liverpool twice a week, always on a tight schedule. Times might be slightly different, but in my time with A.C.L. the 'outward vessel' arrived on a Friday to both load and discharge, sailing 24 hours later. The 'homeward bound vessel' would arrive on a Monday, this time, sailing twelve hours later. Obviously, bad weather conditions or the southern extremity of the summer ice flows in the North Atlantic could lead to minor delays in the schedule, but this was the basic weekly plan for these five vessels in Liverpool.

Weather conditions permitting, these vessels are always boarded with their pilot at Point Lynas and when possible, four hours before their lock, docking time at Gladstone Lock. Two hours are allowed for the thirty five mile passage to the Bar Light Float.

This is ideal for a seventeen and a half knot ship with the tide behind them and gives plenty of time to ease back and make a timed approach for the shallows at the Formby Safe Water Buoy. (Latest name for the Formby Light Float).

A further two hours is allowed for the channel and river approaches to the lock and includes time for both the 180 degree swing off the lock to stem the flood prior to locking in and time to make the tugs fast for docking. Bottom line is that you cannot hurry a big ship! The bigger the ship, the further ahead the pilot has to think to be travelling at the right speed at the right time in the right place.

The final two hours of the total, approximately six hour passage is the time taken for the vessel to be run up to dock level once in the lock, the time taken to proceed from the lock through Gladstone Dock and the Seaforth Cut into Seaforth, a swing to the west, backing up onto the berth, (usually S3) and finally the time it takes for the crew to secure the vessel with ropes to the berth. The actual passage time will, water in the channel permitting, normally take much less time than this for the vessel being 'All Fast' on the berth, approximately one hour before high water Liverpool.

The pilot boards and if the vessel is on her E.T.A., the ship will proceed at full speed towards the Bar Light Float. The ship's speed is then adjusted so that she may creep over the shallows in the Formby Strait in the main channel approaches as soon as she has water underneath the keel to safely do so. A reduction in speed is required so that there is no increase in the draft, which could be caused by the phenomenon known as 'squat', which has been explained earlier in this chapter, see footnote [13].

Once across the shallows, the A.C.L. will increase speed to round the bend into the Crosby Channel before regulating her speed again for the approach to the north river. Here with the flood tide behind her, she will make a controlled swing to port just to the north of the Brazil Buoy, with or without tug assistance, depending upon numerous variables including the vessel's actual draft and existing weather conditions.

Having completed the swing, if the pilot's judgement has been correct, the vessel should be in the optimum position for docking. If the lock is on river level ready to accept her, she will continue with tug assistance, 'dropping across the tide,' before slowly moving ahead and edging safely into position to make fast in the lock, ready to be run up in the lock to the dock level.

There were occasions when there were problems with designated tugs possibly still operating on other vessels, or even perhaps for some reason still 'locked in the system' when there were no tugs available. When these occasions occurred, weather and tidal conditions permitting, I have docked A.C.L. vessels without tugs, using only the ship's main engine, steering rudder and her bow and stern thrusters. This could also happen when the vessel was outward bound, but rarely.

A.C.L. control panel.

With the main engine power capable of driving the ship at a speed in excess of seventeen knots, a handy, swift-moving rudder, a bow thruster of two thousand horse power and a stern thruster of two thousand five hundred horsepower, the G3 A.C.L's were incredibly versatile and safe handling ships. They were the finest ships, which I personally ever handled. For docking, the pilot would be on the starboard side of the bridge with the well organised control panel to his left with all the controls at his fingertips. At the forward end of the control panel was the bow thrust control, behind that the stern thrust control, then the main engine control and finally, behind that in the line, the tiller.

The visibility down the side of the ship looking ahead, to the side and astern from this control position was superb. At this point I always think of my reply to taxi drivers taking me from the Woodside Pilot's Rooms over to an outward bound A.C.L. in Seaforth, when they would ask me what it was like to handle such a vessel and I would reply: "Actually it is a bit like driving a car, but the road is moving and you haven't got any brakes!" This may sound a bit of a glib reply, but in reality it is not far from the truth.

Another piece of practical pilotage here, with the beam of the vessel being not much less than the width of the lock, there was no time for the pilot to run from one side to the other. (A distance of 32.5 metres and the lock being 39.62 metres wide). This 'run' would be to see if the other side to that, on which the pilot was standing, was getting close and in danger of striking the dock wall. We would say; if looking forward down the side of the vessel, that, if it was becoming possible to 'fit' one of the containers on deck into the space before you in your mind's eye, then the other side was nearing a collision point with the other side of the lock!

Much has been written and recorded in photography with regard to the G3s, but here I will make a brief reference to these magnificent vessels. The Atlantic Container Line was originally formed as a conglomerate with British, French and Swedish interests. All three provided vessels to the company. By the time the G3s were running, (actually they were G2's lengthened) there were five vessels operating 'the conveyor belt' service on a round trip across the Atlantic. I intend what follows to be simply a 'not in depth' pilot's tribute to these fine vessels.

By the time that I was involved in piloting the A.C.L's, the original format had been altered and all the vessels were registered in Stockholm and were sailing with Swedish officers and Filipino crews. The British contribution in my time as an A.C.L. pilot was the *Atlantic Conveyor*, which had replaced the original *Atlantic Conveyor*, the latter being the vessel, which was to be sunk during the Falkland's War. The French provided the *Atlantic Cartier* and the Swedes provided three vessels: *Atlantic Companion, Atlantic Concert* and *Atlantic Compass*.

Dear John !

So glad to hear from you.
Yes your good colleuge Gary pilot us both in and out Liverpool this call.
Professionally done as always !

Understand you are busy now , only days left on your long long career as a pilot.
Must be with mixed feelings , both a relief and with a feeling of giving up something you love doing.
Because I know you dont see your profession only as a pilot but also as a way of living.

I can ashore you , you will be remembered and missed .
As you said , we have both had our tough times in redundant weather condition but have come out winning.
Times I never will forget , experiences I had with you . I am privileged to have worked and learn from you John.

I trust you will have a pleasant trip with Ulf and his crew across the big blue Atlantic.
Wish you all the best and a good stay onboard and your time in New York.

Dont fortget us on the ACL ship's please keep in contact John

Best regards:
Leif Holmberg

Letter from Leif, Master of the Atlantic Compass

Each of these vessels had two crews, alternating for each round trip. We, the A.C.L. pilots, got to know the masters of these vessels as good friends, sailing in all weathers, fair and foul, trusting each other implicitly to achieve the safe passage of these vessels both to and from this most difficult of ports, to which they made both frequent and regular visits.

From time to time, the G3 A.C.L. vessels passed in the dock system in a manoeuvre, which pilots came to call the A.C.L. 'Waltz'. There was little space for this to be accomplished, but if both were moving on the same tide when it was necessary for the inward bound vessel to be on the loading and discharging berth and necessary for the outward bound vessel to reach the lock and be on her way out to sea, there was no alternative but to employ this manoeuvre. With the advent of the G4s with the increased size and draft, this option is apparently no longer available if two of these ships are moving on the same tide.

Inward bound G3 A.C.L. passing through C. 4th cut.

In the days when it was possible to pass in the system, when the inward bound vessel was leaving the lock, the outward bound vessel would leave the berth and proceed on a 'lazy' swing to the west of the line of the Seaforth Cut to end up heading south for the Cut. The inward vessel would leave the lock and proceed through into Seaforth before making a port swing to head west, then she would back up onto the berth vacated by the outward bound vessel. When the Cut was clear the outward vessel would proceed on her way. If the manoeuvre was timed correctly, neither vessel actually stopped moving. There was not much room, but it was beautiful to watch and there was also an enormous amount of job satisfaction for the pilots on board both of the vessels 'waltzing.'

Two A.C.L's. commencing the 'Waltz!'

We have always said, as pilots, that no matter what their size, all ships need looking after whether the charge is an A.C.L. container vessel, a tanker for Tranmere Oil Stages or a coaster bound for Birkenhead, Garston, or Eastham Locks. It is also a fact, as in so many walks of life, that the pilot is: "only as good as his last job." "

The above article in 'Ships Monthly' was accompanied by a shorter article, which I include here. It was in effect, a brief description of the Port of Liverpool at that time: December 2005.

"Every evening, visitors to New Brighton can look across the River Mersey at the huge expanse of the Royal Seaforth Dock and note its empty quays and idle gantry cranes. (Now too, they may note the addition of the huge, red, post Panamax gantry cranes of the Liverpool 2 river container terminal to the west of Gladstone Dock). They will probably conclude that the port is dead and not what it was in 'the good old days.' What they will not have taken into account is that maybe more than half a dozen container ships will have passed through the dock system on the intervening tides. The port will also have handled more cargoes from ports all over the world than numerous general cargo ships could have loaded and discharged in more than a week only a few decades ago.

Five Liebherr container gantries are each able to cope with in excess of thirty five containers per hour on Seaforth's three main container berths, which handle trade from the Continent, the Mediterranean and the Americas. The smaller gantries on the S1 and S2 berths are in almost constant use with the Irish trade. There is another Ro-Ro terminal located on S1 as well as one at S3 within the Seaforth Dock System and there is also a Ro-Ro berth at the tidal river berth of Twelve Quays across the river at Birkenhead.

Gladstone Lock, the main entrance to the modern Port of Liverpool was opened in 1927 and at that time could accommodate four 'large' vessels of the day. Thankfully the architects who designed the lock took the Panama lock dimensions into consideration and so Liverpool is able to handle Panamax (Maximum for the Panama Canal) bulkers, the largest, of which are more than twenty metres longer than the *Titanic* was. As I write, now of course, 2021, the Panama Canal locks have been increased in size to accommodate 'Post Panamax' size vessels). In addition to the container berths, the dock offers two extensive grain berths, scrap berths and four large vessel berths for handling bulk cargoes as varied as timber, copper, paper, stone and zinc.

In the older dock system to the south, there are facilities for many different types of cargoes. Coal is landed at Gladstone No. 1 branch dock from Australia, South America and South Africa. Cement from Greece was landed (until comparatively recently) at the old Palm Line berths in the South Huskisson No. 1 Branch Dock. The former 'sugar berth' in 'Husky 3' (Huskisson 3), along with other berths in the vicinity now host vessels from all over the world with diverse cargoes including cars. Gladstone No. 1 Branch also berths the large car carriers from Japan, which carry second hand, right hand drive vehicles. From Langton Lock and Dock, south in the system, the port handles smaller bulk carriers such as those bound for the vegetable oil terminals or the scrap berths to load that cargo, which is now fondly known to the German Captains as: "Englische Stückgut," which translates quite simply as: "English General Cargo!"

Located across the River Mersey from the Port of Liverpool is the Port of Birkenhead, an enclosed dock system built on the inlet of the River Birkett. This system, once the home of the big general cargo companies, with two locks handling sometimes as many as seven vessels in and seven vessels out on the tide, all 'five hatch' jobs and big ships in their day, now only operates one lock and is limited to the dimensions of that, the North Lock and its tidal basin. Today large bulkers of 180 metres in length with cargoes such as animal feed are handled. Caustic soda and oils pass through as well as large amounts of pit props from the Western Isles and steel plates. Once, Birkenhead was the home to Manganese Bronze, the company, which cast ship's propellers of all sizes. Sadly this company is no longer in operation.

To the south of Birkenhead are the ship repair yards and dry docks of Cammell Laird, now back in business under new ownership. Further south on what used to be the Cheshire bank are the

Tranmere Oil Terminals. V.L.C.Cs and U.L.C.Cs, albeit part loaded, have berthed at Tranmere. The present imports of crude oil are mainly from the North Sea Oil fields and are carried in small, modern, doubled-hulled tankers of around 130,000 deadweight tons servicing the North Sea fields.

Further south again lies the entrance to the Manchester Ship Canal, Eastham Locks, now no longer handling 'large' general cargo ships, but still busy with smaller tankers to the Stanlow Oil Refinery itself and with many other commodities carried by smaller vessel both to and from the canal.

Across the river from Eastham Locks, lies the Associated British Ports: Port of Garston.

Liverpool may no longer have the volume of traffic navigating the Mersey as in the post war period, but the amount of cargo handled exceeds previous levels and is steadily increasing year after year.

Since I wrote the article, the Liverpool Cruise Terminal, operated by Liverpool City Council has become very popular with cruise liners visiting the beautiful, 'Collage[15]' City of Liverpool. Indeed I 'opened' the terminal in 2009 when I piloted the *Seven Seas Voyager* both to and from the terminal on 'opening day.' We trust that when Covid 19 has finally passed, that the terminal will be as busy as it ever was before, that was at least handling one vessel a week. We may think of Seamus Heaney's words from the time of the 'The Troubles' in Ireland to give us all hope on the issue of Covid 19: "If we can winter this one out, we can summer anywhere."

Liverpool still operates as a major port for the United Kingdom.

---

15 The Liverpool poet Adrian Henry's description of the City.

The Seven Seas Voyager at Liverpool passenger terminal September 2007.

The Seven Seas Voyager

PILOTAGE REORGANISATION IN THE PORT OF LIVERPOOL

With the advent of containerisation, shipping trade was completely revolutionised almost overnight. The container revolution followed the tanker revolution, which took place after the Suez Canal Crisis in 1956, when, following the canal's closure during the conflict, the move was to build ever bigger tankers to carry the precious commodity of oil in ever larger parcels sailing round the Cape of Good Hope to the south of the African continent.

These developments both contributed to the fact that goods, both solid and liquid, were being carried in ever 'larger parcels' and whether these parcels were liquids or gas in tanks, or solids in containers, the vessels carrying them could be ever increased in size. This meant bigger vessels to carry more, but naturally this was to lead to fewer vessels afloat and the need for fewer marine pilots worldwide. As the container revolution marched on, it was in the early 1970s that it was universally recognised that the profession would have to adapt and slim down in numbers.

Liverpool had reached the highest number of pilots in service ever, (apart from when a number of temporary pilots were employed during the Second World War) when I became one of one hundred and eighty six licensed pilots as explained in an earlier chapter.

As all United Kingdom pilots were self-employed, it meant that we ourselves realised that we had a big problem with fewer ships to pilot, not only locally but internationally. The Government was to move necessarily to bring about a new Pilotage Act in 1987. But political changes, such as were necessary need time, the pilots who were alerted recognised the necessity for change and took action themselves. Those who wished to be temporarily released from duty without pay were allowed to go. A reasonable number of United Kingdom pilots, including pilots from Liverpool, took up positions in ports such as Jeddah and other Gulf ports where they were very much in demand.

In 1980, Liverpool pilots took action, knowing that the Pilotage Act of 1913 was to be 'opened up' for both revision and renewal. The pilots representatives chose 'twelve good men and true' to convene at the pilot office every Thursday to examine in detail the Pilotage Act and to determine, what, when the act was opened up, we would like, if it were possible, to have included in the new act. I say pointedly 'if it were possible' with feeling, for in reality little pilot input made its way into the new act.

At this time Liverpool was operating a launch system from the land down at the Western Station at Point Lynas and still had the 179' (55 metres) No. 3 pilot boat *Arnet Robinson* operational at the Bar Light Vessel. This station boat was served by a launch system taking pilots both to and from the operational area, clear of the main channels.

As we sat discussing the future through the examination of the Bye-Laws from the 1913 Pilotage Act, I began to formulate some ideas about the future of the service of my own. Ideas came to me and I would scribble them down along with the notes, which I was making during these Thursday meetings.

Lunchtimes were interesting on these Thursdays, for the idea of the pilots traditional lunchtime 'pie and a pint,' for this committee did not seem appropriate under the circumstances. I came up with the idea that we proceed from the Pier Head up to Hope Street and the renowned Everyman Bistro, which was under the Everyman Theatre itself. The Everyman Theatre did not normally take bookings, but the idea of twelve Liverpool marine pilots having lunch with them every Thursday must have had a certain appeal, for we were able to book one of the large 'round the pillar' tables for every Thursday lunch time for all the many months, during which we were to meet.

My scribblings, which included a pen sketch of a pilot boat in
No.2 Canning Graving Dock situated behind the old 'purpose
built' pilot office on Canning Pier Head, helped my thoughts to
be positive about the concept of exploring ways to operate a new
streamlined service in the future. Like minded colleagues such as
John Westwood, John Tebay and Geoff Topp, along with many
others, were all looking towards our future.

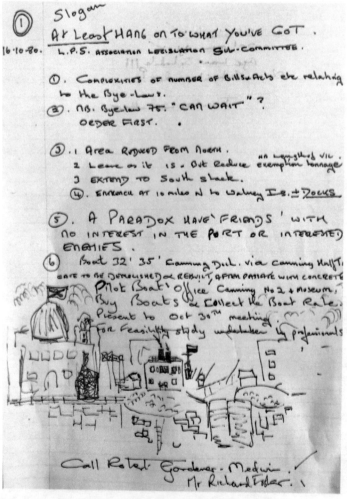

Sketch of the pilot boat in Canning Dry Dock.

My thoughts led me back in time before the advent of first steam pilot boat the S.S. *Francis Henderson*, which was introduced in 1896. Prior to this event, the pilots owned the sailing pilot boats themselves. They apparently did not want the responsibility of 'owning' a concern as complicated and expensive as a steam pilot boat. The 'ownership' of course was questionable as we shall see later in the chapter and formed one of my arguments for what I called an 'Independent Pilotage Authority' in the Port of Liverpool.

I believed that the Humber Pilots were operating their own 'Boat Service' at that time and that the Milford Haven Pilots were operating their own 'independent pilot service,' in that, for example, the pilots themselves collected their own pilotage dues from the shipping agents for services rendered. These pilots would meet once a month to share out these earnings equally. Basically these two operations were to form the basis for an investigation into the future of our own service.

I was not a member of our executive committee at that time and needed to present myself before them to ask permission for the service to commence an official investigation into the possibilities of the realisation of my ideas. The start of such an investigation I could see was to be with a visit to both pilot services then operating on the Humber and in the Bristol Channel.

The executive readily agreed to the idea and authorised myself as the one who would undertake these visits, understanding that a volunteer with some ideas was possibly going to be best positioned to offer options for our future in these troubled times. A young member of the executive committee was appointed to accompany me and thus make the visits 'official.'

At the end of 1980, Liverpool was hosting the United Kingdom Pilot's Association[16] Conference at the Adelphi Hotel and there

---

16 Now the United Kingdom Maritime Pilot's Association. This addition was made not to confuse us with airline pilots and even though we were on the sea long before they were in the air, we changed!

I was able to meet the Senior Representatives of both ports. Following this introduction, I was invited to make a visit to both ports.

Both of these visits were made in the December of 1980 and the resulting paper, which I wrote was presented to the Liverpool Pilot Service early in the January of 1981. The date would indicate that this report was written on a typewriter in days sometime before word processors and, indeed, the duplication was achieved on a photocopier at the pilot office. In all it was a painstaking process.

Each pilot received a copy of the paper by post. On the evening tide on the day of the postal delivery, I was outward bound from Eastham Locks on a coaster and John Westwood was inward bound for the QEII Lock on a Shell tanker. I both valued and respected John's opinion on pilotage politics of the day. We were to pass in the Eastham channel. With trepidation, I called him up on the V.H.F. radio channel, which I knew he was using to direct his tug boats and asked him what he thought of my efforts. His reply gave me great pleasure. In a very stern 'John Westwood voice' he said: "John, I have read the paper and you have gone well beyond your brief..." This was followed by the truly heartening words expressed in a much warmer tone: "... and God bless you for it!"

The following pages contain an amended transcript of that paper. The rest of this chapter may be considered as 'hard going' for the casual reader, if this proves to be the case for you, my apologies and may I suggest that you move on to the following chapter. I wish, however for the chapter to remain as it is for the record of the history contained within it. (J.L.C.)

"Pilotage Reorganisation in the Port of Liverpool."

Stage 1: A REPORT TOWARDS THE SETTING UP OF A PROFFESSIONAL INVESTIGATION INTO THE LEGAL AND FINANCIAL VIABILITY OF ESTABLISHING AN INDEPENDENT PILOTAGE AUTHORITY IN THE PORT.

Prepared by J. L. Curry, Pilot. Presented January 1981.

Acknowledgements.

For whatever interest or value this report contains, may I thank the Liverpool Pilot's Association for their support in the passing of the original proposition regarding the permission necessary, for me to undertake this venture. May I also thank Clive Wilkin on the Humber and Ian Evans of Milford Haven for both their hospitality and for their cooperation in supplying me with invaluable information on the subject of setting up an independent pilotage authority.

A Preface.

Gentlemen, as we are aware this is our business. As better men than myself have said before me, may I say that in times of expansion or in times of recession, in a rising port or in a port in decline, perhaps the most desirable situation for pilots to be in is to be in control of all that appertains to their destinies, so far as control is possible.

Looking to both the Humber and to Milford Haven, two ports as separate and distinct from each other even as they are from Liverpool, we have examples of two ports, whose pilots have already become convinced that this is the case and they have taken the first steps to achieve this control in the form of independent pilotage authorities.

It is to these two ports, which I have turned to for the groundwork for our possible professional investigation. Milford Haven have from the 1st of November 1980, been operating an independent pilotage authority, but have had to relinquish claims to either the management or 'ownership' of the 'Pilot Boat Company' for six years as part of their negotiations with Trinity House and Milford Haven Conservancy Board.

The Humber, on the other hand, now has both management control of and pilot directors on the board of the 'Humber Pilot Cutter Company.' They are negotiating for 'ownership' of the company, which will lead to the establishment of a Humber independent pilotage authority.

As we are aware from our representatives, from reports from members of the Liverpool Pilot Association's Legislation Sub-Committee (The 'twelve good men and true' mentioned earlier). and from reports in the national press, the 'battle lines' are drawn up. The battlefield will prove and only after fierce struggles, decisive to our very existence and right to be on the bridge of a ship. I trust that international fears for the safety of lives, both ashore and afloat and fears for the safety of the environment, coupled with sound common sense will eventually give pilots the victory.

The national battleground, however, must not be divorced from our own situation and the strength of the Liverpool Pilot Service that is vital to the national effort. If our strength may be concentrated through independence, I suggest we may well find a resulting efficiency that will benefit all pilots in general and the safety of all users of this port in particular.

My own convictions are not strictly relevant to this report for I do not possess a crystal ball, merely I wish to be as objective as I can be in presenting certain facts of information that I have learned from financial accounts provided by the Humber and from legal files provided by Milford Haven along with some ideas of my own, which have developed from the study of these documents.

With the present Pilotage Order and Bye-Laws laying open before us for revision, the possibility of radical change is probably nearer than it ever will be again this century. With our long served pilot cutters, 'boat dinosaurs', obsolete as they float in their present condition and in desperate need of some form of refit or replacement, perhaps the desirability for independence is also with us. This is what our investigation will prove and after that the choice will be ours.

A brief résumé so far:

Having started literally from scratch at the first compulsory meeting of the Liverpool Pilots Association's sub-committee for legislation with a few ideas based on the principle: 'At least hang on to what you've got', I progressed through the emotions of the special general meeting held on October 30th, to the general meeting in November. Here I was referred to the November executive meeting where a proposition contained within my letter was taken to the vote and carried by 17 to 4 with 3 abstentions. The proposition was as follows: 'That this Association agrees to involve itself in a professional investigation into both the legal and financial aspects of the viability of establishing, what is in effect, an independent pilotage authority in the Port of Liverpool.'

I had offered both my time and efforts should the Association so wish it and it was decided that I should indeed be given the task of carrying out stage 1 assisted by a member of the executive committee, to be decided, as I was at that time not a member.

From the executive I then had the good fortune to be introduced to both Clive Wilkin and Ian Evans at the reception held for the U.K. pilot's conference, which was being held at the Adelphi hotel in Liverpool later that week. (as mentioned earlier) Both gentlemen cordially invited me to visit them and observe their pilotage operations and also offered their co-operation in whatever I was seeking.

Back to the December general meeting for further support from the Association and there a unanimous decision granted me both the time and expenses to undertake the acceptance of both invitations. With some good fortune and with the total co-operation of both the Humber and Milford Haven, the visits were completed within ten days of that meeting. At the December executive meeting, I expressed the hope of completing a comprehensive Stage 1 report by mid-January 1981.

Observations from the Humber visit on 05: 12: 1980.

I observed a very efficient pilotage operation organised by pilots. The service with a compliment of 150 pilots is not far removed from our own in numbers. The operation is under the supervision of a Pilot Manager who is himself a licence holder. Two outside managers had been found unsuitable for the task. Apart from administrative duties, which concern most of his working life, the pilotage manager occasionally takes 'a turn' on the rota list. There is only a rota list, appropriation has been dispensed with, the V.L.C.Cs being piloted on a 'middle cut' basis.

A pilot office is situated at Hull with all the amenities, which our own pilot office affords with the exception of the shore master's office. Humber Radio is installed above the pilot office, whilst thirty miles downstream is situated the most impressive part of the Humber operation: Pilot Control. The Humber pilots have built a tower, not dissimilar to the M.D.H.C. tower at Seaforth. Beneath the tower lies a wartime gun emplacement, which has been converted into the Spurn pilot station, which is very similar to and indeed incorporates ideas from our own Point Lynas pilot station.

The secret of the success of the Humber operation lies in the control tower on Spurn Point. I believe that the secret of our future here in Liverpool also lies in a control tower. This need not necessarily be the Seaforth control tower, but having that one already built at great expense and it being only partially occupied, it would seem, that with the supposed good relations between ourselves and the port, that to build another would be beyond the common sense, to which I have already referred to.

Humber pilots began 'port control', now operated from the purpose built tower, by bringing their last remaining pilot cutter, (our own No. 4, the *William M Clark*), into dock by themselves. From her they took the radars and installed them in a caravan lashed down against both wind and sea on Spurn Point. Further examples of pilot involvement in Port control are to be found elsewhere and I cite Hamburg as one. No one can deny the efficiency of either the Humber or Hamburg following pilot participation in port control. I trust that Liverpool, unlike these two quoted ports, objections, if any, would be minimal. Should the case prove otherwise, we have the tenacity shown by both of these ports as an example towards Liverpool pilots achieving ultimate success in this venture.

Spurn Pilot Control is both manned and sited as our shore master's office should be manned and sited. It is manned by a licensed pilot master, but for twenty four hours a day and is situated at a great height overlooking the seaward, pilot operation. The pilot master is one of seven. Six of these are catered for on the work index, the seventh being subsidised by the pilots themselves. The pilot master is assisted by a rota pilot who is manned in his own turn from the working list. The two are further assisted by a clerk.

The control tower is equipped with V.H.F. radios, radars, which include Decca Spot[17] in their function, Telex, which receives E.T.A.s and with G.P.O. telephones. Pilots may phone into a four line answering service, which gives a full disposition broadcast of ship's movements, pilots turns on the working list, weather reports, forecasts and navigation warnings, which is updated every hour.

Every inward bound vessel is boarded by one of either six anchorage pilots who are on a twenty four hour duty period at

---

17 Decca Spot: One of the many sophisticated radar surveillance systems being developed at this time.

Spurn, or by a pilot brought to the pilot station to board a vessel on her E.T.A if the vessel is docking on arrival. Vessels riding to an anchor, awaiting docking orders are maned for docking according to their anchorage times and docking pilots are brought to Spurn by road in good time to board their ships by fast launch before the regulated docking time or for the tide.

Three launches are based at the Spurn jetty and are fully manned at all times. A fourth is based at Hull to deal with vessels bound further upriver to Goole or bound for the Trent.

The Humber pilots are engaged in a fierce battle over the granting of exemption certificates. The first Dutch master has been granted an exemption certificate for a 13,000 ton ferry in January of this year. (1979). Loss of piloting this vessel, will lead to severe financial loss to each licensed pilot per annum. This will also lead to the inevitable reduction in numbers of pilots as other E.E.C. vessels apply for exemption certificates. We have lived with exemption in Liverpool for many years, but may I stress the vital importance of establishing a realistic limit to the number of certificates allowed. Also in the interests of safety the importance of the necessity to restrict Bye-Law, with a maximum acceptable size, draught and also acceptable nature of hazardous cargoes, vessels eligible.

Despite the implications of what exemption could mean to the Humber, Humber pilots are convinced of the advantage of both the ownership of the 'Cutter Company' and of the establishment of an independent pilotage authority.

Observations from the Milford Haven visit on 08: 12: 1980.

Here I observed a very efficient body of pilots operating in the first weeks of establishing their independent pilotage authority. Milford Haven Pilots had overcome all objections and were able to offer full details of the entire legal procedure that was followed to 'independence' in Milford Haven.

The new statutory instrument, which bears the title: "The Milford Haven Pilotage Order 1980," is impressive and the Milford Haven pilots talked me through the process, which covers the period commencing with the first letters on the subject through to the completion of the order itself.

The 'Authority' consists of nine members of whom three are elected by the pilots themselves, two are appointed by the Milford Haven Conservancy Board, two are appointed by the General Council of Shipping, one is appointed by the statutory authorities in Milford Haven and one is an independent member, at present a master mariner chosen by the pilots. The Chairman of the Authority is a pilot and a young solicitor has been appointed by the Authority as full time secretary.

Ian Evans confirmed my belief that the legal proceedings would be easier, if considered desirable, with the existing Pilotage Order and the Bye-Laws appertaining to the order being open for revision. Milford Haven pilots are also engaged, as the Humber pilots are, in a fierce battle concerned with the granting of exemption certificates. For Milford Haven's independent pilotage authority it is early days and for them the possibility of reorganisation of the launch system (The Boat Rate Company). and of a 'pilot control' for the port is ostensibly six years away, yet their conviction is absolute.

Ground Work for the Legal Aspect.

I have been fortunate enough to have the legal advice of a marine solicitor friend who has in confidence, assisted me in my deliberations so far. Both he and Ian Evans accepted my analogy of a sextant sun sight[18] in relation to the procedure. The decision is taken to proceed as a sextant altitude is taken by observation. The 'sights' are worked up and result in a position of the ship on

---

18 Sextant sun sight: Satellite navigation was still in its early days and mariners were still well used to fixing their position on the Earth's surface by the use of astronomical navigation with sextants.

the Earth's surface, which in the legal procedure results in an independent pilotage authority.

At this point let us bear in mind that in our present order: 'The pilot boat rate shall be payable to the Authority[19]...' and that: The Authority may (from time to time) build, purchase or hire and employ in the pilotage service as many boats or vessels (of whatever kind and however propelled) as shall in their opinion be required for that service[20]...'

Here then are the simple legal steps, which I understand must be taken to establish an independent pilotage authority. The steps themselves are 'simple,' although obviously Gentlemen, the effort to achieve each one may possibly require both great strength and fortitude:

1) Signatures from pilots requesting a reorganisation of the Pilotage Authority are presented to an official body. (In Milford's case all pilots signed the request and 'the official body' was the United Kingdom's Pilot Association).

2) The 'official body' presents the request to the Department of Trade[21].

3) The D.O.T then sends in an independent commission chairman who forms a committee to consider the case. (At Milford Haven the committee consisted of the D.O.T. chairman, pilots, ship owners and Milford Haven Conservancy Board representatives).

4) The committee produces an order.

---

19 Authority: In those days the Port Authority, which changed to the: Competent Harbour Authority (C.H.A.) in the wording of the 1987 Pilotage Act.

20 Possibly self-explanatory, but referring to the provision of the necessary means of transport for the conveying of pilots to and from their charges.

21 D.O.T: Government body, name subsequently changed to D.T.I. (Department of Trade and Industry.) now all changed again...

5) The order is presented to the Secretary of State. (Trinity House presented the Milford Haven order).

6) The order progresses through both Houses of Parliament, with a final six weeks objection period followed by a further six week petition period.

Thereafter the 'sun sight' analogy position is obtained in the form of an independent pilotage authority. Dare I add: Q.E.D?

Ground work for the Financial Aspect.

This one is possibly the most difficult problem of the two as we may imagine Gentlemen. The Humber reorganisation is based on the concept that the secret lies in the accounts. I was allowed to sight copies of both the proposed estimated accounts of the 1974 Humber Pilotage Organisation Sub-Committee and the actual accounts for the year ending December 31st 1979. The Humber accounts proved an increased efficiency in the existing 'Cutter Company,' which was replaced by a new company with pilots as directors.

With regard to our own 'Boat Rate Company,' I am convinced that with offers such as the use of a computer[22] and with contacts offering the use of dry docks and oil supplies from our colleagues already on the books, together with the memory of episodes in our history such as the *Girl Jean*[23], how can any doubt the ability to succeed in increasing the efficiency of the 'Boat Rate Company?' The Service is, however, thankfully composed of 'devil's advocates,' whose energies, I trust, will eventually unite to achieve whatever we decide we wish to achieve.

---

22 A fact possibly difficult to comprehend now, but computers were only in their early stages of development and few were privately owned!

23 *Girl Jean* was an ex-fishing boat owned privately by a group of Liverpool pilots under the leadership of Pilot Alan Lang and had been used as a pilot boat down at Point Lynas during a strike action taken by the floating plant of the M.D.H.B (Mersey Docks and Harbour Board) in the sixties.

I have been fortunate to have had the advice of a chartered accountant friend, who like my marine solicitor friend has in confidence assisted me in my deliberations so far. We have obtained a set of the eight basic questions regarding the financing of a new company from another friend who is the District Corporate Manager of one of the large banks. To 'buy' the company we should have to answer all eight questions satisfactorily.

However, before even asking these questions, I would like to examine the 'Guardianship Argument' at present being employed by the Humber. The Humber pilots gave over the ownership of the assets of the 'Cutter Company' to the Humber Conservancy Board in 1948. The Board in turn 'handed over' the ownership of the said assets to the British Transport Dock Board in 1968.

In 1974 the Humber found that they were faced with the need for major changes in pilotage operations, even as we are now faced with the same necessity. The estimated accounts for the proposed new company were accepted by the B.T.D.B., (British Transport Dock Board) but ownership of the 'Cutter Company' was denied unless the sum of 1.1 million pounds was paid to them for the existing assets of the company.

The ship owners, when asked to assist in the raising of the necessary sum, not unreasonably pointed out the fact that they had already paid for these assets through the payment of the Landing and Boarding Rate! (The ship owner pays a twofold bill for any act of pilotage in the United Kingdom. The one: for the act of pilotage itself and the other: for the necessary means to transport the pilot to or from a vessel).

At present, an application for 'guardianship' of what I shall now describe as the 'Boat Rate Company' of the Humber has been made on behalf of the Humber Pilots to Parliament and they await the decision, which they hope will simply 'give back the guardianship' that the pilots had prior to 1948.

Our present 'Boat Rate Company' has been in the hands of the M.D.H.B (now M.D.H.C.) since the 'Mersey Docks Act of 1881'. The written down assets for the year ending December 31st 1979, plus the addition of further radar equipment during 1980, are valued in the region of 0.75 million. Our present authority may well be delighted to concur with the 'Guardianship Argument' to allow us to improve the efficiency of a pilotage operation in Liverpool, which like the Humber operation, now faces major changes.

Handling our own business would allow us to use our own monies to our advantage rather than accept quarterly settlements from the M.D.H.C with regard to pilotage dues. With this point in mind let us remember that the main object of the financial exercise of a 'Boat Rate Company' is to minimise that boat rate to maximise dues. A pilotage authority 'Boat Rate Company', we know must not make money, but let us not forget that the Humber's operation has increased efficiency and minimised the boat rate for the ship owners. Should we not also 'Take up the Slack' and minimise the boat rate to maximise dues?

Toward Stage II.

'Legally' we must now ask a firm of solicitors to confirm my own findings and consider their application to the Port of Liverpool.

'Financially' we should employ a chartered accountant to assist pilots to produce an estimate of accounts for a twelve month period for a 'Boat Rate Company' owned by an independent pilotage authority. I would suggest that incorporated in such accounts must be carefully 'checked out' ideas from a pool of pilot's contributions regarding contacts and offers such as the computer already mentioned.

Eventually an official pilot, organisation sub-committee would have to be set up, which included pilots and representatives of both M.D.H.C. and ship owners to consider the implications of our own findings if we should discover that we are convinced of both the viability and of the desirability of establishing an independent pilotage authority in the Port of Liverpool.

Ideas on what we might expect to achieve:

We would expect to achieve efficiency, which we could well wish for in this new era of pilotage which will follow the introduction of the new act. We have already acknowledged that a cruising pilot cutter is extremely expensive, both to buy and to maintain. Reorganisation could well influence any replacement more strongly in favour of pilot's wishes, to serve the port as we have done for over two hundred years.

I believe that the secret of our future operations lies in an operation based in a "Control Tower." A shore based station, which is manned twenty for hours a day by a shore master assisted by a rota pilot and a clerk. Radar coverage of the Bar Anchorage, of the channel approaches and of the river should be considered essential. Pilotage participation in Port Control would then be constant and not simply as an 'emergency measure' as it is now.

With our own company, strike action of crews would not cripple our boarding and landing facilities as it does now. The Humber launches are manned by pilots in times of strike action much in the same way as we both provided and manned the *Girl Jean* as mentioned earlier.

With major changes in legislation still undecided, we should ensure that safety is our main concern as it always has been. Safety after all is the very essence of pilotage. To do this we should insist on pilot surveillance over all traffic moving through both channel approaches and in the river itself.

We should consider the present Lynas Pilot Station, with its proven efficiency as our vital western outpost. We should man it with a team of anchorage pilots on a 24 hour tour of duty. We too should board every ship upon its arrival. Those not docking on arrival would be anchored at Lynas and Liverpool informed so that a docking pilot might be manned off in time for a regulated docking time or for a particular tide. Those docking on arrival would be catered for on an E.T.A. manning from Liverpool, a system, which would be assisted by the new E.T.A, Bye-Law, which is reaching its final stage as I write. (1980)

Ships arriving from the north would either be boarded to anchor on arrival to await a regulated docking time or for the tide as at Point Lynas. Boarding at the Bar must either be 'on arrival' of an E.T.A. from a 50' launch in suitable weather conditions, or from a tidal cutter, which the boat rate must provide for. I appreciate that a replacement for our present cruising pilot cutter is being negotiated and I trust that a craft that may operate in similar conditions during tide time will be the result. I have previously mentioned at meetings the Le Havre tidal cutter. This is 'one of a type', which, yet to be confirmed, are 'off the peg' jobs, built in Holland. It occurs to me that we may pursue the idea of a quote into the conversion of a North Sea trawler, many, of which are virtually new and barely used, laid up since the decline in the fishing industry.

May we not also consider that at no great expense, as our 40' launches are replaced in time that one could be 'mothballed' in Douglas, where, in the shelter of the Isle of Man, even northerly storm force ten would hold no stresses for such a craft as would even be normally expected in operational conditions at Point Lynas?

Pilot services need recruits from youth and I would like to believe that with our moral obligation to 54 young men who are now on our 'closed list' for Liverpool, that we might endeavour to make renewed efforts to support John Tebay's concept of "Early Pilotage Involvement" for all prospective United Kingdom pilots of the future. We, through lack of understanding, have inadvertently lost what we all believe to be the finest pilot training scheme possible. Interest in our own independence could well result in our own boathand's interests being catered for too[24].

Finally to the concept of a disused pilot cutter serving as both a superb pilot office, as well as being a treasure for prosperity. I have been in contact with the Director of Liverpool Museums and he has expressed great interest in the possibility of a pilot cutter in the Canning Graving Docks.

We know from our representatives that the figure placed on No. 2 Pilot Boat, the *Edmund Gardner*, would not build a new pilot office. Yet would not a cutter so placed in Canning Dry Dock provide a magnificent office for pilots? I am certain that an architect of our acquaintance would produce a splendid adaptation of a pilot cutter, which at minimum draught, with our expertise, could be floated into Canning via Canning Half Tide Gateway on a ten meter tide at minimum expense. From such an office, our administration block could once again view the river and assist in bringing life back to the South Dock System[25].

Conclusion.

Tradition and radical change in balance are what I believe is necessary within our Service in 1981. Pilotage participation in Port Control is essential for the future. Boarding off the Rock Lighthouse is not a new idea and remember the magnificent painting by J. Witham: "Follow the Leader?" Let us determine 'to lead' our pilotage operation into the 1980s, taking up any slack ourselves in order to offer a continued tradition of both safety

---

24 The 'boathand' training scheme for Liverpool has been described through my own career path in earlier pages of this book and more comprehensively in "East a Half South."

25 The Liverpool Pilots had been moved out of their purpose built pilot office by the M.D.H.C. and into the only known 'Underground pilot office' in the basement of the M.D.H.B. building some years earlier. The old pilot office, however, I like to think was the 'spark,' which ignited the flame, which brought the derelict South Dock System back to life. The building was the first in the system to be utilised by Liverpool Museums.

and efficiency, yet in addition controlling our own destinies more closely than pilots have been able to do for almost a century.

Events were to overtake our efforts to achieve an independent pilotage authority in Liverpool. We were to be taken into employment as one of the results of the Pilotage Act of 1987 when it came into force. I have covered our battle to return to self-employment and indeed what could be loosely described as an independence that Milford Haven had achieved in 1979 in the forming of the 'Liverpool Pilots Company' Limited in "East Half South." This 'independence' was achieved in the July of 1997 when we returned to self-employment.

What we were able to achieve before 1987, was pilot involvement in the radar tower and better than a 'floating dinosaur' of a floating, pilot cutter renewal as depicted in my report, but a far more efficient total launch boarding and disembarking operation from the Liverpool Pier Head and Woodside Stage on the Birkenhead side of the river to where we moved our pilot office 'above ground!'

I worked on the system along with others and was, indeed the first 'Pilot Master' on duty in the radar tower on the day the system was implemented and the *Arnet Robinson* was withdrawn from station for the very last time and was put into 'mothballs' on the 1st July 1982.

We did not convert a pilot cutter into a pilot office, but the chairman of the time, John Tebay and myself, did have lunch with the then Director of Liverpool Museums, Richard Foster (later Sir Richard Foster) and as a result of that meeting, Liverpool Museums paid £7000 (a nominal amount to cover the cost of the relatively new galley stoves) for the then laid up No.2 Pilot Boat *Edmund Gardner*. Not long after, a crew of volunteer pilots (who voted me as captain!) shifted the vessel from her lay-by berth in the North Dock System, dead ship (with no engines) with two tug boats assisting, south to a berth in Princes Dock near to the

Pier Head. Here she was prepared for visitors and indeed, first opened there to the public as part of the museum.

Subsequently, *Edmund Gardner* was shifted again under her own power from Princes Dock via the river to Canning Dry Dock No.2 in the South Dock system, again with volunteer pilots as her crew where she is now both kept and maintained by the Liverpool Maritime Museum and where she may be visited by the public. When I visit her myself on the 'Unofficial Leadsman[26]' outings, or simply pass by, I think of that rough pen sketch made in my notes at that meeting so many years ago.

No.2 Pilot Boat, Edmund Gardner in Canning Dry Dock.

---

26 'The Unofficial Leadsman': The guided tour around the *Edmund Gardner*, on which I take newly authorised pilots as part of their induction into the service. It is in effect 'a visit into all our histories.' The explanation as to how this 'leadsman' came about is covered in "East a Half South." To me it sometimes seems that I am a living dinosaur and that the pilot boat is my cave!

(Whilst visiting the Humber, Clive Wilkin was to make me a present of a Humber Pilot's tie. The motif on the tie was a pilot flag on a staff, superimposed upon a foul anchor. (A 'foul or fouled' anchor is the artistic depiction of an anchor with a rope cable wrapped around the shank). Both above and below the design was a white over red band all on a navy blue background. Later I was to modify this design by replacing the anchor with a Liver Bird. This tie is the one still worn by Liverpool Pilots as I write).

The Liverpool Pilot's Tie.

"TO WHOM IT MAY CONCERN..."

Marine Pilot's Injustice.

Who can I write to?
Who can I tell?

When the charge is committed,
Still afloat,
Not yet subject to the Lutine Bell,
'Though she may be,
Were it not for the pilot's hands
Keeping her away from the grasping sands.
All's well, when it goes well.
No problem,
No need for a professional man,
'Til the tide turns
And 'the shit hits the fan...'
Then: with one or no tugs,
Main engines gone, thrusters too,
Who will it be then
Who carries the can?

Chlorine, methane, propane gasses,
Released so simply by: possibly a Greek,
Straying too far up an unknown creek,
Striking the gas carrier with her prow
"How fares the wind for England" now?
Conservation, preservation,
The planet's already a wreck.
Don't sink it simply for the sake
Of a licensed pilot's check.

Worthless or worthwhile,
We have guarded you

For more tha two centuries,
Whilst you slept, peacefully,
My hands care for you,
Will bring you flowers in the morning,
Not only in the spring time
But in the winter too.

Who can I write to?
Who can I tell?

Written following a near disastrous breakdown aboard a Polish, sulphur tanker in-bound for the Manchester Ship Canal on the 28th October 1987. In the early 1980s during the period that "The Twelve Good Men and True" were meeting in Liverpool and after the port's visits and the report mentioned previously, I was to write a letter to the press following a newspaper article by a certain Stephen Aris in December 1984. I sent copies to my local M.P., David Hunt and I also sent copies to all M.Ps of the constituencies bordering the River Mersey. I reproduce the letter here believing that it is as relevant today as it was then and will be still in the future, when and if ever again, pilotage in the United Kingdom should come up for revision.

Dear Sir,

As one of 'the few' who is at present proud to protect my country's shoreline by virtue of the responsibility entrusted to me by licence, I would like to reply to Stephen Aris' article: "Dropping the Pilot[27]" of the 7th inst.

My last charge as a marine pilot, a vessel of less than 1600 tons carrying heavy fuel oil, has recently been reduced in crew numbers by three during the preceding twelve months: one engineer, one

---

27 Dropping the pilot: A reference to the famous cartoon by Sir John Tenniel, 'Punch' magazine 1980, where *Bismark* is depicted as a marine pilot 'going overboard' and leaving the German people to their fate.

donkey-man and one pantry boy. Job losses appear to be necessary during the present recession and throughout this era of increasing unemployment. Do we now propose to take away the marine pilot and his insurance from the ship's master thus increasing the stress upon ship's masters further?

Having had the good fortune to have been licensed as a marine pilot at the tender age of twenty four and thus now being forty years of age, with sixteen years of both experience and pleasure in my vocation as a pilot, I wish to point out to both the ship owner and the general public the danger of: "Trimming the pilot's sails." (The latter term a quote from the article).

Now although being forty years of age, I am accorded a "Peter Pan" status by some of my more elderly colleagues. "You are only a young man" they say. My sad reply to them and my message to the country is that we have no 'young' pilots training at present, as I did, to continue protecting the shores of the United Kingdom.

"Without the sap rising, the old tree will wither and die" is an acceptable concept in all fields of expertise. We need marine pilots, the *Amoco Cadiz*[28] was not fiction and £20,000, the average earnings (of a marine pilot at that time) as quoted by Stephen Aris, would not even begin to pay for the effluents necessary to commence a 'mopping up operation' following an oil spill caused by an error of judgement in the treacherous waters of the Liverpool Pilotage District, or indeed in any of the other thirty nine pilotage districts in the United Kingdom.

It is true to say that whilst the general public work, or whilst they sleep, marine pilots, who are both highly skilled and highly trained, guide vessels safely in and out of our ports. Cargoes such as chlorine gas and other 'nasties' in such quantities that many would not sleep at night if they knew that these cargoes were

---

28 Amoco Cadiz : One of several marine catastrophes of the 20th century, which resulted in an oil spillage with extensive pollution and damage to both wildlife and the environment.

passing 'so close to their beds', are dealt with, with a dedication that is normal for we "proud men with no humility." (Another quote from Stephen's article).

At present we are asking for nothing other than to preserve that, which we have for the safety of all and of the environment: our Pilotage Districts. Our exemption from pilotage certificates, which are granted to regular users of the ports after both tuition and guidance followed by examination, are also under fire.

We are few in number, but we are the insurance that trade between the United Kingdom and the rest of the world may continue with the maximum of safety possible in the future as it has done in the past.

May I recommend that during discussions re: the green paper[29] the government of Margaret Thatcher considers an extension of the operations of marine pilotage rather than the reduction in the limits of pilotage areas, a foolish act that would simply serve to line the 'ship owning pockets' further whilst risking both our shoreline and our heritage.

Yours Sincerely,

John Curry. Liverpool Pilot

---

29 The 'green paper' referred to was the forerunner of the white paper, which resulted in the Pilotage Act of 1987.

Sir John Tenniel's sketch: 'Dropping the Pilot.'

When the dust settled after the publication of the act and after a great deal of local political fighting in all ports, eventually the necessary reduction in numbers, as was always understood to be the prime objective of the exercise, was achieved and resulted in the desired streamlined pilot services. Some of the other unwanted outcomes, which were feared and did come about, took longer to resolve. Liverpool after being employed as a result of the act finally returned to self-employment in 1997 with the setting up of the co-operative: Liverpool Pilot's Limited.

An Exclusive Club?

Now that it is 'all over,'
Laughter has died,
Even as the ebb has flowed far
Leaving a stench of cigar smoke
Clinging to the non-smoker's clothes,
A still, stale-spilled, beer-scent
Lingering around the ash trays
In the dawn light.

The wooden tables are not so well polished,
Nor the carpets so luxuriously piled
As they appeared to be
In the magical 'candle-light' of the evening
Before the last launch ferried the members
Back to a final, distant shore.

The accountant's bottom line is more important now
Than sandy, rock bottoms,
Which we avoided to further a cargo, safely.
Cargo, not only financial, but one,
Including the lives of those guarding it
And those downwind of Chlorine gas
And other hazardous cargoes,
Which pass the Pier head by night.

The cruel hands of the Crosby Sands
Are no less cruel than they ever were,
Even with pilot's at the helm,
But "East a Half South,"
A compass course, means little to a politician.

Shakespeare's Moor
Arrived on stage during a Tempest.

One of the three witches cut off a pilot's thumb.
"Left hand down a bit," or "Port Easy"
Is not a radio joke
When the charge 'kisses' an unfriendly wall of stone,
But gently.
Captain and pilot make their farewells
Safely, as safely sleep all those on land
When prizes may be torn from a trusty, steady hand.
Bright fares the morrow, but "how fares the wind for England"
now?
Will the last one out, please close the door?

TREVOR'S TAXIS

When I was a boathand, (that is a pilot apprentice) pilots, including my father, would often travel from Birkenhead to Bangor by train. Initially the trains ran from the L.M.S. built, overland, train station at Woodside to Chester. At Chester a change of train would mean then that the pilots would be travelling on the London to Holyhead train. Quite often this would be the renowned *Emerald Isle Express*. Following the reduction in the numbers of pilot boats from four to three and therefore, when there was no longer a 'running boat', travelling by train was the most frequent means of pilot transport down to the western station. (That is before the late nineteen eighties when travel became exclusively overland by taxi[30]).

At Bangor Station pilots would be met by Jones' Taxis for the drive across Menai Bridge and then on over the Island of Anglesey to the Port of Amlwch, where they would be picked up by a boarding punt to be taken out to the waiting pilot cutter offshore. When outward bound, the pilots would land either at Amlwch, or if the winds were to the north of west-north-west, in the shelter of Moelfre Bay at the R.N.L.I. Lifeboat Slip.

When I first became a pilot, this was the usual way that pilots would make the journeys both to and from Point Lynas Station. That is except for 'changeover day' when the pilot boat relieving the station boat would carry the complement of pilots for that day from the Prince's Landing Stage at lunch time with her to the west. Just occasionally taxis would be employed from Birkenhead, Woodside to the island. In the August of 1973, when I became a first class pilot, the system for a five weeks tour of duty was for three weeks 'sea turns', (bringing the ships inbound) followed by

---

30 When Liverpool pilots became employed, The M.D.H.C. realised that it was cheaper to pay for taxis than for more numbers of pilots, if the existing pilots could be whisked swiftly to and from the Western Station by road, thus making them available for duty sooner. An arrangement the pilots themselves welcomed as mentioned in the text.

two weeks 'longshore,' (taking the ships outward bound).

Pilots were organised in groups and I was placed in Group 1, Black, Section A, sub-section e. My other immediate colleagues holding the other letters were John Cowen, Bill Wood and Sam Couch. Sam had held both of the letters 'd' and 'e' until I joined the group. We would usually commence the tour by travelling together by train down to the Western Station. Twenty four hours later after completing our first inward passage, there we would almost certainly be together again on the train bound for the Lynas Station. So often was this the case, that we often referred to ourselves as the 'Railway Children.'

Early on in the 'dark period' of the M.D.H.C. employment, when we were operating a one list system, each pilot was asked what we thought of the idea of travelling by taxi both ways? Every single pilot said: 'Great idea!' It would be true to say that none of us had really thought the idea through, for what it meant in reality was that, for instance: if the pilot had landed in Anglesey after it was possible to catch the last train back to Birkenhead, there would be no 'all night' in bed at the hostel, followed by breakfast before the homeward journey, but rather it meant that a taxi would be waiting engine revving, ready to whisk the pilot back home in approximately two hours so that as soon as he reached there he would be back on the eligible list, ready to go again.

That of course meant the need for fewer pilots, which kept the cost down for the employers. When this came into operation, however, not one of us would have had the new system of travel changed.

Also when I was a boathand, I remember Mr. and Mrs Jones who both drove taxis in what was their company, based at Bangor Station. One of the additional taxi drivers, whom they employed, was a young man who was my age by the name of Trevor Roberts. Trevor was to inherit the taxi firm from the Jones' family when they retired and gave sterling service until well after I myself had retired as a serving pilot. It is true to say that Trevor was dedicated to his commitment to drive pilots.

There were many journeys and of course many stories of, or from these journeys. The first one, which comes to mind, is a story of a train journey from Chester to Bangor one evening. There were three pilots including myself making the journey. One of the three had just returned from a secondment piloting ships out in Papua New Guinea.

The train slowed to a halt just before Llandudno Junction. The pilot who had just returned from Papua New Guinea was telling a story, which should have been interesting, but for some reason, as so many of his other stories, it was not. He had flown from one part of the island to another by sea-plane to pilot the famed Cunard Liner M.V. *QE II*. He had reached the point where, as far as we could understand, he had had to improvise moorings by using palm trees to make the ropes fast to...

The voice of the story teller could now be heard by the rest of the passengers in the full carriage. Just then, the guard came through the carriage and announced in a welsh lilt, that there was a problem, for there was a flock of sheep on the line. The guard continued through the inter-connecting door of the carriage, but as it closed behind him and thankfully before the *QE II* story could be resumed, the *Emerald Isle Express* came thundering down the track from the opposite direction and hurtled past. The interconnecting door reopened and the guard stuck his head back into the carriage announcing now in a very strong welsh accent: "That should have cleared them!"

Trevor, along with his drivers, who included members of his own family, were always on hand when required to ferry pilots either way, to or from the Western Station. Trevor's wife Nancy, his two sons, Young Trevor and Malcolm, as well as Claire, one of his two daughters, along with a great team of drivers whom we got to know so well, all drove pilots thousands upon thousands of miles to and from Anglesey at all times of the day and night.

There was one, sadly fatal accident, which I feel I have to mention and that was when a driver misread activity on a set of roadworks on the North Wales coast road and crashed killing the pilot in the passenger seat as well as badly injuring the two pilots in the back seats. I remember it well for it was not long after we had established a pilot control in the Radar Tower (as mentioned in a previous chapter). I was on duty as the pilot master in the tower on the evening when the call came through from the Lynas Station asking for my assistance to re-allocate pilots for the ships, which the three pilots involved in the accident had been booked for.

I reasoned that two were relatively small vessels, which could well miss the tide if they were to be delayed and so I ordered them both to be instructed to proceed on into the Bar Station where I was able to have pilots sent out on a launch in good time to meet them and catch the tide. The third was a large vessel also running for the tide, but her E.T.A. was later and indeed there was time to send a local taxi to the relief pilot's home to transport him down to the Western Station to board the vessel on her arrival. No ship was to miss the tide, but we were to lose a good friend and colleague.

Long before this event, one summer's evening, John Cowen and myself, were making the journey by train and had arrived in Chester to find that the Holyhead Boat Train was delayed for over an hour. Ever ready to 'Live the Moment' we left our piloting bags in a 'lock up,' left-luggage box, (which were still in operation then) and chose to stroll down to the River Dee and the hostelry known as the 'Boathouse' where we stopped by on the river bank for a half of bitter beer before strolling back in good time for the delayed train.

We recovered our bags and stood on the platform along with many other frustrated passengers. The *Emerald Isle Express'* arrival was clearly announced and a train pulled in to the main through platform. All the waiting passengers were ordered to board the train, which we all duly did and off we went with only one stop before Bangor at Llandudno Junction. John and myself were deep in conversation as the train pulled out of the junction. I was facing forwards and noticed that the train was 'going off to the right' from the main line. 'It will be for some necessary shunt or other,' John voiced.

The train pulled into Deganwy Junction. All the doors of the train opened and crowds of passengers leapt out demanding an explanation. A bewildered, yet shrewd station master, ordered everyone back on board the train saying that: 'it would all be sorted.' (But not by that stationmaster!)

The train set off again and duly arrived in Llandudno where we discovered that the error had been made in Chester. The train, which we had all boarded there was not the *Emerald Isle Express* but rather a 'day shopping excursion' from Llandudno return. This train had somehow, because of the express train's delay, overtaken her and had been announced as the 'Boat Train.' Our train had actually pulled up just after we had left Llandudno Junction and the *Emerald Isle Express*, the train, which we should have been on, went thundering past on its delayed journey to Bangor and then on to Holyhead.

As pilots are ever resourceful, we were straight across the road from the station to find a telephone box to make a phone call to Trevor. (These were days long before mobile telephones). Once knowing that a taxi was on its way from Bangor for us, we adjourned to the nearest pub where we were soon to be picked up by a Trevor's taxi before being safely driven down to the pilot's hostel on Lynas Point. Both of us were booked for ships, which were arriving after breakfast the following morning, so a full night's sleep was before us after our adventure on the North Wales' coast railway line.

There were many memorable journeys both to and from Anglesey with Trevor's taxis. When I was operating as an A.C.L. pilot, the journey would be made at all hours of the day. We would talk with the drivers about all topics of conversation. On one outward journey with Trevor, he put on a disc, which he had recently bought. We played it over and over again, not only on that journey, but on many others. The song was: 'Dance with my father' by Luther Vandross. Somehow the haunting tune and the wistful lyrics evoked childhood memories of both our fathers for the two of us.

One morning journey with Trevor was almost a disaster regarding the timing to dock ships. I was booked to dock an Independent Container Line ship at Gladstone Lock late in the afternoon. I arrived at the pilot's rooms at Woodside in good time for the taxi. Trevor was already there with a Mercedes and so too was a young pilot who had inadvertently left his 'floatacoat' (pilots coat with built in lifejacket) at his home in Chester. The omission was something to do with having cleaned out his car and having left the coat in the hallway.

Trevor was backing the young pilot's wishes to make our journey via Chester to collect the coat. I argued that the young man could use one of the lifejackets kept as spares on the pilot launch when he boarded his ship, so there was no safety issue. I should have been more assertive, but there was seemingly time to make the detour and Trevor was persuasive, wanting to please.

We made the diversion to collect the coat in good time and then set off for the remainder of the journey. What Trevor had not been aware of was that there were miles of major road works on the A55 immediately out of Chester. The Mercedes crawled along, stop starting and the time flew past. We sent a message to Lynas via Liverpool that we were running late and finally arrived at Point Lynas one hour after my designated boarding time.

On the bridge, the German captain, who I knew, was, not surprisingly, not in a good mood. "Captain, please, I apologise for my late arrival due to circumstances beyond my control." (Not strictly true, but I did have my fingers crossed!) "Please, however, do not say anything yet, just give me maximum full sea speed and I will try to make amends." This was all in my best German, although I did not in fact feel like speaking in any language at all.

Fortunately, she was a fast ship and there was little traffic on the tide as well as the clear visibility of a summer's afternoon so that we were able to maintain full sea speed all the way up to the Bar Light Ship and on up the channel to just short of Gladstone Lock, our destination. The engines were such that the engineer could change from sea speed to manoeuvring speed without any delay. We crossed the outer sill of the lock spot on our docking time and the captain was more than placated. I personally was relieved, but had learned another lesson about timing and I had been lucky.

The other ship did manage to dock on the tide, but was somewhat late as she did not have our speed to make up the 'floatacoat' lost time. I do not believe that the pilot would ever forget his coat again!

Trevor and his family were to serve the Liverpool pilots faithfully as a family (Liverpool pilots being part of that family) for some years after I had retired before modern operation overruled his loyalty to the pilots and his services were abruptly dispensed with. An act, understandably, which Trevor was sadly never able to come to terms with.

A homeward bound taxi story is one, which took place after I had been boarded at Point Lynas on a British coaster bound for Llandulas Stone Jetty. I was boarded on the inward bound coaster *Penelope Everard* on the evening of 23rd September 1982. She was bound for Llandulas Stone Jetty to load a cargo of stone to be taken to the Thames for the purpose of road building around London.

The Robert's Family. Malcolm, Claire, Trevor, Nancy,
Young Trevor and Angela

As we approached the jetty in the dark on the flood of the tide, the captain was not impressed with what looks from seawards as if the ship is running into a sheer cliff. There is in fact a beach and then an incline, before the steeper rise to the quarry above and behind the A56 coast road. "I do not like the look of this jetty Pilot. How do I take my ship back off again?"

"It really is straightforward Captain. The tide will be on the ebb and you literally 'let go' all ropes, give the vessel a touch astern on the main engine to have her moving physically astern when the tide will push you clear of the jetty. Your right-handed propeller should bring your bow round to starboard (with the transverse thrust[31]) and you can then go ahead on the engines and clear with a course to the north-west."

---

31 Ship's main propellers are either cast 'right handed or left handed'. That is the direction they turn when the engines are in forward gear. This means that the stern will be pushed up to starboard and the bow to port. If the helm is left mid-ships and the engine is engaged astern with a right handed propeller, the movement will take the stern 'up' to port and the bow will swing to starboard as the ship gathers stern way.

"I do not like the sound of that Pilot, particularly as there is a strong westerly wind forecast. Are you able to stay with me and take me safely away?"

A pilot is always pleased to be wanted and happy to have more work and my reply was in the affirmative. That settled, after putting the ship safely alongside the jetty on the flood of the tide, I was shown to the pilot's cabin where I was able to manage a few hours of much needed sleep, before being awakened in good time for the departure when the ship had completed loading the stone in the early hours of the following day.

I did exactly as I had advised and we were soon on our way to the west down to an anchorage in Moelfre Bay where the captain had decided to wait until the strong westerly winds that had been forecast had abated. I was to be taken off the ship by launch and landed at the jetty to the south-east of Point Lynas, from where I had boarded the night before, to a waiting Trevor taxi. The taxi was to take me to Bangor Station in time for the first train to Chester.

I had somehow come across a bottle of rum on my travels and had borrowed a glass and had taken a slice of lemon from the Lynas pilot hostel before we had set off on the homeward journey. Sitting on the train in my carriage, I thought of the coaster last seen in the dawn from my taxi. I thought of how often when working with time and tide, the pilot's life timings can be so different to the majority of people's working lives. I wrote the following poem on the homeward journey.

Rest Now.

Day turned upside down,
The returning train
Turning south towards north.
Rum on the breakfast table,
A bitter taste
Of lemon in the mouth.

Through carriage windows
Ragged rocks surround the Orme,
Whose serpent head rests
Upon rough, calmed wind-waters.

A rusting coaster lies to an anchor,
Patched yellow,
A hold full of stone
In the cliff-dark lee,
Storm-sheltered
As the Norse keel-bird, long-ships once were
When they flew over this Celtic sea.

The sky,
Deep red with black cloud,
Crimsons
As the evening dawn
Breaks over the empty house.

I notice from my tide tables that this month was my first as a full time undergraduate student at the University of Liverpool, reading a Joint Honours Degree in French and German. I was keeping a record of my hours at the University to see if the venture was a viable proposition. I note that on the day of the boarding of the ship, I was at University from 0900 Hrs. to 1100 Hrs., (two lectures).

On the following day, the day of the return and the writing of the poem, there is a full tick, indicating that I was home in time to change bags and be over at the University for a full-day of lectures. I believe that I must have been made of 'strong stuff' at the time. Indeed over my four year course, I was to miss on average only one hour's lecture per week for the whole degree course. I missed no ships! I must emphasise again that, because of containerisation, we were overmanned and whilst waiting for reform needed to reduce our numbers, we had time on our hands between ships.

There are so many taxi stories, but for the purpose of this short chapter, I believe that I have written sufficient stories to give a flavour of the necessity for, and to show our debt to, Trevor and the taxi involvement travelling both to and from the Western Station.

"ALL'S WELL THAT ENDS WELL"

We have all used Shakespeare's play title many times in our lives to express the relief felt after a trying time or a close call, but I think that the very nature of the pilot's calling must bring the individual pilot to use the expression possibly more than most during the course of his or her career.

My memory is good for pilotage stories from the past as hopefully my writing illustrates, but I do not have a memory for jokes. I do remember a few like the story of the Liverpool pilot who met a mermaid on the tide line on the beach at Caldy below the golf course, but I doubt that I shall tell that one within these pages!

There is another, which I will paraphrase, for it is somewhat of a 'shaggy dog' story, but I feel that it is appropriate in relation to the stories in this chapter. It is the one about that occasion when both the Archbishop of Canterbury and the Pope were to die at the same time.

The two found themselves in a very long queue before the golden gates. Each walks up individually to speak to Saint Peter to put forward their case as to why, because of their calling, they should be admitted without any waiting. Both requests are turned down.

Sometime later, an individual wearing a 'floatacoat' and carrying a bag goes past. He is admitted on arrival. The two again present themselves at the gates demanding to know why this individual has been allowed in. They are told that whatever their calling, there was no doubt that the individual who was a Liverpool pilot in life had put 'the fear of God' into more people in the course of his career than the two of them had together.

I know from personal experience that there were many occasions when this 'joke' actually had more than a ring of truth about it. An additional comment is necessary, however, for without a doubt, in many instances, that fear was deep within me too.

I have related the horror story of the *Rhine Ore* in my first book "East a Half South," which perhaps was, without doubt, one of the most fearful occasions, which I experienced in the whole of my sea going career. There were many others perhaps, but not quite so harrowing. Dense fog or falling snow can bring about conditions, which will often heighten the senses to put it mildly.

If a ship was equipped with good radars, I was always happy to attempt a passage through the channel approaches and the river. One reason being that, particularly in times when the river was busy with large numbers of vessels as it was before containerisation, it was a fact that fewer ships would be moving in restricted visibility.

One such occasion was when I was manned to relieve an older colleague who had been taken off a tanker of about five thousand tons gross bound for the QE II Oil Dock at Eastham. The vessel would have been about 120 metres in length. The colleague had anchored the vessel out at the Bar Anchorage to await docking on the evening tide, having brought her in from the Point Lynas Station. The pilot had then requested a relief because of a serious family problem back home. I was to proceed outwards by launch to board the vessel in time for the evening tide.

The visibility was misty as it had been all day, but as I boarded the vessel, the fog closed in to a visibility of less than half a mile. This was to deteriorate to 'hands in front of the face stuff,' which was a light hearted way, we as pilots, would describe really dense fog. Discussing the situation with the captain and having ascertained that very little traffic was to move on the tide, I made the decision to make the passage.

The ship's radars were superb with high definition and she was fitted with a bow thruster for manoeuvring when she was close to the lock itself. We heaved up the anchor and proceeded inward bound, lookouts posted and my head in the radar.

The passage was made safely through the channel approaches, the river and eventually up the Eastham Channel to the entrance to the QE II lock. Once in front of the lock with the ebb tide away, we edged up, right on time to berth in the lock itself about half an hour after the high water. It was a relief to see something, even though it was only the glow of the faint yellow illumination of the lights on the west side of the lock seen through the haze of the fog. Directly below me, I could make out the coping stones[32] on top of the edge of the lock wall.

The captain shook my hand thankfully and I had a sense of relief that my decision had been the right one and as a result the ship was safely in. My job was done. I reported in by V.H.F. radio to the Liverpool control to be told that Eastham control wished to speak to me on their V.H.F. channel.

I called in and was both amazed and horrified to be told that the ship could not stay in the lock because of some essential repairs, which were to be carried out on a gate over the coming low water period of the tide and that it had been decided that it was 'too dangerous' to move the ship in the dense fog across the dock to her berth on the opposite, south side.

The captain was in disbelief and like me, fearful of the thought of backing from the safety of the lock out into the swirling waters of the ebb of a spring tide, then to swing somewhere and make another dense fog passage out to the safety of an anchorage.

I managed to maintain a cool, professional attitude before I made my reply. I found myself calmly saying words to this effect:

"Eastham Control, I have brought this vessel safely inwards over a distance of more than twenty miles without seeing anything

---

32 Coping Stones: The top, rounded, block of stone 'topping off' the horizontal to the vertical plane of a lock wall.

visually and have moored her, without damage, safely in your lock. The thought of taking her back out from a place of safety into danger is both unthinkable and un-seamanlike. I realise that we cannot stay here, but I request that you open the inner gate and we will edge out of the lock leaving lines from both quarters astern on the last bollards on either side of the lock. We will slack the lines easily away as we edge our way across the dock until the chief officer on the foredeck sights the wall below the bow. Then we will drop the ship safely on to it and into her required position. Now that we are out of the tideway and there is no wind, we have all the time in the world."

There was at first silence, then a request for me to standby.

Five minutes later a Manchester pilot, who would normally have been employed to take the vessel from the lock to the berth, boarded the vessel from the quay. He arrived on the bridge full of apologies that we had been advised so badly, but he had no explanation as why this had been so.

The captain shook my hand again, this time for much longer than the first time and I left the bridge happily with the pilot's orders ringing in my ears: "Captain, put stern lines out onto the last bollards on either side of the lock!"

When Gracechurch Container Line were using Garston North Dock as their home port and I was one of their two Gracechurch appropriated pilots, there were many situations when I would either step aboard a launch out at sea or step onto the quay at Garston remembering Shakespeare's play title. On one occasion after I had 'fought' the 117 metres long container vessel through the lock and through both of the narrow gates in the system in an easterly 'near gale' force wind in late spring, I found myself confronted with an unusual wildlife emergency.

There was some problem with the bow thruster and it was going to be difficult to manoeuvre the vessel, which was loaded high on her decks with containers, up against the wind, which was blowing off the quay. I had ordered a rope boat and she was in attendance to ferry our ropes to the berth. We were blown westwards almost onto the empty quay there before we had mooring ropes out both fore and aft by courtesy of the rope boat. They however, stretched almost the full width of the Garston North Dock. At this point we began the long haul back up against the wind using both the windless forward and the capstan aft to heave on the ropes. This, along with what assistance I could give with the main engine and the Becker rudder[33].

After some time and after great efforts on everybody's part, we were within a few feet of the quayside when I looked down into the water from my position on the bridge aft into the water in the narrow space now left between the ship's side and the quay. There to my horror was a female mallard duck and her brood of seven ducklings.

"Slack away Captain, slack away fore and aft and quickly."

I was speaking in German at the time so the actual order would have been: "Weglockern Kapitän, Weglockern Sie vor und achter, schnell, schenell."

The captain had sighted the mallards almost at the same time as I did. Without hesitation the orders were given, the ropes were slacked away and the ship flew off the quay, blown by the strong easterly wind. Thankfully, the gap widened and the mallard cleared the bow to safety with her brood and our battle to fight the vessel back up to wind wards and our long haul back to the berth began all over again.

That was without a doubt another occasion when I left my charge knowing that: "All's well that ends well!"

---

33 Becker Rudder. A German designed type of hinged rudder, which gives the rudder an extra control to enhance its turning efficiency, particularly when manoeuvring.

Another inward bound passage in my early years as a pilot, when there was both an element of fear and, after the event, the feeling of 'all ending well,' occurred after an unusually busy tide up at Eastham Locks. The reason for this was that there had been a strike on the canal. This was one of many such strikes, which took place in the late sixties and the early seventies on the docks in the United Kingdom, when the work force was fighting many issues including decasualisation/casualisation. This one in 1967 had lasted over several tides causing a backlog of traffic.

When the strike was over, those in control, had for some reason, 'best known to themselves,' decided that instead of making a timed order for vessels both sailing and docking over consecutive tides, quite simply announced that it was 'First come First served'. That was except for the larger vessels requiring tug assistance, both outward and inward bound.

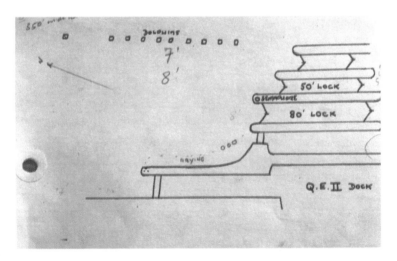

A diagram of Eastham Locks from my boathand's mark book.

I believe that there were four such vessels inward bound, which had been allocated a turn for the big lock[34]. There were some forty ships inward bound and around thirty ships outward bound. (There always seemed to be more vessels inward bound than there were outwards at Eastham Locks for some reason, which I was never able to work out).

I had been boarded on what we referred to as a 'Flying Finn' inbound from the Lynas Station earlier in the day. The *Poseidon* was a small, but fast vessel of some 1600 tons gross, belonging to a Finnish company. Along with the Dutch owned 'Stroom boats', particularly the latest ones the *Spaarnestroom* and the *Texelstroom*, they were the fastest small ships afloat. As a young, newly licensed pilot, known as a 'short hand' (as opposed to a 'full hand' i.e: one fully qualified) it was always a pleasure to be manned on one of these fine vessels for you were assured of a swift passage, being able to overtake most other traffic on a tide providing it was safe to do so. With a bridge amidships (in the middle) they always looked much bigger than they actually were.

This passage, however, was going to be far from swift. Under the circumstances, it would have been possible to order tugs for the vessel and be allocated fifth ship for the big lock, based on our draught. There was little wind and I felt that the expense of tugs for the size of the vessel was unwarranted. Therefore, along with many others, I opted to enter the Eastham Channel late on the flood tide in the hope of docking at one hour to the high water when the flood tide's strength had eased off. This was not to be the case. We were finally to literally 'slide' into the big lock at five hours ebb, very close to the bottom, (that is close to grounding on the river bed) some six hours later.

---

34 Throughout my career as a pilot there were only two of the three locks built at Eastham in operation. From the diagram there is the East, or 'small lock' and the West or 'big lock.' The lock to the furthest east was once the 'barge lock,' but this was not operational in my time.

Some ships turned out and went back to an anchorage to wait for the next tide. Some ran fully aground, indeed the coaster ahead of me into the lock actually touched the bottom as the pilot entered the lock and I was of a deeper draught then he was! Perhaps his keel gouged a channel for my ship to float in! Whatever, we were finally in and I was feeling like the proverbial wet rag.

The whole of this long period of time was spent keeping the vessel safe from drifting out of the channel on the ebb of the tide onto a sand bank. In addition, I had to make sure that we did not collide with, or go alongside another of the many ships queuing up, all hoping, as we were, to dock on the tide. (Some of the others did both!)

I was monitoring the tide gauges and the time to be aware of the state of tide throughout the whole operation to make sure that my vessel did have enough water to float in. Although this tide had reached around the thirty foot mark, (ten metres), when the tide starts to ebb after the high water, the tide falls at the rate of two centimetres a minute. I have often likened this to pulling the plug out of a bath tub. The big lock had opened for us to be one of the last four ships to be taken in, just in time before we would have had to turn out and make for the safety of deeper water.

This docking took place on the ebb of a spring tide with the high water being in the middle of the day. I remember that I must have looked (and have been) exhausted, for after I had arrived home later on that evening, Gill was concerned and asked me if I was alright and what sort of day I had had which had caused me to look so shattered? I believe that I sank into an arm chair, replying simply: "Long" and promptly fell asleep.

The penultimate tale for this chapter is one of an incident, which could have been a disaster save for providence and a matter of luck as well as chance timing. I will relate the tale withholding names and dates in due deference to the fact that despite the negligence of certain officers: "All's well that ends well!"

During my career there were times when ferry companies, which ran regular services to and from Irish ports for example, in some cases were not allowed exemption cerificates[35] or possibly did not have an officer with an exemption certificate on board a vessel for a particular crossing. Naturally, a pilot would be required for safety if this was the case.

The horror story, which I am about to relate took place on a ferry. At the time, a pilot was often manned to pilot the vessel outward bound and then stay on board the vessel to the Irish port, coming back with her to pilot the vessel inward bound when she re-entered the pilotage district.

I was flown to Belfast to take the place of a pilot who was going on leave and because of the fact that the vessel had been delayed a tide, this meant that he would have been going into his leave period had he stayed with the ship.

I arrived on board and was made welcome being shown to my cabin, which fortunately for us all was forward of the accommodation on the starboard side of the bridge housing with a window facing forwards. The ferry was to sail soon after my arrival on board as it was to be an overnight crossing. I went up onto the bridge for sailing to meet the Belfast pilot and then observed the outward passage until the pilot disembarked. I then went below to the restaurant for an evening meal before 'turning in' for a reasonable night's sleep.

I had left strict instructions that I was to be called ten miles west of the Bar Light Ship and had witnessed the captain write these orders clearly in his night order book for the officer of the watch.

---

35 As mentioned several time in Chapter 8, these certificates were issued to regular visitors to the port following a candidate having completed a specified number of trips on board the same vessel under pilotage supervision. Then, following a 'Check Ride,' (candidates were observed operating on an inward passage by an authorised pilot (a 'licensed' pilot before 1987) along with a representative of the port) this would be followed up with an oral exam.

A call ten miles west of the Bar would give me time to take a quick shower and dress to be on the bridge in good time to take over command of the navigation well before we were to enter the channel on our inward passage for the lock and docking.

I slept well until there was a knock on my cabin door and a mumbled call, which I took to be the 'Ten miles west of the Bar' call, which I had ordered. I was out of my bunk immediately and into the shower. A quick shower and I was out drying myself, walking (fortunately) to look out of the cabin window, which I have said faced forwards.

I had a sense of well-being. I had taken a flight to Belfast on a summer's evening, eaten a good meal followed by most of the night in bed. A day time job was to follow on a fine ship... I took a deep intake of gasped breath, for, as I looked out at the beauty of the misty, grey, early morning light, there to port was a green conical buoy marking the starboard side of the Formby Strait. The ship had 'missed the channel!'

A split second decision of what to do, dash up onto the bridge naked, which I suppose for the safety of the ship I should have done for speed, possibly with a towel wrapped round me for the ship was hurtling at seventeen knots towards the sands of the Burbo Bank. This would not have been for modesty, but I reasoned rather for authority. (I feared that nobody might take any notice of a 'gibbering naked man' arriving into the ordered calm of the wheelhouse). I chose rather to 'throw on my clothes' without fastening any buttons or zipping zips, grabbed my 'floatacoat' and briefcase as I dashed out of the cabin and up the two flights of stairs leading to the bridge.

I literally burst onto the bridge, dropped my coat and bag on the deck before shoulder charging the helmsman so that he flew from the wheel to land in a heap on the port side of the wheelhouse. This action was necessary for I was out of breath and thus was unable to give any orders.

I spun the wheel hard over to port, which would take the ship's head towards the north and the channel. The vessel was twin screw (two main engines and two propellers) and I brought both to 'stop.' Then I had to wait for seconds for the revolutions of the engines to decrease. These seconds seemed like hours, but the ship's head was swinging to port away from the bank. I rang the port engine to full astern and the starboard engine to full ahead. This manoeuvre with the type of propellers that the ship was equipped with, would I hoped, accelerate a swing to port away from the danger lying not far ahead.

At this point I noticed that both the captain and the officer of the watch were standing together in the starboard, foreward corner of the wheelhouse. I also remember that both were staring at me with their mouths wide open.

Then, looking to the west and the entrance to the channel, I was horrified to see that there was a fast, German, coastal-container ship whose captain had an exemption certificate, in bound and closing from port.

I called the vessel on the V.H.F. to establish contact, thankful that I had my breath back. The captain on the container ship was well aware that something was not quite as it should be with my vessel being so far to the south and offered to slow down to allow me to regain the channel.

I assessed the situation swiftly and judged that the best course of action was for the other vessel to continue with both course and speed. I thanked the captain for his offer, but requested that he did keep his course and speed to get passed and clear, leaving me to sort out our safe entry into the Formby Strait. The captain of the container ship wished me well and continued as agreed.

My charge was now heading north for the channel and safety about to enter the Formby Strait, which I would do when the other vessel was safely passed. I adjusted the engines and spun the wheel hard over to starboard to bring the vessel back onto the correct course before handing the wheel back to the helmsman with an apology for his necessary rough handling.

Not one of the three crew members who were on the bridge when I had first arrived said a word during the whole incident.

"Right Captain, we shall be up at the lock within the hour, ready to dock at our appointed time. We shall carry on as normal, but you and I will have a de-briefing in your cabin when we are on our berth. For now, carry on."

At this point V.T.S. control called me on the radio and asked if all was well on board. I replied calmly that all was well and that we had just entered the main channel on passage on schedule for our lock time. I gave all the necessary ship's details of an inward bound ship's report: draught, with hazardous cargo and no reported defects, all in fact in order!

After we were safely on the berth, I accompanied the captain down to his cabin and we closed the door.

"Well Captain, perhaps you would like to explain to me what happened?"

He was quite obviously upset and rightly so. His reply was honest and quite simple: "I can only say that I am truly sorry John, but I thought that you were on the bridge."

"Well Captain, I was not on the bridge having been called not where I had left my instructions to be called, but instead only when the ship was not far off the channel entrance. As a result, between you and the officer of the watch, you were not only unaware that you had missed the channel entrance, but were also totally unaware that you were proceeding at a speed of around seventeen knots and were so close to running aground on the Burbo Bank."

I found myself saying, yet again in Shakespeare's immortal words:

"All's well that ends well Captain, but although you are a very experienced man, it is never too late to learn a lesson and there is certainly a lesson for you to learn following this morning's near disaster. Unless I am asked to explain the incident Captain I will not make a report providing that you promise me that you will never let such an error happen on board any of your commands again."

The captain thanked me profusely on all counts appearing to be both suitably humbled and thankful for his deliverance. We parted as friends. I was never officially asked to explain the events of that passage and I kept my word.

There is however, a sequel to this near horror story. My elder brother Brian Curry was also a pilot with me and the following week rang to tell me that he had made the round trip on the same ferry. He told me that when he had boarded the vessel in Liverpool, he had sat in the captain's cabin before the sailing and that he and the captain had chatted about this and that including discussing the various pilots who had piloted the vessel before him.

Brian mentioned my name, to which the captain replied: "John Curry? No pilot, we have never had a pilot of that name here before."

The week after this telephone conversation, I was manned on the same ship, this time for the round trip. I arrived early and went to the captain's cabin. I knocked politely on the cabin door and was invited in.

"Good evening John," was the welcome I received as I entered the cabin.

"John is it Captain? Only last week you met my brother Brian and on that occasion you denied all knowledge of my very existence. I am a pilot, not a psychologist and I have not studied the subject formerly, but Captain, I believe that the experience, which you and I had together on the last inward passage when I was with you, which so nearly ended in disaster with a possible loss of life, was one which you wanted to forget because of your own personal failings on that occasion. I suggest Captain, that you never 'forget' me again or the incident, for if you do not guard against it a similar error could be made and the next time you may not be so lucky."

The captain was reduced to a suitably chastened man and he apologised profusely. I was certain that he would never forget me again.

My final story chosen for this chapter takes us away from the Mersey and Liverpool, but although at one stage the probable outcome could well have been another kind of disaster, it was because I was a Liverpool Pilot that it did all end well!

The adventure took place right at the beginning of my annual leave in 1976. At this time Gill and myself had four children, Paul and John James, blood brothers who were at that time fostered, (later to be adopted) Becky, our adopted daughter and Nathan our biological son.

Our 'car' at that time was a brand new Volkswagen van, a Devon 'Sundowner,' camper conversion. This had replaced a Fiat 850, 'Farina,' camping wagon converted to a camper from the Italian small commercial vehicle, often used as a bread van. For us the 'Sundowner' was our luxury mobile home and with tents we could roam wherever our fancy took us throughout Europe.

Our Swedish student friend Lena was referred to in Chapter 4, when I wrote about how I met her again, much later in our lives, when I was in Stockholm with Stan Frith. Lena had been the first of many young Swedish students whom we had hosted in our home for some years in the month of June. They came over to perfect, as far as I could judge, their already perfect English! Lena was only eighteen when she stayed with us and we were in our late twenties. With so little age difference we became firm friends.

Lena's close friend Marguerita was staying close by that year with other friends and we were to take them both, along with our two boys, over to stay with Brian and Pat McShane in his family home in Glenarm, Northern Ireland. Brian, as recorded earlier in my writings, was to become Marine Operation's Manager of the Port of Liverpool, but at that time he was still in the lower ranks of the 'Floating Plant.'

As a result of our friendship, Marguerita's family invited us over to stay in their Summer House, which was situated by a trout stream at Hindös, inland from Gothenburg. We accepted the invitation, loaded up our highly polished and spotlessly clean, almost brand new camping wagon with all necessary equipment and the four children and set off one July morning for the summer holiday. Later that day another, unexpected adventure began.

We had friends who lived in the village of Winterton, just outside of Scunthorpe and they had invited us for lunch on our way over to the ferry at Immingham. They had a big house with gardens. We had lunch and played croquet on the lawn sipping gin and tonics. In good time, (or so we thought) we set off for the Tor Line Terminal at Immingham for the twenty four hour sailing over to Gothenburg.

The weather was beautiful. It was the start of that very hot summer of 1976, which was so hot that people died as a result of the heat. We were in a great frame of mind. We had been given a splendid lunch by friends and we were looking forward to almost a whole month in a Swedish summer house, which had been loaned to us. We had a safe crossing over a calm North Sea to look forward to. We had made the crossing before when we had just the two boys before Becky and Nathan were born and we knew that the vessel was luxurious. She was fitted out with all first class facilities including a sauna, which I was particularly looking forward to.

About a mile down the road the earlier 'joie de vivre' was to vanish in an instant. I asked Gill to please just check on the sailing time. We will not say how it came about, but an error had been made on our behalf and so instead of having plenty of time to join the vessel, we were running not late, but very late.

We arrived at the ferry terminal to discover that the ferry was actually 'running down' to river level in the lock and was about to proceed to sea. I drove the shining, spotlessly clean Volkswagen van through the coal tips at speed round to the lock. The children had picked up that there was something wrong and so there were tears in the back seats.

What was in my mind when I drove round to the lock, I am not quite sure, but I believe that I had the ridiculous idea that I could have persuaded the captain to return back to the berth to pick up we latecomers. Fortunately for me, as we arrived at the lock, the ferry was swinging out into the tideway and was on her way.

What now? Resourceful as ever, I surveyed the dock system and spotted a Roll-On Roll-off ferry of the same company loading vehicles on the opposite side of the dock. I set off again at speed in our now coal-dust-blackened, camping wagon. We arrived up above the Ro-Ro berth and I left Gill and the children, asking her to keep her fingers tightly crossed. I believe that she had a vague idea of what I was hoping could be achieved.

I boarded the vessel with no challenge and proceeded up to the captain's cabin. I knocked on the door and was invited in. There before me was familiar sight. Both the captain and the agent were sitting having a beer whilst completing the papers for sailing.

"Good Afternoon Captain, I am a Liverpool Pilot somewhat out of my district, but more importantly today, I am on holiday with my wife and four children. Suffice to say, for whatever reason, we have missed our sailing over to Gothenburg. The next sailing, I believe is in five days. I am desperately wondering if you would be kind enough to take us over the North Sea, to wherever you are bound. With you being the same company as the ferry, I may be able to transfer my tickets or at least recover some of the cost from the company. More importantly, we will be on our way to Sweden, even if we have to drive there."

The two men looked at each other, both somewhat mystified and amused by this sudden unexpected apparition in the captain's cabin. The captain faced the agent whilst stroking his chin thoughtfully. I cannot remember, which one of them spoke first, but I was told that the vessel was bound for Rotterdam. (A fair way from Gothenburg!) I was told to return to my vehicle and wait.

This I did, not relishing the next decision if we could not board the Ro-Ro. The choice was off to a hotel, or back over the Pennines to return for the next sailing to Gothenburg.

Neither of these choices was necessary, however and the day soon began, very definitely to improve. The agent strolled off the vessel down the ramp at the stern door with his jacket over his shoulder, briefcase in hand and walked up to my driver's window.

"Right Pilot, no questions, but keep your eye on the last forty footer, which was loaded onto the ferry. In a few minutes from now it will drive back ashore. As we told you, the ferry is bound for Rotterdam, docking in the morning, but if you want to sail with her, the lorry will wait, only for a few minutes, just long enough to give you the time you will need to drive on before it will drive back aboard behind you. There will be space for you between that lorry and the lorry ahead of it. Whatever you decide Pilot, have a good holiday." He shook my hand through the window and was gone.

The forty footer rolled back ashore as promised moments later and the Volkswagen camper rolled up the ramp and into the position indicated by the officer of the watch. The lorry rolled back aboard and the stern door closed behind. Another, unexpected, life-adventure had begun.

Gill and myself, along with the two youngest children were shown to a vacant electrician's cabin, whilst the two elder boys were to share one of the lorry driver's vacant cabins. We were invited up onto the bridge once the ship had left the lock at Immingham and we enjoyed the sail down the Humber River before being invited down to the crew's mess for an evening meal. The captain's daughter was making the trip and she was about the same age as our two elder boys, they became friends.

We slept well and arrived at around breakfast time on the berth in the busy port of Rotterdam. We made our farewell to the kind and most generous captain and set off at speed for Amsterdam. The reason for this was that at that time, Tor Line ran the ferry service from Immingham to Gothenburg. The same ferry then sailed from Gothenburg to Amsterdam, and then back to Gothenburg before returning to Immingham.

We covered the sixty miles or so from Rotterdam to Amsterdam in about an hour and a half and arrived at the Tor Line offices there just after they had opened. Bearing in mind that 'our own ship' was still crossing the North Sea, I asked to see the manager.

I explained that, for whatever reason, which was now history, my family had missed the crossing we were booked on the evening before. I did not state that we had, in effect, 'hitch hiked' across the North Sea, but rather I said that we had managed to find a passage from Immingham to Rotterdam and upon arrival had driven straight to Amsterdam. I requested that, if it were possible, I would like to rebook the camper and the family back to Gothenburg on the ship's return journey.

The manager looked both understanding and sympathetic. He asked for my tickets and disappeared with them into the back office. It did not take him very long before he returned bearing with him replacement tickets.

"I am delighted to tell you that I have been able to book you on the crossing and have even been able to secure the same cabins, which you were allocated before. It is a simple transfer of a booking in my opinion, there will be no charge."

Well, here we were in one piece with almost two days to spend in Amsterdam, a booking we may have included in the original holiday, if we had been able to afford it. As I have said, our ferry had not yet arrived in Gothenburg and we were able to telephone our Swedish friends who fortunately happened to be at their home in Gothenburg briefly that morning. (Again, days of no mobile phones). We were able to inform them of the delay. Thankfully, this caused no problems for them.

Finding a hotel was possibly going to be a problem at that time of year, but we opted for one room for us all for the one night. Having booked the room we set off, much to Gill's artistic delight, to spend the afternoon at the recently opened Vincent Van Gogh Museum in the heart of the city.

There is a rider to this tale. Nathan, our own child and the youngest, was not an easy child when it came to staying quiet for a full night's sleep. As I write this, years later, I do realise that I am putting that fact mildly. He slept fitfully during the night, but in the early morning at first light, his fretfulness was causing disruption. So, I opted to rise, dress quickly and bundle Nathan into his push chair before setting off to walk the streets by the canals of Amsterdam.

Nathan was out like a light in minutes and I was able to witness the dawn mists as they rose from the waters of the canals in a peace and quiet, which was strikingly beautiful. Amusingly, as I had no map with me, just my inbuilt compass for direction, which would eventually guide me back to the hotel in time for breakfast, I found myself pushing Nathan, inadvertently, through the Red Light District! Some of the girls were still in their shop windows and some even came out, somewhat bleary eyed to exclaim what a beautiful, blonde baby Nathan was. I smiled and thanked them for their compliments, whilst muttering under my breath:

"You girls do not know the other half, which is why I am pushing this pram over your cobbled streets at this ridiculous time of the morning instead of being where I should be... fast asleep in bed."

(An aside here having made mention of these 'Ladies of the Night,' in Liverpool it used to be said that in the early hours, between one and six, you were likely only to see the three 'p's:' Police, Pilots and Prostitutes!)

I was back in time for breakfast. We had a morning in a park and a picnic lunch. I can also assure you that we were in particularly good time down at the ferry terminal from where we were to set off to regain our original holiday plans.

I remember wading in the trout stream near this idyllic summer house where we were staying and catching trout for the evening meal as the sun was setting during the 'evening rise.' I found myself reflecting back on this somewhat dreamlike sequence, which was the start of the holiday and thinking yet again: "All's well that ends well."

SHARING THE PILOTING EXPERIENCE

In Chapter 3, the chapter about my father and also in "East a Half South," I have mentioned that I was to accompany Dad on both dock and river shifts, often in school holidays, from a very early age.

This practice was fairly general amongst pilots who took both friends and relations with them on suitable occasions, which apart from being a personal experience, enabled many to gain some understanding of what a pilot's calling was about. Obviously this could only happen if the pilot believed that it was safe to do so and the captain of the vessel gave his permission.

Over the years, I was to take a great many friends and relations of all ages with me when a favourable opportunity presented itself. It is not my intention to relate the stories of all these accompanied pilotages, but rather to write about some of the most notable.

The first person to accompany me was my nephew, Timothy, who came with me on board the *Hemsley I*, which was a small bunkering tanker. The *Hemsley I* had run regularly from fuel oil storage berths around the area bunkering larger vessels. When I was a child, she was one of the vessels, which my father had taken me on board numerous times.

Captain Roy Kilby-Leonard was still the master and always helped the younger pilots to learn more about ship handling even after they were qualified. The nature of her work meant that she was one of those 'shifting jobs,' which did not require pilot boat 'boardings,' but was rather a passage from berth to berth. This meant that for safety, it was possible to take a guest along if the captain was in agreement.

Timothy was my sister Vivienne's son who was intending to follow in his father's footsteps and join the Royal Navy. The date was April 9th 1969, so Timothy would have been thirteen years old. The passage was from the QE II Lock over to berth in the North Liverpool dock system via Langton Lock. I remember that it was a fine evening and was notable not only because of Timothy's obvious enjoyment of having the opportunity to be on board the vessel, but also because of an exclamation made by the captain, whilst waiting off Langton Lock to gain entry into the North System.

There was a delay in the outer lock gate opening and when I called the lockmaster on the V.H.F. radio to inquire what the delay was for, he informed me that there was a problem with the water levels in the pipes. Upon hearing this Roy made us all laugh, the thirteen year old Timothy in particular with his outburst of: "Oh what a b---icks, he's lost his hydraulics!"

The lockmaster 'got them back,' the hydraulics that is, before too long and we were to complete the assignment without further incident.

The *Hemsley I* had been built as a Royal Navy bunkering tanker, launched in Scotland as R.F.A. *Scotal* in 1906 as a steam engined, coastal tanker and had operated on the south coast until 1949 when she was sold to Hemsley Bell Ltd. She was renamed *Hemsley I* and then operated mainly on the River Mersey for the rest of her days.

I mention this fact because the month after Timothy had made the trip with me, she sailed on her final voyage bound for the breaker's yard in Holland. Sadly, after such a long and illustrious career, she was to be caught in dense fog off Porth Cothan in Cornwall and was wrecked six nautical miles south of Padstow.

I remember watching the T.V. news the following day after the crew had been taken off by lifeboat and Captain Roy kilby-Leonard had returned to the wreck by the cliff path. The camera crew filmed him making his way laboriously back up the steep, cliff path. After he had reached the top, somewhat breathless and obviously devastated by the loss of his command to shipwreck, a microphone was thrust in front of his face and he was asked if he had any comments to make. Not surprisingly, the captain had no comment to make and I was left to think how cruel some can be in trying to capitalise on the misfortunes of others for the sake of news.

The second shared pilot experience, I recall was with a small British coaster called the *Ardglen*. I remember minor details of the vessel: she was painted grey, both hull and superstructure and she had a red funnel with a black top. On this pilotage in June 1969, during my first full summer as a third class pilot, I had brought the ship into the river to an anchorage prior to docking at Brunswick Lock in the South dock system on the following late, evening tide.

I left the ship safely at anchor and went ashore to move my car over to the berth so that I might have transport home in the early hours of the following day. I had promised a childhood friend, Graham Taylor, a keen yachtsman, that if ever the opportunity arose, I would take him with me. I rang Graham and he was delighted to accept the offer.

I had ordered the river launch[36] to take me back to the anchored ship in good time for the tide and Graham joined me at the landing stage to board with me. I had cleared the arrangement with the captain before I had gone ashore and so the docking was made with Graham as an observer and I know that he was suitably impressed.

I had both the honour and the pleasure to take my father with me on an occasion when I had anchored a small coaster in the Middle Deep Anchorage, an anchorage mid-river between Bromborough

---

36 River Launch: A small motor launch serving the needs of pilots within the boundaries of the river between the hours of 0900Hrs. and sunset throughout the year. She was manned by two pilot service boathands.

and the Dingle. This anchorage was south of a line, which was marked on the chart and was where vessels could be left in a safe anchorage without it being a legal requirement for the pilot to remain on board.

My father had retired and this, although sometime after the retirement, was still in my early years as a pilot. We boarded from the river launch in good time to heave up the anchor and proceeded north to dock at Alfred Locks, the entrance to Birkenhead Docks, on the day tide. The coaster was bound for a berth in the West Float. I was relieved that all was to go well. This was a fairly straight forward manoeuvre in good visibility with little wind, but having my father with all his experience and ability alongside me, it would have been a disaster if I had made the slightest error with him as an observer. With our positions reversed after all the years since he first took me with him as a child, I believe that both of us were proud, each in our own way.

I was to take my own son Nathan with me twice much later on in my career. One is covered fully in "East a Half South," a passage from Liverpool to LLandulas stone jetty on a Dutch coaster. This was the trip, on which we 'rescued' a budgerigar from the vicious beaks of a flock of gulls. The bird must have escaped and with the easterly wind have been blown offshore. The gull attack was taking place in the vicinity of the Bar Light vessel, miles out to sea. The other occasion Nathan came with me was on board a Roebottom's tanker transporting from Eastham Locks to Birkenhead via a river anchorage south.

My daughter Becky was to join me in Alfred Locks on board the Sail Training Association vessel *Sir Winston Churchill* to accompany me to Esparto Quay, a berth in the East Float.

During the summer of 1983 when we were not busy, having too many pilots referred to earlier and indeed during the time I was both a full time pilot and a full time student at the University of

Liverpool, I had a telephone consultation on a Tuesday about a tanker, which had experienced difficulties whilst docking at the QE II Oil Dock.

My daughter Becky with my V.H.F. on board Sir Winston Churchill.

The tanker was the *Philmac Venture* (60,000 tons) later to be renamed the *Vanessa*, chartered to carry a particularly nasty grade of fuel oil from South America to the QE II Oil Dock en route for the power station at Fiddler's Ferry. The vessel had been transported over to Gladstone Dock for repairs to the bow section and my consultation was regarding the safe return trip back to the QE II Lock. Looking at her draught noted in my tide tables, 8.4 metres, would indicate that there had been no discharge of cargo after the damage and that she was still fully laden.

The damage had been done on the very first of the many planned trips carrying the fuel from South America over to supply the power station with an alternative to coal. The downside of this alternative, as I recall, is that there was no filter fine enough to trap the waste product once it had been burned. The booked return was on the day tide of the following Sunday, which was a spring tide at 1740 Hrs. B.S.T. with a predicted height of a little over eight metres, Liverpool.

On the Saturday evening, a family of five came to dinner with our family in West Kirby. Kathy Humphries, the mother and a good friend, expressed an interest in my profession and a wish that she could accompany me some day. The following morning the agent rang me to assure me that the vessel was all ready for the move and that the tugs, which I had requested had been ordered.

Whilst he was on the phone and as he was still on the ship, I asked him if he would be kind enough to ask the captain if I may bring a guest along with me, promising that she would not be in the way. The reply came back that Kathy would be most welcome. There was then additional information for me that the superintendent of the company would also be making the passage to observe the operation. I remember thinking that I hoped that he would not get in the way either! I rang Kathy and she was delighted to accept the invitation.

The weather was fine, clear blue skies and very little wind. The whole operation from the sailing out of Liverpool to the docking went remarkably smoothly and according to plan. As we approached the QE II Lock, there are two memories, which I have in mind: One is that both Kathy's and my family were on the old jetty at Eastham waving as we went past. The other is that the superintendent could not understand why I was standing calmly on the starboard wing of the bridge directing operations when the damage had been done on the port bow. (That is diagonally opposite to my position). Politely asking him to give me room, I explained that by making sure that the vessel was flat alongside on the starboard side and stayed there, she could not possibly touch anywhere on the other side and do damage.

As we slid safely into the lock, the superintendent understood my explanation and was delighted that all went so well and exactly as he had been promised. After we were safely alongside and the job was over, Kathy and myself, walked up to the Eastham Ferry Hotel for a family, evening meal in the hotel's gardens overlooking the river, whilst the children played in the woods nearby.

Two shifting jobs, which were similar, one to the other and which meant that I was able to take an observer with me, were both scrap ships, partly laden moving from the Langton system north to the Gladstone system. Both ships were too wide to pass through the Hornby Passageway in the system, which meant that it was necessary to take them out into the river via Langton Lock before returning into the docks via Gladstone Lock.

Both moves were in daylight. The second of the two was the bulker *Yick Luk* in July 2008, transporting from South Alexander Dock II Branch Dock scrap berth to the Minor Quay in Seaforth. The ship was part loaded with scrap, but because of the draught limitations at Langton, it was necessary for her to proceed to Seaforth to 'top up' to achieve maximum draught. Our sailing draught was 8.6 metres (28 feet). These shifts involved fairly large ships, maximum for the space in Alexander Dock and there was little room for manoeuvres with them in that system.

Alan Forster, a friend with whom I share an interest in Hornby trains and who had been kind to me with a wagon repair, whilst I was recovering from my double hip operation earlier in the year had, expressed a wish to accompany me on a ship if it was at all possible.

Alan came with me and, as a keen photographer, took a splendid set of photographs of the whole exercise. Those taken within the Langton system, were later to be sent to the agents E.M.R. in Liverpool at their request so that they might send them to ship owners for them to better appreciate the delicate manoeuvring required for the safety of such vessels in that system.

Myself, the Captain and Alan Forster on the bridge of the Yick Luk.
Photo: Alan Forster

On another earlier such shift, again in daylight in the January of 2008, it was an honour for me to have another friend, David Dodd, retired local fisherman and retired coxswain of the Hoylake 'All Weather Lifeboat' with me. The ship I believe was the *Surmene 4*, of a similar size to the *Yick Luk*, same draft but bound on this shift to West Gladstone Dock. Again all went well and the captain insisted on taking a photograph of the three of us when the ship was finally moored on her berth.

A guest who I was able to officially ask permission to accompany me on the full passage from Point Lynas to the berth on S3 on board the A.C.L. container ship the *Atlantic Cartier* was the then serving coxswain of the Hoylake Lifeboat, David Whiteley. I was granted permission from both the Liverpool Pilots and the Mersey Docks and Harbour Company when I presented the case that as a coxswain of an 'All Weather Lifeboat' operating in the pilotage district, the experience might help him in the future if he was ever to be called out to a casualty on board a large vessel.

David Dodd, the Captain and myself on the bridge of the Surmene 4.

David accompanied me in one of Trevor's Mercedes taxis down to the pilot's hostel at Point Lynas. We were to have supper, followed by a full night's sleep before being boarded at breakfast time the following morning to dock in the early afternoon. I would say that this was 'the full hit', the ultimate in showing a lay person the wonderful life, on occasions, that was to be experienced in the course of the daily duties of a Liverpool pilot.

After I had taken David home, I returned to the ship and picked up Jonas, the captain, who then came back to dinner at my home. Jonas was a keen golfer and before we went back to Devonshire Road, I was able to take him to sight both the Caldy Golf Club and the Royal Liverpool Golf Club. In addition we were to visit the Hoylake Lifeboat Station and show him the Mersey Class Lifeboat: *Lady of Hilbre*, David's command, then stationed in the old lifeboat station at Hoylake.

This story reminds me of the many occasions when I found myself piloting a vessel, which passed the Hoylake Lifeboat when she was out on exercise. I would take the opportunity, if it were safe to do so, of calling her to come alongside the moving vessel to take a 'simulated' stretcher case overboard, or possibly we would throw a lifebelt, representing a 'man overboard,' over the side to be recovered and returned to the ship.

Two more friends were to make the 'full trip' with me. These 'full trips' were both outward bound from Eastham Locks to the Liverpool Bar Station, returning by pilot launch. The first was both a friend and a neighbour, Hugh Dalzell. Some years later, after I had spent part of my University 'year abroad' at the Marine Research and Training Centre at Port Revel near Grenoble, France, the second was to be Jean Graaf, the director of Port Revel. Jean came to stay with us for a few days whilst on a tour of the British Isles.

Hugh was a marine solicitor who was to act for me sometime later following the epic of the *Khudoznik Romas*. This epic took place when the engines failed and I lost one of her anchors in saving the ship from running aground on the stones of the Queen's North Training Wall. A story covered in full in "East a Half South."

Hugh had asked me if it was possible to accompany me on a passage out to sea to assist with his knowledge and work as a recently appointed marine solicitor at one of the big law firms in Liverpool. I arranged to take Hugh with me on a coaster out of Eastham Locks to sea on an afternoon tide. The ship was the *Patria* of about 2000 tons. We sailed on a summer's evening in July 1981. As we were passing abeam of (at right angles to) Seaforth, I noticed a large grain ship on the grain terminal. Her name was the *Jhansi K I Rani*. I made the observation that I would love to take him with me on such a large vessel. He agreed that such an experience would be of great interest.

That passage took place on Saturday 11th July 1981. The following Monday morning, I was manned for my next ship following the *Patria* on the *Jahnsi K I Rani*! I rang Hugh and he was delighted to follow up with the somewhat larger ship experience.

He was able to accompany me from the berth to the lock where he had to disembark having a commitment at home that evening. Hugh vowed that after that experience of watching the manoeuvres on board such a huge ship, in his mind he would always walk five paces behind me! (To observe such an operation is impressive). Hugh also booked tickets to take both Gill and myself to the opera: Bizet's 'Pearl Fishers,' sung by the Welsh National Opera at the Liverpool Empire Theatre as a 'Thank You.' He did not have to, but we did all enjoy the performance.

Jean Graaf's trip, sometime after I had graduated, was similar to Hugh's first passage, but there was to be no follow up as there was in Hugh's case.

After completing my first year at University, I had made many new friends among both students and lecturers (including Carol Chapman), many of the latter being of a similar age to myself. One of these was John Reddick, my Professor of German. John was a keen sailor with a large yacht based in the Brunswick Yacht Marina on the Mersey. Gill and myself, had sailed with him on the river. An opportunity arose in the first summer vacation from my studies at the University to take John with me on a Chinese cargo ship, the *Darquinshan*, a conventional five hatch cargo ship. My booking was to shift her from Birkenhead over to West Langton Dock, early one June evening.

I borrowed a 'floatacoat' from a colleague of similar size to John who was a tall man. When we arrived on the bridge of the vessel the captain rushed past me to shake hands with the obviously more impressive figure. (I am only five feet four inches.) He turned back when he heard my outburst of uncontrolled laughter and I explained politely that although John was of taller stature, he would be better off accepting me as his pilot.

There were many others over the forty plus years, during which I served as a pilot, possible thirty or more. I hope that my guests were able to appreciate from their experience, something of what it entails in being a marine pilot.

Gill came with me on several occasions, one of which was unintended. That was on board the U25, the German submarine, which was in attendance at the fiftieth anniversary of the Battle of the Atlantic and the end of the Second World War. The U-Boat was moored in the West Float Birkenhead.

I piloted two other warships during the anniversary and had been manned on the U-Boat on her outward passage, partly because I spoke German. Like the 'Tall Ship's' visits, the pilots who were on the warships were on leave and had volunteered for the bookings because with the volume of the increased traffic, the operational pilots were covering the normal flow of commercial traffic. Unlike the 'Tall Ships' where our services were given free of charge, with the warships, they were not.

I was Chairman of the Liverpool Pilots at that time and Gill had accompanied me to a number of functions held in the City of Liverpool celebrating the visit of the warships. We had met the commander of U25 several times and he had invited Gill to bring me down to the vessel half an hour before our sailing time so that she may come on board.

We were welcomed on board and showed up to the conning tower. The commander indicated that Gill was to climb down the ladder inside the conning tower for a tour of the submarine. Gill vanished and before I could say a word the commander ordered all ropes to be let go and we were off.

The commander had the bit between his teeth, possibly because so much interest and fascination had been shown during the week in the submarine by the many visitors who had been on board. I ordered him in my best German to proceed at a very slow speed for nothing was ready for him. The lock was down to river level and the two bridges, which we had to pass through, would not be opened for some time. The commander did as he was ordered from then on. Even so we were to spend hours in the lock when it was ready for us. Below is a photograph of Gill 'in command!'

Gill on the conning tower of U25. In Alfred Lock.

Gill's final guest passage and indeed the final guest, which I was to have with me in my career was to be with me on my last act of pilotage on board *Atlantic Compass* when I sailed her outward bound and remained on board for the voyage over to New York, a voyage, which was in effect into my retirement in the May of 2009.

SIMULATION BY PHYSICAL MODELS AT PORT REVEL

An article with the above title was commissioned by Jean Graaf, then Managing Director at Port Revel, in 1985. Port Revel is the 'model simulator' centre established by Esso with the advent of the large tankers, which took place after the closure of the Suez Canal. The company found it difficult to recruit trainees from other companies and gave the centre over to the French firm Sogreah who had built both the centre and the models, which operated at the 'Marine Research and Training Centre' near Grenoble.

I believe that a personal comment on navigational aids to training is in order here, for as an apprenticed, 'hands on,' trained pilot in the Port of Liverpool, I have always been sceptical of the value of both simulators and models.

That is not to say that both do not have a place in training programmes, but rather, having operated on both simulators and scale models, I personally found that once I had mastered the 'parameters' of the particular 'model,' be it simulated or scale, I could execute manoeuvres that I knew would be impossible in real life. I have written these words as a preamble to the commissioned article because I believe that my personal, professional opinion is evident within its content.

'Autumn 1985.'

High in the mountains, some sixty kilometres north-north-west of Grenoble, Isère, France, is the Marine Research and Training Centre of Port Revel. With the advent of the V.L.C.C. (Very Large Crude Carrier) Port Revel was established as a training centre for masters in command and licensed pilots of the world to experience, in simulation, the handling features of these hitherto unknown leviathans. As we experienced ship handlers of the 1980s know, all problems in all extremes of conditions have been overcome on the bridges of the ships themselves.

We may acknowledge that the era of the 500,000 tonners is over and that we never reached the era of the 1,000,000 ton tanker. The trend would appear to be that the size of the remaining V.L.C.Cs is diminishing toward an optimum size, which is concentrating on a tonnage of around 120,000 tons. At present Port Revel, under the excellent jurisdiction of Sogreah, offers in particular 'specialised training' for handling large crude carriers and large gas carriers.

There is a superb fleet of 8 1/25 scale models representing real ships ranging from 17,000 tons up to 400,000 tons. The 'time scale' for the models is approximately five times faster than reality, but since the ship handler is himself 'in scale' with the models, this has the advantage of allowing him or her to carry out five times the number of manoeuvres during the training period.

Like other simulators, Port Revel exists as a result of both high technology and great expense. That it simply exists perhaps is of paramount importance to ourselves as professionals. There are two main possibilities, in which we as ship handlers may utilise the facilities at Port Revel in the future. The first possibility is for the experienced ship handler to 'try out' new and untried manoeuvres. If successful, these manoeuvres may be practised to perfection before attempting the real-life manoeuvre on the bridge of a ship.

It is worth noting here, that Sogreah at their research centre in Grenoble itself are able to simulate in scale, all kinds of harbours, complete with shallows and deeps, along with tidal sets, currents, not to mention both wind and waves to go with them.

The second possibility is for 'genuine trainees,' that is ship's officers and unlicensed trainee pilots to supplement real life 'on board' experience with model command. As we are well aware, with certificates and licences at stake, trainee ship handlers learn mainly by observation and store a multitude of manoeuvres in their brains. These 'possible' manoeuvres arm the newly qualified ship handler for his or her future professional expertise. This expertise may only develop as a result of personal experience with no other expert present to rely on to confirm decision making. All simulators offer the trainee 'decision making' command to varying degrees with their inevitable results.

Port Revel offers the trainee the opportunity to 'play' with scale model ships and 'get a feel' of a vessel being solely in their command. Playing as a child plays to gain life experience is invaluable. Those qualified persons who dare to step foot on board the models at Port Revel with the idea that 'it is only a model' may well risk the indignity of being 're-floated' after running aground in their travels around the lake by an instructor with the aid of a boathook!

Those of us, who pride ourselves on our expertise, alone can know what a dent in our professional pride that must be if we take Port Revel seriously and relate the models to the real thing. (One course I was teaching on a rare day of strong winds at Port Revel, had me physically exhausted at the end of the session in the afternoon, for each crew ran their model aground in the narrow strait known as the Suez Canal and pushing them off with a boathook was hard going).

From my personal observations at Port Revel, I have noticed that the ability of professionals to adapt to 'Port Revel Scale' reflects their own particular field very early on during the first morning afloat. Masters in command, ship's officers, pilots and lecturers in navigation are obvious to the discerning eye ashore. Last but not least, our pilot colleagues may be further identified as those who are sea pilots, river pilots, harbour pilots, or those who are a combination of all three. Surely this in itself, a reflection on the realism embodied in Port Revel's scale facilities.

Considering the problems facing the existing operations with regard to navigation, safety and the environment (and who amongst us would deny that all three are synonymous?), to present a paper on training is somewhat difficult[37]. However, we as fully trained and experienced pilots must not lose sight of the fact that new blood must be trained to replace us and every pilot involvement is vital to the future safe ship handling of the officers and pilots of the marine world.

Port Revel exists. Radar and other forms of simulation exist. Let us use them as best we may with the cooperation of professional expertise, which produced them, so that those who follow us are capable of being the 'Lightning Pilots' described by Mark Twain in 'Life on the Mississippi.'

We may describe such facilities as Port Revel as an expensive luxury, which the world cannot afford, or we may incorporate them into our training schemes and look towards the future. The future, in which we, as responsible members of society, must continue to justify our very existence,

I may now say that whilst I was at Port Revel, Sogreah was having increased difficulty in attracting "éstagiers" (trainees) to pay for what was an expensive course. The cost included full board at the Hôtel Bonôit down in the valley. It has to be said that the food was superb. However, Jean Graaf wanted my opinion as to how the course could be made more attractive to the marine world.

In addition to the paper, which as I have said was commissioned, I offered several more suggestions, which may or may not have been taken up. Sogreah had taken the 'Exxon' name away from the names of the models when they took them over leaving the main name only. For example the 400,000 tonner *Exxon Antifer* became the *Antifer*. This was to attract other companies to send trainees there. Since then and after my time many changes have been made.

---

37 This paper was first written in 1985 when the pilot services of the United Kingdom were under attack, brought about by the necessary proposed legislation of the Thatcher government referred to earlier.

My observations to Jean were that the models were only oil tankers with the exception of one gas carrier. I believed that the addition of both a container vessel, and with the growing popularity of cruising, a passenger liner would enhance the appeal of the training fleet. I am aware that Port Revel has examples of both now, but I do not know if either of them were directly influenced by my comments.

I also know that model, remote-control tugs have been added to the facility. These will make the operation more realistic than the original 'transverse bow and stern thrusters,' which the models were first fitted with to simulate tugs. Another of my suggestions was that the facility (along with the benefits of the superb cuisine of the Hôtel Bônoit!) could be used in the future for businesses engaged in 'team building' exercises.

Another of my suggestions, which I do not believe was ever taken up, was that as the team of technician's 'handling of the models' was superb, they could perhaps, under supervision, be put in command of the 'real thing,' possibly at the oil terminal at Fos, Marseille. Now that really would prove a point!

A NORWEGIAN ADVENTURE

In 1979, following an inward bound passage on a 30,000 ton tanker fitted with a 'Norcontrol' computerised navigation system, what could only be described as a Norwegian adventure took place, which, in part is described in the article below. The short 'official' article was commissioned by the Marine Pilot's Branch of the Transport and General Workers Union. The main interest in the subject matter is that the experience took place in the early days of computerised navigational system's experimentation and before the advent of satellite navigation systems.

Marine Pilotage Branch. Technical Developments Sub-Committee.

Computerised Navigational Systems as an aid to Navigation in Confined Waters.

J. L. Curry. Liverpool Pilot.

Arriving on the bridge of a 30,000 ton tanker in the early hours of a dark March morning, I was asked: "May we proceed by computer Pilot?" A question, which, without doubt is likely to be asked as a matter of course in the not too distant future. A matter of course providing that the mariner is prepared to accept the computer as an aid to navigation rather than a threat to his rôle of decision-making controller of the navigational situation.

As a young first class pilot in the Port of Liverpool, I gazed in the darkness of the tanker's wheel house. There were two huge consoles bristling with knobs, buttons and switches. They were glowing with dials and indicator lights. My immediate response was that I considered the ship was large enough and of sufficient draught to present enough problems for me docking at the QE II Oil Dock on the day tide without me having any interference from a computer.

However, having given the course to steer and having asked for the speed required for the thirty five miles of sea pilotage to the Bar anchorage, I turned my attention to the idea of coming to terms with a computerised navigation system.

The particular computerised navigation system fitted on board the brand new *Texaco Stockholm* was the 'Norcontrol Databridge DB-4.' The system incorporates anti-collision, navigation and auto-pilot systems. The vessel was also fitted with condition monitoring and maintenance, engine-room automation in the form of 'Norcontrol Datachief.' The two systems with all their instrumentation accounted largely for the huge double console and 'space age quality' of the navigation bridge[38].

I assured myself that we are in the 'Space Age' and having further assurance from the captain that the mere flick of a switch would redeliver the ship back into my own hands, I submitted to the computer.

I soon realised the value of 'Databridge' and rather than a submission, I had availed myself of an aid to navigation that would enable me to carry out my duties as a pilot with greater efficiency by making use of the local knowledge gained from the system . Such knowledge may be used by the navigator either to influence or confirm navigational judgement.

On the inward course from Point Lynas to the Bar anchorage, the collision avoidance system alerted me three times. Each time, as it was clear visibility, I had already sighted the target visually and was already deliberating upon the necessary avoiding action to be taken. In each case the use of the inbuilt simulator confirmed the safety of my own actions.

I was encouraged to operate the system myself and was surprised how quickly I came to be conversant with the comparatively small area incorporated in the 'Databridge' system.

---

38 'A bridge Layout,' which was to become all too familiar very soon after the experience.

The system consists of the following systems: ' Dataradar', an anti-collision system, 'Datapilot', an adaptive automatic pilot, (that is an automatic steering system), 'Datasailing', a navigational system based upon signals from both the log and from the gyro compass and finally 'Dataposition', an automatic navigational system based upon information from electronic receivers, including 'Doppler Sonar Systems[39] Dataradar makes use of the ship's main radar without interfering with the latter's function. Thus the operation of the main radar is completely independent of the 'Dataradar' system's operation. This is a vital point, with which to reassure those of us who have become navigators during the age of radar.

It is possible to track twenty four targets on the 'Dataradar' and to obtain data regarding the nature of a target's course and speed simply by pressing a button. The information is presented on a digital readout, which is an integral part of the consul. A point to mention here for future additional safety at sea is the possibility of a vessel being fitted with a transmitter, as aircraft are, which not only would positively identify the target, but could provide further detailed information about the target identified[40]. Such identification, whether on the open sea or in confined waters, would enable V.H.F radio to be used to establish contact between vessels.

I do not wish to involve myself in explanations of vectors and other computer controlled symbols, which the indicator can show, or indeed explain presentation modes. Suffice to say that it is impressive to have a radar display, which can provide information to supplement that provided by a 'normal' radar display. The

---

39 This 'positioning' and its accuracy was the questionable part of any of these early computerised navigational systems and it was not until the advent of 'satellite positioning' on the earth's surface that this aspect of these systems could be positively relied on.

40 The 2002 'IMO SOLAS Agreement' included a mandate that required most vessels over 300 Gross tonnage to fit an AIS (Automatic Identification System) transponder. This was a direct result of the advent of 'satellite navigation' along with the early research and developments described above. The satellite system became available through the auspices of the United States in 1993.

operation of such a system is a pleasure and I must emphasise that it is in no way complicated or requiring skills, which the navigator is not already in possession of.

Texaco Stockholm was to anchor for some hours and as we approached the relatively crowded anchorage, I requested that the vessel should proceed in manual control before reducing speed. I confess at this point to the practical navigator's suspicions of computers and felt safer reverting to the safety of my known world of human control.

The computer's digital control read out was still available to supply me with information such as distance and course to steer to the latitude and longitude that had been fed into the computer for our selected anchorage position.

I was impressed by the accuracy of our final anchored position. By using the computer as an aid to my specialist pilotage knowledge of the area and by using it to check both visual and radar bearings, the vessel was 'brought up' (finally anchored) with five shackles of anchor cable in the water, -0.01 of a mile from the desired position. That is 61 feet 'out' on a ship herself over 600 feet long.

I declined the offer to feed courses and distances from the anchorage to the lock into the computer. My polite refusal was made without hesitation as problems of timing, tidal sets and strengths of currents along with many other difficulties presented by a confined waters situation flickered across the grey matter of this human brain.

I had realised that the accuracy of the computer position depended upon the accuracy of the system, which was being fed into the computer. As we know, 'Decca', 'Omega, 'Sat Nav' and other such systems vary in their degree of accuracy and although we may accept a degree of some error in the open sea, or in an open, deep water anchorage, it is impossible to entertain such errors in the confines of a narrow channel.

An aside here as I write is that my concerns were well founded, for it was some years after the advent of 'satellite navigation' mentioned overleaf before such a system was brought to safer and more reliable parameters, particularly of positioning of a body on the Earth's surface.

Texaco Stockholm (which was a Norwegian registered ship) berthed successfully on the day's tide, relying on her pilot, master, officers and crew using knowledge and expertise gained from training that has been accepted in the marine world and by using equipment that has been evolved by technological development over centuries. For myself, I was grateful to have had my first experience of computerised navigational aids.

Only a week or so later, whilst attending the 'Third World Symposium of Marine Traffic Systems' held in Liverpool in the April of 1978, in the role of French Interpreter, I was struck by the number of controversies that arose from the phrase 'Remote Control' being used in varying contexts. (All related to computerised navigation systems).

During the symposium I was introduced to a representative of 'Norcontrol' by Alan Bole who had been one of my radar lecturers at Liverpool, Byrom Street, Polytechnic, Marine Department. (Now a department of the John Moore's University). Alan introduced me as a young pilot who had recently been aboard a vessel fitted with the 'Norcontrol' system.

Following my 'positive' comments regarding my experience with 'Databridge,' I was invited as a 'practical navigator,' to visit the development centre of 'Databridge' at Horten in Norway.

I accepted and being on leave within the next few days, found myself crossing the North sea as 'Norcontrol's' guest with Tor Line from Felixstowe to Gothenburg. *Tor Britannia* and *Tor Scandinavia* were among the first ships to be fitted with the earliest versions of 'Databridge' some four years before.

I was impressed with the officer's acceptance of 'Databridge' as an aid to navigation and by the officer's competent use of the information gained from the computer. Their efficiency was not dependent on the system, which was used in conjunction with other navigational aids and never in preference to, or with the exclusion of them. When the system was inoperative at any time they were quite content to navigate with only the more conventional instruments, commenting that if all else failed, they still had the magnetic compass! (Officers after my own heart!)

Such a professional attitude relieved any doubts in my mind about fears of 'computerised dependency' that might well result in a development towards 'human robots operating under remote control.'

At Horten I discussed the problems of 'the practical navigator' in confined pilotage waters with 'Norcontrol' technocrats and learned something of their problems in research development. They assured me that 'Remote Control' is far from their minds as it is far from being desirable in the marine world. Their interest was in marketing navigational aids, which the ship owner and more importantly, the mariner desire in the concerns of safety at sea.

In confined waters with narrow channels and strong tides they indicated the dangers of the computer being overloaded with parameters, which could lead to the computer failing to interpret the situation presented in an acceptable navigational appreciation of existing conditions for a safe passage.

The technocrats at Horten did offer the idea of a 'predictor system,' as an answer to positioning in confined waters. Such a system would be based on a vessel navigating around a fixed beacon, relying on reflected radar waves to supply information for a computer to interpret position on time and distance from the beacon for accuracy. The 'Predictor System' has been tested in both British and American waters and findings may be studied on the Exxon report on the trials.

Another aside from the original publication: I was asked if there was anywhere where this 'Predictor System' might work in the Liverpool Bay. I had taken my charts with me and pointed out the possibility of placing a beacon on the Burbo Bank so that if its position was such that it was the 'centre point' in an outer circle on the Crosby Bend, then vessels may be able to use the information supplied to navigate the bend.

This would be a useful source of information particularly in reduced visibility or even in dense fog. My concerns expressed at the time were for the 'ever changing' parameters, which the strength and direction of the tide would present to such a system. As 'Norcontrol' never requested permission from the M.D.H.C. to establish such a beacon on the Burbo Bank and experiment with the idea, I believe that my concerns were probably an accurate assessment of possibly an insurmountable problem.

In conclusion, may I say that as I flew south from Oslo, a few terms used in computerised navigation systems had been made clearer to me. More importantly, I knew that although it may not be a general opinion at the present time, I believe that in the future, many navigators would, like myself, consider themselves fortunate to operate on the bridge of a vessel equipped with a computerised navigation system such as 'Databridge.' This, especially in days when relatively few vessels are so equipped. Obviously if all ships become computerised (as most have become since this article was written) new dangers will present themselves, but no doubt this fact will be born in mind by research technocrats and navigators alike.

Another aside: in my latter days as a serving pilot with most vessels then fitted with computerised navigation systems, it is hard to believe, but true, that it was still possible to hear on the

V.H.F. radio the desperate voice of a concerned officer of the watch mouthing words such as: "Vessel on my starboard bow…!"

With safety at sea as our number one criterion and the possibilities regarding safety resulting from the implementation of such developments as the 'Predictor System,' and target triggered transponders, I urge that we consider the advantages of computerised navigation in the light of an aid to present day navigation. With such positive thinking, perhaps at the 'Fourth World Symposium of Marine Traffic Services,' the phrase 'Remote Control' will not cause the same consternation that 'Steam' caused in the days of sail. End.

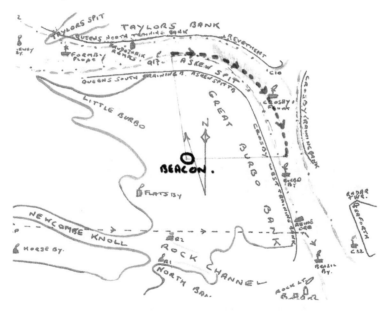

Chart of the Formby and Crosby Channels with a 'Predictor System' sketched in.

A postscript: I attended the 'Fourth World Symposium of Marine Traffic Services,' which was held in Marseille and I am pleased to say that the attitude towards computerised navigation systems was far more favourable than it had been at the one held in Liverpool.

Over forty years on, as I write this book, computers, robots and automated intelligence have become essential parts of our lives, but in 1979 they were very much in their infancy. Last week, on February 18th 2021, NASA's *Perseverance* touched down safely on Mars. We have come a long way since my first experience with a computerised navigation system!

After I had been introduced to the representative from 'Norcontrol' in Liverpool and accepted the invitation over to Horten, two days later a pack of tickets dropped through the letterbox. First class rail fare to Felixtowe, First class passage on Tor Line over to Gothenburg, followed by a rail ticket up to Moss on the Oslo Fjord. I arrived at Moss late in the evening and it was dark. After I had arrived at the railway station and was making my way to board the ferry, I remember feeling like as if I was a wartime agent crossing the fjord over to Horten.

At Horten I was picked up by taxi. The driver had the instructions to take me to the Hotel Klubben at Tønsberg . There the driver dropped me off. The hotel was expecting me but still no sign of any representative from Norcontrol. The receptionist told me I was to make myself comfortable in my room and that dinner was being served. Someone would pick me up after breakfast the following day.

Whilst I ate dinner, a female singer with a beautiful voice sang. She gave a particularly moving rendition of the song 'We are Sailing,' which was particularly poignant with its association with *Ark Royal* and the fact that the aircraft carrier was being decommissioned at that time. As noted earlier in the book, my father had been one of the pilots on board her when she came down the slip on the day of her launch.

The following morning I was duly collected and I spent the next two days in discussions with the engineers and developers at

Horten. The only cost, which I insisted that I should pay, was for a beer for six of us at dinner on the first evening. I was horrified when I was given the bill by the waiter. I had forgotten the cost of alcohol in Norway. I did not offer again.

For the return trip my flight was booked later on the third day from Oslo to Manchester via Copenhagen. The train took me up the west side of the Oslo Fjord to Oslo. Before I bade farewell to my friends at Horten, I was asked what I would like to see in the time I was to wait in Oslo before my evening flight. I had two possibilities in mind: one was to visit *Kon Tiki*, Thor Heyerdal's raft, or the other was to pay a visit to the art gallery to see the work of Edvard Munch. The latter won.

From the station a taxi took me to the art gallery where I was at first stopped from going in. Disappointed I asked why, to be told that I must wait for half an hour because the King of Norway was due to give a Japanese diplomat a tour of the gallery. I was assured that as soon as the Royal Party was in, I would be allowed to follow.

The Munch Museum.

As good as their word, I was called in and was virtually a member of the party, even looking at Munch's perhaps most famous painting 'The Scream[41]' at the same time as the King!

My flight home was uneventful and I was soon home safely after my totally unexpected Norwegian Adventure.

WILDLIFE ENCOUNTERED IN THE COURSE OF DUTY

Memories and extracts from a sea-going log book.

From hearing tigers roaring to the stars on the banks of the Pussar River, watching elephants bathing in the Katagastota River, or observing albatross gliding in our wake in the Indian Ocean, throughout my life I have always had an interest in wildlife wherever and whenever I have had the fortune to encounter it. This chapter is necessarily fragmented, but, I trust will make up a further life experience.

One afternoon whilst serving as a boathand, I remember the watch keeper on the bridge spotting a basking shark lazily drifting near to the surface on a flat-calm, summer-sea close alongside the pilot boat on station at the Bar Light Vessel. The pilot boat was lying to an anchor. We, the afternoon watch on deck, lowered one of the boarding punts and gently motored up alongside the magnificent, giant. We cut the motor and drifted westwards on the ebb of the tide away from the pilot boat in company with the leviathan. We estimated the shark to be well over twenty feet (seven metres) long. A memorable experience lasting about half an hour before the creature sank slowly out of sight back into the depths.

In the summer months, whilst 'standing by a line,' (that is being the crew member attending to the boarding punt from the mother ship, the pilot boat herself) during the dark of the short nights, it was possible to sight both sea horses and pipe fish, which were attracted to the glare of the boat's working lights and would be seen swimming close to the surface of a calm sea.

On an occasion when I was a young pilot inward bound from Point Lynas on board a coaster in the dawn of an early Spring morning, the officer of the watch and myself were amazed to realise that in that grey dawn we were literally surrounded by huge shoals of dolphins/porpoises (I am not sure, which of the two) but they were not in their hundreds, but rather I believe, in their thousands. That was both an amazing and an exhilarating experience.

The creatures were heading east so that we were on a parallel course. There were pods close to the ship and, indeed pods visible as far as the horizon all around us. Again, sadly, no camera. I did write a report of the sighting, which I sent to the marine department of the University of Liverpool. At that time the University had a marine base in the Isle of Man. The beauty of that morning sighting is etched in my mind forever.

In "East a Half South", I related the tale of Mr. Blue, a budgerigar, which after being attacked by gulls out near the Bar Light Ship, took refuge on the after end of the bridge deck of a coaster I was piloting from Liverpool down to LLandulas stone jetty with Nathan, my son, on board for the passage. The coaster was the *Lady Rhoda*, which I had brought into Liverpool from Point Lynas a day or so before. We caught the bird in the captain's hat, and brought 'Mr. Blue' home with us in a cardboard box. Sadly, the bird was to die the following day, no doubt from his exertions resulting from him having been blown out to sea by an easterly breeze.

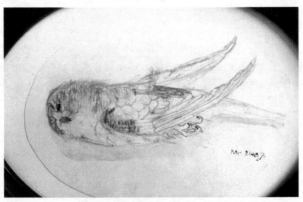

Nathan's watercolour of Mr. Blue.

Mr. Blue.

Flitting over
The wild, white wave crests,
Of the estuary,
You came,
For all the world
Flying like a little tern.

Fluttering, exhausted onto
The floating, island haven
Of our ship to escape
The snapping, sharp,
Deadly beaks of gulls,
Skuas and shearwaters,
You enhanced our boyish dreams.

For the late Mr. Blue, a 'seagoing budgerigar' and Nathan. 31st August 1987.

Another wildlife story told in that volume is the story, with photograph, of the seal cub, which had been rescued by the R.S.P.C.A. off the mud banks up at Garston. They had taken the pup in a sack down to the Liverpool Princes Landing Stage where they had asked the crew of a pilot launch to take the creature out to sea and release it.

I was landing on the ebb of the afternoon tide, having left my ship safely anchored in the Sloyne off Birkenhead, in order to move my car to the berth so that I might be able to drive home after docking the ship on the coming flood tide in the early hours of the morning. I took the seal pup, which was ignominiously tied in a sack, ashore with me. The launch crew and myself, both believed that the animal would have more chance of survival if it were to be released onto the West Hoyle Bank in the Dee Estuary where there is a colony of seals. We favoured this option rather than the one of the pup being dropped overboard out at sea on the flood of a spring tide, which we reasoned would probably bring him back to the mud flats off Garston the following morning.

I had time to whip home with the sack to show the tiny seal to my young family. Then I drove him to Hoylake and gave him into the care of Harry Jones, the then coxswain of the Hoylake lifeboat who had agreed to take the seal out to the colony on the West Hoyle Bank.

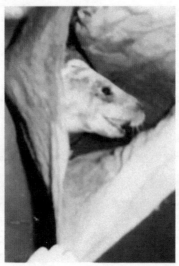

The seal in a sack.

Trawling through my memories and my Clan Line, Cadet Log Book, which was continued when I sailed as third officer with Booker Line, I come across many references to fish, whales, birds and animals sighted out at sea. There are also references to birds and animals sighted on land in faraway places.

In chronological order, my first reference in the log book whilst on board the *Clan Brodie* in 1960 was made to: "porpoises leaping under the bow..." and to: "...many sea birds, including gannets, circling the ship off Gibraltar." These references evoke the memory of my first full day at sea when, clear of Lands' End and all the way across the Bay of Biscay, I was amazed as to the amount the vessel rolled lazily in the Atlantic swell. The *Brodie* rolled some twenty to thirty degrees in a regular movement during that period and I remember the first morning, sitting, gripping on to No.3 hatch watching the port side, dip then rise again and thinking that I had 'made it:', "I am really at sea, a member of a deep sea ship's crew."

My interest in nature had always been strong from early on in my childhood and continues to the present day. I can still sense the excitement of first sighting flying fish under the bow of the ship and, indeed, alongside the vessel after we had passed through the Suez Canal and were proceeding down the Arabian Sea. In all ports visited, I record the problem of flies and how troublesome they were.

In India, I make mention of seeing in ports, what I refer to as: 'Bombay Canaries.' There were large grasshopper/cricket type insects. Research reveals that a 'Bombay Canary' is also the name given to an American cockroach. This creature is described as being brown with a yellow collar and can reach two inches (5 cms,) in length.

This creature, despite being called a ship's cockroach is not my 'Bombay Canary.' The 'beast,' which I saw was about five inches (almost 13 cms) in length. Always travelling alone they looked like large, colourful grasshoppers, which hurled themselves down the length of the ship's alleyways with a loud whirring noise. They were quite frightening for they came along unexpectedly. On one occasion I was on cargo watch in Bombay (now Mumbai) and decided that another cargo lamp was needed to help illuminate No. 3 hold. I fetched one from the focs'le-head stores and proceeded back to an electric socket at the forward end of the mid-ships accommodation. The actual socket was just for'd of the door to the cadet's cabin on the port side of the ship.

It was the same type of vaguely sexual, wooden, male plug, which fitted into the vaguely female socket as the one described in Andy, my fellow cadet's streaming of the log tale on board the *Clan Macleod* story in "East a Half South." I was about to push the plug into the socket when I was shocked by the realisation that one of these so called 'Bombay Canaries' was vertically resting on the junction box of the plug. The insect became aware of me at about the same time as I became aware of it and took flight, whirring off aft, along the alleyway of the mid-ships accommodation.

In the Indian Ocean it was possible to see not only flying fish, but frequently small fish could be observed being chased by larger fish under the ship's bow. Quite often I make note in my log of sightings of porpoises, dolphins, whales, and occasionally I refer quite simply to a 'large fin' visible in the distance, breaking an otherwise calm sea.

Whilst anchored in the rivers of what was East Pakistan, now Bangladesh, I refer to 'shite hawks', which frequently circled the ship hoping for scraps. I believe that the term 'shite hawk' came from the sailor's ignorance of the true identification of a bird and his wish to use a name, which had an air of 'bravado' about it, that is a name, which was familiar and accepted in the nautical fraternity.

My present research would have me believe that these magnificent raptors were probably flocks made up of a mixture of bald eagles, Pallas' fish eagles and ospreys. These, mixed with black kites and no doubt other birds of prey, made for an exciting flock of 'scavengers' present every day and so easily observed in great numbers from the decks of the ship.

I saw elephants bathing in the Katagastota River on my excursion from Colombo around what was then Ceylon in the Seaman's Mission Bus and no doubt monkeys, but I am amazed that there is no reference to them in my log book. I believe, however, that I must have sighted both langurs and macaques. In both India and East Pakistan there would have been both the former two as well as other 'old world monkeys', almost certainly in the trees on the banks of the rivers we navigated. (Ceylon now Sri Lanka, East Pakistan now Bangladesh).

I am personally not keen on snakes, but I do remember snake charmers with their flutes, known as 'pungi' and the baskets with live cobras waiting to be 'charmed' near the Temple of the Tooth in Kandy, Ceylon. (Sri Lanka)

I did not see tigers in the jungles, but I did hear them howling in the dark of night when keeping anchor watch on what was then the Pussar River near Chalna.

My final observation of wildlife on my first trip to sea was of a porpoise playing around the ship on the 9th of February 1961 when we were homeward bound, heading north in the Red Sea.

Along with these memories of sightings, I have a vivid recollection of the many scents of the east, which were to assail my nostrils at the time, not all of them either 'mystical' or pleasant.

My first recorded sighting of nature on my second voyage aboard the *Clan Macleod* bound for Australia was of a 'fin' spotted on the 16th March 1961: "Saw fin about 200 yards off on the starboard side. Possibly a whale or a shark." We were sailing south in the north of the Bay of Biscay.

My recent research into both whale and sharks in the Bay suggests that the fin could have been a great white shark. The Bay of Biscay is also reported to be a whale watching 'hotspot' for whales in general and amongst others sperm whales may be sighted. There are, however, possibly as many as thirty species, to which the fin could have belonged to including a killer whale and possibly even a blue whale. My sighting, however is the simple one recorded above and my only other firm belief is that it was not moving like a dolphin or porpoise, but rather was it on a steady course with the fin cutting through the surface of the water.

The next wildlife recordings are made when the ship was in the Indian Ocean. The first was of a single albatross that was circling the ship. The weather was fresh, but we were on our intended course for Australia and were south of the Equator. Not having a vast knowledge of albatross, I recorded it as a 'young albatross.'

Several days later, when we were running before storm force winds south of our designated course line, I record that: "Two albatross with wingspans of about 'ten feet' (3.1 metres) have been following the ship throughout the day, gliding through the wave troughs and skimming over the wave crests."

There have been 22 species of albatross recorded in this part of the ocean, of which 17 are 'Globally Threatened.' (2021) I cannot be sure of which of the 22 species I saw, but I can be fairly certain that they were of two different species by the difference in the size of the birds. Thus two different species of albatross to be found in the northerly latitudes of the southern Indian Ocean, the first smaller than the other two, which, because of their wing span, could well have been 'wandering albatross.'

The day after the first albatross was sighted the storm was strengthening and a great many gannets were circling the ship. In addition to the gannets, before breakfast on the same day, I sighted a water spout, which covered an area of about: 'one hundred square feet.'

We arrived in Sydney on the 21st April and moored on the discharging berth having passed under the Sydney Harbour Bridge the following day. The ship was to stay in Sydney discharging until the 30th of April before moving north to Brisbane. We were to return to Sydney for a brief loading period before going back to Brisbane to load the majority of the cargo for the homeward trip.

Whilst in Sydney the first time, Andy and myself made a train journey inland to the Blue Mountains. Herewith the account as recorded in my log book:

Tuesday 25th April. Anzac Day, Sydney.

"Went up into the Blue Mountains by train to Katoomba, 3336 feet, (1017 metres) above sea-level. We walked from Queen Elizabeth's Lookout, down the Giant Staircase and along the valley to the scenic railway. After travelling up on the railway, we crossed over the Jamison Valley in the 'skyway aerial car.' At one point we were 1000 feet (305 metres) above the valley floor.

The notable landmarks, which we saw were "The Three Sisters," (Rock formations) "Katoomba Falls" and "Orphan Rock." The mountains in the distance appeared to be of a brilliant-blue in colour.

Whiplash birds and Pee Wee birds could be heard in the valley. There were many strange trees and plants including gum trees and 'bottle brush plants.' The scenery was really beautiful."

Above we have a sixteen year old's account of a reasonably adventurous day ashore for two young cadet officers who found themselves on the other side of the world!

Andy Douglas, the fourth engineer, myself and the fifth engineer at Taronga Park Zoo.

On the 29th April, a Sunday, a small number of the ship's officers, (five I believe) went ashore in Sydney to visit Taronga Park Zoo. There I record seeing: Koala bears, kangaroos, wallabies, wallaroos and emus as well as other Australian animals and birds. Sadly, I did not keep a record of exactly what these species were.

Later when I made a journey north from Brisbane to Surfer's Paradise on the Gold Coast with friends, (Here I was to be chased out of the water at Currumbin Beach by the shark alarm bell being rung by the 'wedged-shaped', beach guard, not sure which breed of shark, but I was still 'swimming' some five yards up the beach!) Also on that day we visited Currumbin Bird Sanctuary. The latter is particularly famous for the huge flocks of 'free-flying' rainbow parakeets, which come to the sanctuary to feed.

Another of my observations from the southern hemisphere is of the 'different sky at night' with the beauty of the 'Southern Cross' constellation to the south. I have always believed that the best two places to sight the stars on a clear night are either on a mountain top or from the bridge of a ship.

On our homeward voyage, a 'long tailed' bird was spotted near the equator out in the ocean, which I believe now was almost certainly a white-tailed tropic bird. I also have recordings of sighting frigate birds. In my recent research, I was surprised to find that these ocean wanderers do not have waterproof feathers and if they were to land on water it would be fatal and yet they wander over thousands of miles of ocean.

My final log entry from my second trip to sea, referring to wildlife, is of sightings of both 'sharks and dolphins' when we were north bound, homewards through the Red Sea.

This voyage ended my initial wanderings deep sea, for I was called in to start serving my time on board the Liverpool pilot boats and to commence training to become a Liverpool Pilot.

My Cadet Log Book

Between the 12th of November 1967 and the 3rd of April 1968, I was released from the Liverpool Pilot Service to complete my sea time for my 'ticket' (marine qualification) requirement and sailed with Booker Line as third officer from the Thames on board the M.V. *Booker Venture*. I was to make three voyages with the *Venture*: The first two, from the Thames were straight forward trips outward bound in ballast to Georgetown, Guyana for full cargoes of sugar. We called in at Bridgetown, Barbados, for bunkers on our homeward passage.

On the third voyage, which was 'out of season' for the sugar in Guyana, we sailed from the Thames for Bremen to load phosphates to carry over to Jacksonville and Tampa in Florida before proceeding south to load sugar in Jamaica, 'topping up' at St. Kitts and then taking bunkers in Antigua before proceeding back to Slivertown on the Thames.

On the first voyage we sailed in early November and I sighted gannets on the 14th of November as well as 'a large unidentified raptor' off the Spanish coast. Flying fish were to appear around the vessel in the mid-Atlantic. The *Booker Venture* was not the fastest of ships. Her official speed was 12 knots, but the slightest wave and she slowed considerably, without doubt preferring to go 'through' both wave and swell rather than 'riding' them. She was affectionately known as the 'Booker Line submarine', which speaks volumes!

On the 23rd of November and we were 'still out there' I note that two of 'Mother Carey's Chickens', those delightful, small birds of the oceans, stormy (storm) petrels were resting on the deck of the ship. One flew off by itself the following morning. The other needed gentle, 'cupped hands' assistance before it too took flight. I considered it to have been both a wonderful and a privileged experience to hold this tiny, 'little bigger than a sparrow', bird in my hands. No weight to speak of, just a tiny bundle of black and white feathers flying off over the ocean waters with no land in sight.

Two more, petrels, (maybe the same two?) were on the deck in the same place, just forward of the lifeboat on the starboard side of the boat deck the following night, but neither needed help to leave the next morning, but I did watch them fly on my way up to the bridge to take my watch at 0800 Hours.

On Friday the 1st December, when we were homeward bound and had left Barbados where we had taken bunkers, I made an entry in my log book, which I will reproduce here:

"0800 -1200 Hrs, on watch. We have had a strong NE'ly wind since leaving Barbados. The trade wind, but the strength has decreased during the day to force 2-3. The sunset tonight was quite beautiful, a pale light in the western sky, very slowly changing from pink to a deep red long after the sun had set.

2000–2400 Hrs, on watch. A flat calm sea and a slight breeze. Observed a violent electric storm away to the north. Phosphorescence in evidence in the water. This is the first time that I have noticed it in any great profusion during this voyage."

On all three of my voyages with Booker line, I was to sight the weed in the Sargasso Sea in mid Atlantic. The first time was on the 5th December 1967 and I was surprised how thick the weed is in these waters of the North Atlantic Ocean.

This Sargasso weed, 'sargassum,' is home to a multitude of marine organisms, which set up home and live in this weed, which is always afloat in rafts in mid Atlantic. One larger variety of marine life, which spawns in the Sargasso weed are European eels, which have a complex lifecycle beginning as a tiny egg actually laid by the adult eel in the Sargasso weed.

After the eggs hatch, the young eels, known as elvers, drift inland with the ocean currents and after travelling for a long period of time, possibly many years, by which time they have covered over three thousand miles, they enter the rivers and lakes of Europe where they spend most of their lives. They return to the weed in the Sargasso to spawn and die.

Sadly, as with so many species on our beautiful planet, the records are showing a drastic decline in numbers and eels are now on the world's list of endangered species. I can remember fishing for sea trout on late summer's evenings down on the River Clwyd when I was a young pilot in the 1970's and sighting eels slithering through the grass moving seawards, which I was told was the beginning of the spawning migration. Let us hope that their numbers will increase again.

On the homeward trip we were visited by stormy petrels again on the night of the 6th of November. The following day, I did not see it being taken, but I am fairly certain that the impeller on the end of our log line[42] was taken by a shark, much as a salmon or sea trout will take a spinner. The 'log line' had definitely been bitten through and frayed. We replaced the lost impeller.

The log impeller 'sets' came in a wooden box with two impellers along with the log line and a clock. Being in charge of this instrument as third officer, the captain instructed me to order a new set after we had brought in the impeller's replacement for the last time that trip, adding that as I was in charge of the equipment, I could do what I wished with the remaining brass piece. (It is now on a wall in my home!)

There are no further 'wildlife' recordings on that first trip with the *Venture*. I will make mention here (for a further relevant interesting comment later about landing from the anchored ship after 'signing off' for a short leave) of the fact that Booker's brought our relief crew out to us on board a launch and the 'sailing crew' were landed at Southend Pier on board the same launch before travelling up to London by train to Euston and then on home to Liverpool.

As indicated at the beginning of "The Clearing Tide," my intention was to be 'outward bound' into literary seas, as it were and my thoughts were to let the currents of the mind take me where they would and indeed, so far, I believe that is exactly how the book has progressed. Now, I am staying with my deep-sea voyages to complete this chapter. This means that we have two more Booker Line voyages and my final voyage into retirement with A.C.L. on board Atlantic Compass to cover with regard to the wildlife and other aspects of nature encountered.

---

42 Log line. On board ships, it was usual to 'stream the log' to gather a rough idea of distance travelled. An impeller (rather like a small brass propeller) attached to the end of a 'log line' attached to a 'log clock' on board the ship would spin and clock up a calibrated distance, which would appear on a repeater on the bridge. This gave a 'log-distance', which together with sun sights/star sights would help to verify the ship's position on the earth's surface. Now with satellite navigation, the method is virtually obsolete, along with celestial navigation.

After a short leave period the Liverpool members of the crew had agreed to travel on the same train from Liverpool to London, in fact I think that the booking had probably been made by the company. It was on this journey that we met the actor John Gregson in the buffet car and spent most of the journey there chatting to him. An interesting journey.

Blue Sun Calypso

John's gone to the Caribbean
He's gone oh me oh my!
John's gone to the Caribbean
To the blue sun sea and sky.

He's gone on a large bulk carrier
That ploughs her way through the waves,
Her speed will break no sound barrier
For its at twelve knots she slaves.

Blue sun, blue sun
In the yellow of the sky.

They load the sugar in Georgetown man,
Then on to Barbados
With rum in the sun
Certainly that seems no loss.

But, there's someone else who should be around
And thoughts of her make me sad,
It's none too soon we're homeward bound,
Each mile that's lost is bad.

Blue sun, blue sun
In the yellow of the sky

When we're almost home
There's mists and it's so cold
But I'm near my love
And before I'm old…

One day together we'll return
To the rum in the sun,
To the rum in the sun my love,
To the blue sun sea and sky.

Blue sun, blue sun
In the yellow of the sky.

I had taken my guitar with me on board the *Booker Venture* and that 'calypso' was one of several songs, which I wrote whilst I was out at sea. It is to be sung in the key of D. On this Christmas trip, the guitar really came into its own, particularly on Christmas day when even the Captain, Ted Jones played it!

First sighting of dolphins 'playing round the bow' was on the third day out from the Thames. The following day: "Sighted what I believe was a whale at 0900 Hrs. A black hump in the water with the: 'traditional waterspout!' Vanished before I was able to confirm with binoculars."

On Christmas day we were running through 'thick patches of sea weed.' We were back in the Sargasso Sea. Two days later I report 'flying fish weather' and the following day in my evening watch I sighted both a satellite and a shooting star. The latter: "…of intense brilliance, which flashed across the heavens leaving a beautiful, green trail behind before it burned out."

Although the first satellite, *Sputnick 1* had been launched by the Russians in 1957, satellites were still relatively few in number above the Earth even ten years later, which is probably why I thought my sighting worthy of mention. The United States

National Space Science Data Centre catalogued 172 'spacecraft' placed into orbit by launches which took place in 1967. Whereas, at present (February 2021) there are almost 6000 satellites circling above our tiny planet! Only 400 of these are operational, the rest are reported as 'defunct', scrap metal in the dustbin we have made of space.

Two days out from Georgetown, I sight a large shark crossing our bows: "…swimming at a very swift rate indeed, black fin cutting the surface." Later in the watch, I sighted a white tailed tropic bird, like the one, which I had sighted homeward bound from Australia.

Homeward bound flying fish are mentioned. Several days after leaving Barbados, where we had called for bunkers again, some twenty dolphins were jumping ahead of the ship: "… in perfect line formation, which they maintained for more than five minutes before veering away to port and disappearing." Two days later we are back in the Sargasso Sea again with: "large amounts of floating weed around us."

Three days out from the Thames I note that there were: "… a great many gulls circling the ship." I would have thought that this would have been the case on other voyages, but I make no mention of them in my log book.

We anchored in the Thames and the launch brought out our relief crew. I mentioned this on the previous trip for a purpose. When the launch arrived this time, for some reason, she was unable to wait for the crew, who were signing off for their short leave before the next trip, to be landed. We were told that it would be later in the day before she could return. Now leave time was precious and I came up with a plan for me to land, which was inspired by my experience on the Liverpool pilot's river launch when I was serving on her as a boathand.

There were occasions when we, the launch crew of the pilot service launch, would land crew members from anchored ships

who wished to go ashore before their ships docked. I said farewell
to the captain and went down to the head of the accommodation
ladder, which had had been rigged on the starboard side for the
crew transfers. There were many small craft passing up and down
the river beside the *Venture*. The first one, which came close by
was a police launch heading up river. I cheekily 'thumbed' a lift
and to my delight the officers brought the launch alongside. I
explained my position to the officer on deck and he invited me to
'hop aboard.' They kindly landed me in 'the middle of nowhere,'
BUT, I was ashore. The officers told me that, If, I were to crossover
two fields, I would come to a railway station where I could catch a
train to central London.

I caught a train up to London and then a late afternoon train home
in time for Gill and myself to both make it to a fellow boathand's
twenty-first birthday party. He was delighted that: 'I had made the
effort to travel all the way from South America especially to be in
time for the event!'

The third voyage made on the *Venture* as mentioned earlier, was
when the sugar was out of season in Georgetown and we made a
run with phosphates from Bremen to Florida before calling in at
Jamaica and St. Kitts to load sugar for the homeward voyage.

We were to experience bad weather in the Atlantic and the first
nature to be 'logged' apart from the wind and the waves was the
sighting of the sea weed in the Sargasso. The weather improved and
became 'Dolphin Weather' and indeed the day after sighting the
weed I was treated to a ten minutes display in my morning watch
of approximately one hundred dolphins off on the starboard side
of the ship. (The evening before this sighting as we were altering
course to pass north of Bermuda, I noted: "Gorgeous sunset this
day. Deep pink daubed with smoke-grey, wispy clouds. Hopes of
fine weather tomorrow?")

The dolphins: "...were only sixty yards off the side of the ship just below the bridge. So close that they could be seen swimming below the surface between the most magnificent leaps clear of the water into the air, sometimes twisting over onto their backs before re-entry. At the end of the ten minutes display, the leaders, up at the bow, turned and swam back amongst the rest, causing confusion for a minute or so as they circled round beneath the surface, before they all headed off to the north."

The 'Dolphin Weather' was not to last and we were soon in extreme weather conditions with the winds from the WNW in excess of fifty knots. Several days later when the storm had abated, we arrived at Jacksonville. The port is some twenty miles inland and is reached by a pilotage winding through swamps where mangroves grow and pelicans abound.

From Jacksonville we proceeded south along the Florida Keys. Main comments made until we rounded Tortugas Cays into the Gulf of Mexico were about the strength of the Gulf Stream with the *Venture* making only seven knots. We arrived in Tampa having been delayed in the Gulf by storm force winds, which brought the captain onto the bridge during my morning watch when a sea threw us way over to starboard, almost onto our beam ends. The young sailor on the wheel was thrown 'down' to the starboard wheelhouse door. I managed to hang on to the chart table until the vessel came upright again and grabbed the wheel, spinning it hard over to port. The ship responded and clawed her way to being 'end on' to the direction of both wind and sea. The captain arrived on the bridge and ordered 'slow speed ahead' and we 'hove to' for several hours until the wind eased.

Having discharged the remainder of our cargo in Tampa, we set sail for Jamaica where the sugar was back in season. During my evening watch, approaching the Yucatan Channel, I, for some unknown reason shone the Aldis lamp over the starboard side and in its beam I could see dense clouds of tiny, red flies as well as huge shoals of small fish activity near the surface of the clear waters.

Perhaps the fish splashing on the surface, catching the flies, had caught my attention.

On the following Monday, as we were early for our arrival time at Savannah La Mar, (The place where the bird was shot out of the tree in Ian Fleming's, James Bond novel, 'The Man With The Golden Gun') we lay all stopped and drifted south of Negril Point. I was to see many beautiful and strange fish alongside the vessel, which were attracted by the arc lights, which we had hung over the side.

Whilst we were anchored in the bay at Savannah la Mar, as the second mate 'owed me' some hours for being late up on the bridge to relieve me during the Atlantic crossing, he offered to pay me back with a cargo watch whilst we were here. This enabled me to land by motorised canoe early one morning to await a local bus, which was to take me by the coastal route round the western tip of Jamaica, north to Montego Bay.

"Awaited bus for Montego Bay in a strange silence that was loud with the howling of Pye dogs and a hundred cockerels crowing at the first light of early dawn."

The bus was the 'local's bus,' complete with chickens, vegetables and other produce bound for markets in baskets on the roof and ran to Montego bay round the west coast of the island, past Negril Point and Lucea to Montego Bay. The journey took three hours through the most beautiful countryside rich with tropical vegetation and sugar plantations. Through the windows to the left, were the most beautiful white sand beaches and blue sea.

I first wandered round the town and saw amongst other sites: 'The Cage,' which was built in 1806 as a jail for escaped slaves, Lester Art Gallery which houses the work of the retired, Polish born, sea captain, Michael Lester who was to die in 1972 and 'Banana Wharf.'

I bought myself a bathing costume and went to spend the afternoon on Doctor's Cove Beach choosing to go to the 'locals' part of the beach rather than pay the exorbitant price of the tourist's beach. The cruise liner *Bremen* was anchored in the Bay and the prices were 'up' for the American tourists.

I caught another 'local's bus,' back to Savannah la Mar in the early evening. This time the route taken was directly south over the mountains via Montpelier. There was a delay at Montpelier and my kind, friendly fellow passengers shared their food with me. When we eventually arrived at Savannah la Mar, I had to wait three hours for a boatman to ferry me back to the anchored ship.

Captain Armitage and the rest of the crew had become concerned for my safety. There was unrest in Jamaica at the time because of the problems with Ian Smith's government in Rhodesia. (Now Zimbabwe) They feared that harm may have come to me. (In "East a Half South," I recounted the story of piloting the German built, 28 knot, Greek tanker *Johanna V* (built as the *Arietta Venezelos*, which had attempted to beat the British blockade off Beira in 1966).

Having now read 'A Brief History of Seven Killings,' a novel by Marlon James, which tells a story centred round the gang violence in Jamaica, (The plot is woven in the years from 1962 and includes the efforts of the rapper Bob Marley (The 'Singer' in the book) with his failed attempt to stage a 'Peace Concert' in Kingston in 1976, I believe if I had known what I learned from the novel, then, I probably would not have made the journey!) I found only warmth and friendship from my fellow passengers.

There were always many fish in the waters around the anchored ship, attracted by the bright cargo lights hung over her sides. When we moved our loading anchorage to Salt River, closer to Kingston, we anchored just after breakfast and as I was off duty, I asked the pilot if I may accompany him ashore on board the tug taking him ashore. On the passage he was to frighten me by suddeny producing a revolver and firing shots into the water. He was firing at an alligator. He missed and the creature sank into the depths. "Damn, I was hoping for a new pair of shoes," were his words as he pocketed the weapon.

I travelled in the pilot's car the 40 miles through Spanish Town to Kingston. I took my leave of the 'sharp-shooting,' but 'poor shot' pilot in downtown Kingston and wandered through the shopping centre and the harbour. I took a taxi to Port Royal and visited the haunt of the infamous Captain Henry Morgan and other pirates. I visited Fort Charles where Nelson was once stationed. I also viewed the spot where Fort James once stood before it was to sink beneath the waves during the hurricane of 1718. I passed by the Royal Mint and Morgan's Harbour and finally I visited the airport where I sensed shades of James Bond and Dr. No! I returned to the ship by bus for 1800 Hrs. in time for my evening cargo watch. I record: "Feel now as if I have seen a good deal of Jamaica."

Whilst on deck on cargo watch loading the sugar, I was dismayed to find that the Jamaican's loading the sugar were openly hostile to the crew. They were angered by the fact that African's were being hung by the Smith regime in Rhodesia. This was disturbing to find the friendly Jamaican people of 'yesterday', now so aggressive towards us because we are 'white.'

One of the shore-side, night watchmen here, with whom I became friendly whilst on duty, was an old Jamaican who had fought for the United Kingdom in the Second World War. I gave him the nickname of 'Midnight,' which he really liked and we were to discuss Rhodesia and racial problems throughout the world during the night watches. Tarpon were swimming round the ship here, again attracted by the deck lights.

We sailed from Salt River on the 12th March bound for St. Kitts and two days later I note that twenty sharks were following the vessel throughout my morning watch, "keeping station on either quarter." I could not help thinking that they might be hoping that someone would fall overboard!

On Friday 12th March in my evening watch we crossed the Saba Bank. There is an alarming entry in my log. The second officer on board British ships at that time was the navigation officer and responsible for 'laying off' the courses on the ship's charts for the ship to follow. Soon after 2200 Hrs., I became unsettled by the motion and slight 'vibration' of the ship and noticed on the chart that the soundings on the bank were relatively shallow. I therefore switched on the echo sounder, which soon showed me soundings under the keel of as little as 2 fathoms (12 feet or 3.7 metres). I shone the Aldis lamp over the starboard side and in its glare, rocks and sand were clearly visible below the surface. The soundings varied from 2 fathoms to 350 fathoms for almost fifteen minutes whilst we were over the bank.

When Captain Armitage came on the bridge during my following morning watch I reported the shallow patch on our course line to him. He examined the chart before taking a pencil and the parallel rulers and marking an oblong pencil 'boundary' round the bank before writing "Keep Off" in the middle of it. Later he was to have words with George the second mate.

We anchored in Basseterre Roads, St. Kitts to complete loading our full cargo of sugar. This was to take just thirty six hours during, which time I was able to go ashore twice. The first was during the afternoon after my watch. I marvelled at the splendour of this truly beautiful island with huge volcanic rock-mountains, the largest of which is Mount Misery. That morning the peak, almost 4000 feet above sea level, (1220 metres) was shrouded in mist. Sugar cane fields were cultivated as high up the mountain slopes as was possible. Visited Frigate Bay where there is a magnificent white sand beach. On Brimstone Hill there is an impressive fortress built by the British and fought over with the French in the 1600s. From

Basseterre, the capital, the countryside is picaresque with views of the famous fortress.

The following afternoon several of the ship's officers went ashore together and took a taxi to go swimming in Frigate Bay. We were to sail that evening for Antigua. During my watch that evening we passed several island schooners under full sail in the moonlight and the romanticist in me dreamed of Gill and myself returning to sail one of them through these waters in the future.

We bunkered and sailed the following day and set course for home. The visibility was amazing with the islands of Antigua, St Kitts and Nevis, Redonda, Saba, Guadaloupe, Montserrat and Barbuda all visible at once in the early afternoon sun. We headed out into the Atlantic swell with the blue waters of the Caribbean falling away astern in our wake.

On the second day out I observed a pod of some twenty whales ahead of us heading south and spouting frequently, swimming in a flat calm sea. They may possibly have been Right whales, but I am not certain: "These huge creatures passed within a mile of the ship." My final passage through the weed of the Sargasso Sea was on the 24th March when I spotted: "Much gulf weed, trailing in strings to leeward."

There are no further nature sightings recorded other than those of heavy seas, rain and strong winds on this homeward trip but there is another landing by 'thumbing a lift', story, which is worthy of mention.

We had moored the *Booker Venture* at the 'Tilbury Tanker Tier' and the sailing crew were to sign off, me for the last time, for I had completed my sea time and I was to report back to the Liverpool Pilot Service. Again there was not going to be a launch to land the 'sailing crew' until much later in the day. The crew turned to me remembering my 'cheeky' departure from the vessel on the previous voyage and asked if I might possibly be able to 'work the same magic' again.

A group of crew members was a different deal than a single person 'thumbing a lift' on a police launch. I believed that it would be possible, but thought that it would and should 'cost us.' I gathered together the crew who had by now 'signed off' articles and asked if they would be prepared to pay a small fee each (10 shillings in 'old money') in order to be ferried ashore as soon as possible. They all agreed, but although they brought their bags to the head of the gangway, which was rigged over the side, I do not believe that they really believed that there was any chance of my succeeding to get us ferried ashore.

There were many small craft passing up and down the river as on the previous occasion and I went down the accommodation ladder to the bottom step and again literally 'put up my thumb' to the first small oiler which was going past, heading upriver. To both the crew's amazement and delight, the skipper brought her gently alongside the *Venture* and I jumped aboard and explained our position and our wishes to him.

Delighted to be of service and to earn an unexpected amount of money, an agreement was made and the rest of the crew boarded the oiler and we were to be landed at Gravesend. This enabled us to make trains home far earlier than we would have done if we had waited for the official launch. I felt my action had been successful only because, like the crew on board the oiler, I was a 'man of the river,' albeit the Mersey not the Thames!

In 1978, after I had been a pilot for ten years, I was on board the pilot cutter out at the Bar Light Vessel when the *Booker Venture*, now sold off from Booker Line and renamed *Caribbean Memories*, sailed past outward bound from Liverpool for the last time one fine summers evening. A fitting name, I thought, with my own personal memories of the ship in mind.

After nautical school in Liverpool and completing all exams required by the Liverpool pilot service, I returned to 'Senior Lad' (Chief Officer) on board the *Arnet Robinson* for what must have been only one or maybe two cruises, before I was examined for and granted a licence of the third class for the Port of Liverpool on the 21st August 1968.

I was to make one more sea voyage in the May of 2009, but that was with Gill when we were 'passengers' on board my last 'piloted ship' the *Atlantic Compass* when I literally sailed off in to the west and the setting sun on Sunday 24th May 2009, two days before my 65th birthday. The birthday and my retirement were celebrated on the 26th May, SW of Ireland. Gill and myself were to make a Trans-Atlantic crossing, this time together. We left the ship in New York and flew home to a 'new life' after a short stay in Soho.

On the passage over, the weather was not wonderful with mainly strong, but not gale force, westerly winds. On day one, the 25th we sighted a huge whale south of Ireland, but I am not certain of the species. Possibly it was a humpback, as there have been reports of humpbacks off the south coast of Ireland in recent years.

I believe that rough seas prevented us from seeing other fish/sharks/whales for the main part of the Atlantic crossing. We put into Halifax in fog, which apparently is a regular feature in late May. On the voyage south to New York, we were treated to sightings of Right whales. Sadly even since those sightings, falling numbers of the Northern Atlantic Right whales have been reported. They have been on the endangered species list since 1970. There are now in 2021, fewer than 400 whales left with fewer than 100 hundred breeding females.

The threats recorded for these giants are numerous. Entanglement in fishing gear, vessel strikes, habitat degradation, ocean noise, climate change and availability of prey are all possible. These threats and figures are recorded in the NOAA (National Oceanic and Atmospheric Agency) fisheries reports on these baleen whales, which feed on plankton.

There is a slim hope of recovery as this species was hunted to near extinction in the 18th, 19th and 20th centuries. They were only 'saved' from being hunted in 1935 when their numbers may have fallen to less than one hundred. We can only hope that these beautiful creatures may recover again.

Whilst I was still a serving pilot, an A.C.L. vessel came in with a whale impaled upon her bullnose bow. Another example of a 'ship strike' on these relatively 'slow moving' giants, but I am not sure if it was a Right whale. I was not the pilot of the ship.

Whale impaled on the bulbous bow of an A.C.L. vessel, landed in Liverpool. Philip Parker.

I was to experience summers with many jelly fish in the waters of the Liverpool Bay. In the early part of some summers I witnessed incredible displays of phosphorescence in the water. This would be turned to 'green fire' in the bow waves and wakes of ships passing through it. I also remember one winter a jack snipe, frozen, dead on the deck of a ship, which I had anchored in the river south, one dawn, whilst awaiting the tide into Eastham.

On two occasions I witnessed salmon leaping in the Mersey. Once under the bow of a ship docking at Birkenhead and the other time one leaping in the Langton Dock. In Langton Dock, the oil rig supply vessel, which I was piloting was lying alongside the north wall and the captain and myself were leaning over the starboard bridge wing chatting when, right under our gaze below us the ten or twelve pound 'bar of silver', a fresh run fish, leaped clear of the water. Whether it was making an attempt to bring the species back to the Mersey, or whether the fish had missed the River Dee, I do not know, but sadly the fish was to be found dead in the dock system a week or so later.

Apart from the amazing number of dolphins mentioned at the beginning of this chapter, quite often I would see them under the bow of the Point Lynas launches as we made the passage to or from ships down at the western station. They were always both a beautiful and uplifting sight.

As I said at the beginning of this chapter I have always throughout my life, kept an eye out for the wildlife around me and have, as a result been privileged to be granted sightings of some of the world's most magnificent creatures as I have tried to illustrate here.

I have chosen to end this chapter with a poem, which is a tribute to my fellow cadet on board the *Clan Macleod* on my second trip to sea, Andy Douglas. Andy was to become a lifelong friend. He lived in the Isle of Mann, where I was to cross over to by ferry with my car to be present at his all too early funeral in 2010. The poem has lines, which mention wildlife sighted out at sea on our Australian voyage.

Memory of No Return.

Whipped by strong winds,
Manx waters lash rocks, which,
Receding, suck back into darkness
Beneath constant waves, surging seawards,
To lap shores of other islands
Where lie memories.

Fish fly forward, off the bow,
Filling logbooks with thoughts.
Log clocks tick away miles,
Chronometers clock the hours,
Personal tides, ebb and flow.

Gales breeze-blow stories,
Illustrated with fading sepia photographs.
Circling the planet
Gulls scream constantly
And ashes sink into fluid depths,
Halos of blue light
Anchor our thoughts
For just one more fleeting moment.

Sea rolling ever southwards,
Even to the ends of the Earth,
Where albatross glide in troughs,
Haunting oceans
And our dolphin years.

For my shipmate and friend, Andy Douglas. 1943-2010.

'A SMALL CORNER OF SOMEONE ELSE'S COUNTRY'

I have chosen the title for this chapter with the First World War poet Rupert Brook's opening lines from the poem: 'The Soldier' in mind:

"If I should die, think only this of me:
That there's some corner of a foreign field
That is forever England."

Rupert Brook.

Because of those lines, I have often thought of the many foreign ships, which I had the honour to pilot, as being a part of the country they were registered in and myself being the guest visiting that country. The comparison works both ways though, for those small, 'floating corners of foreign fields,' which were the ships themselves, were visiting for them, the foreign Port of Liverpool, England.

Being licensed as a pilot of the third class in the August of 1968 and retiring as a first class pilot in the May of 2009, the years, which I served saw many political struggles and open conflicts throughout the world. I was to pilot ships, which were registered in these countries, or ships, which had recently visited them. I was once asked by a Chilean friend how I could possibly pilot a Chilean registered ship after the Allende coup. I thought carefully about my reply, but answered honestly that in my opinion, in my professional role as a marine pilot, my duty was apolitical and that my responsibility lay with the care of the charge, which I had been entrusted with in the course of my duties.

During 1968 the Vietnamese war was only just over half way through its twenty year life/death span. Many years after the war did end, in the late 1980's, I was to pilot a large bulk carrier registered in Vietnam inwards from Point Lynas to Seaforth Grain

Terminal. The crew were extremely both efficient and pleasant to be with. She was deeply laden and a struggle, having a single propeller and a small rudder. The weather was fine, it was daylight and with the assistance of three tugs, all went well.

Once on the berth the captain insisted on giving me a bottle of whisky as a present. I explained that it was not possible for me to accept such a present and there followed an insistence that was to become heated to the say the least. To avoid 'an international incident', I accepted the gift, which placated the captain. The gangway took a long time to rig, but when it was safely rigged, I descended to the quayside and started to walk along the dock towards the gate. Almost as soon as I set off, a red car appeared in the distance at the far end of the quay and headed straight for me. The vehicle 'stopped' with me almost on the bonnet. A custom's officer came out of each of the front doors and one of them, the 'two ringer', asked me if I had anything to declare.

I was devastated and could only tell the true story including the Vietnamese captain's anger, nay fury, at me for trying not to accept his generous gift. I asked if they would be kind enough to take me back on board to return the bottle and for them to explain to the captain why I could not accept it. To my surprise they both fell about laughing and told me to be on my way together with the bottle! I set off along the quay with my 'booty' somewhat perplexed with their laughter ringing in my ears.

In the January of 1972 I was to pilot the Greek owned vessel the *Captain John*. She, as I was a second class pilot, was a second class ship, around 2000 tons gross. She had been a very 'flash' German vessel by the name of *Poseiden*, but had been sold to a Greek firm and renamed. We were inward bound overnight from the western station in the dark, bound for Liverpool. The captain was a lively individual as I was to find out the following evening, but he went below leaving the officer of the watch on the bridge.

More importantly, the radio officer, a young woman by the name of Georgia Vlipeki was also with me on the bridge.

This was the time of "The Colonel's Greece" and Georgia had been studying law at the University of Athens when the coup took place in April 1967. Because of her political beliefs, she felt that she had no option but to retrain for the foreseeable future and as a result became a ship's radio officer. We talked for the time that the ship was inbound up to the Bar Light vessel in open sea pilotage, which was for a little more than three hours.

As we approached the Bar Light Vessel, I knew that I would soon have to break off our conversation and, knowing that the next evening I would be attending a poetry group called 'Jabberwocky' in Burton village on the Wirral with Gill, I asked if she would like to accompany us there. I also knew that there was going to be a party afterwards in Parkgate and I promised that I would come back to the ship that evening to drive her in my car to both of the events. I assured her that I would take her safely back to the ship when the party was over. Georgia was delighted to accept the invitation as was the captain, who, to my dismay, without me noticing, had arrived on the bridge as I was making the invitation and chose to believe that I was inviting them both.

I had a beer with the captain in his cabin when we were safely made fast on the berth. He ate walnuts the whole time whilst I was waiting for the gangway to be rigged and I even brought a half walnut shell home from one of them that I ate with him. I still have that half in my desk drawer to include it in a story, which, to date, I have never written.

I collected both my guests in good time and took them home to West Kirby to meet Gill and have a meal with us before the poetry. Afterwards, we went on to the party where both Georgia and myself were to be embarrassed when called for the captain having been 'sighted' sitting on the loo and not wanting to miss anything, he had decided to leave the door open! At that point I took them both back to the ship.

Photograph of the walnut shell

Later in that year over Easter, Gill and myself along with our two young, fostered brothers, (later to be our adopted sons, Paul and John James) made a journey to Greece by car including the overnight, sleeper car-train, (which we nearly missed), from Paris to Milan, Italy and then on to Greece by car, a Renault 4, via, what was then, Yugoslavia. We were to travel through Yugoslavia for three days, staying the third night in Skopje. When we arrived there, we had decided to camp and I called in at the Hilton Hotel, which had been rebuilt following the earthquake of July 1963, to ask at the reception desk for directions to the camp site. We had driven passed the station and noticed that the station clock had been left at the time the earthquake had struck.

Whilst inquiring at the reception desk for directions, I was horrified to learn that there was an outbreak of small pox in Yugoslavia and I was told that the border with Greece was closed. Naturally this gave me great cause for concern, for although all four of us in the party had had small pox vaccinations, we had not thought to bring the certificates with us as the news of the outbreak had only broken after we had left, indeed, this was the first that I had heard of it.

Gill wondered why I had taken so long, but when I returned to the car to break the news, I was able to soften it with the announcement that I had booked us into a family room in the rebuilt Hilton Hotel.

I had banked on a good night's sleep for us all without the effort of pitching a tent and setting up camp being the answer to us coming up with a plan to hopefully progress the holiday. The next morning, after breakfast, we set off to find a hospital. There were large posters everywhere depicting people with the disease, which was rather unnerving. We went to more than one but eventually we found a clinic with a doctor who spoke German, with whom I could communicate and we were all four able to be vaccinated again and were given certificates. We then, with a mixture of trepidation and hope, set off for the border where we found a harsh, stern-faced, uniformed soldier who waved us through to the 'no man's land' between the two countries

At the Greek border we were stopped by a character in grey flannel trousers and an open -necked white shirt. I asked him if he spoke English to be told 'no'. I asked him in French if he spoke French to be told 'non'. I asked him in German if he spoke German to be told 'nein'. He put his hand out for our passports. Handing them back he exclaimed: "I am Greek, I speaka za Greek! Come on in, welcome to Greece!" We were in and drove south in high spirits, relieved that we were able to continue on our planned holiday.

Travelling south from the border, we sighted Mount Olympus, 'home of the Gods' with sun on the top and we stopped at Kolynos, the site of the stand of the 300 Spartans at the Pass of Thermopylae. Leonidas, who led the Spartans against the Persians of Xerxes 1, had, along with Odysseus, always been one of my heroes. We also passed through and climbed the hill at Marathon, site of another of the battles of the 'Persian Wars.'

Once in Athens, having Georgia's address, we visited her parent's home. Sadly Georgia was away at sea, but we were invited in for afternoon refreshments including very sweet cakes by the name of baklava. We were only able to correspond by sign language, as neither understood the other's language. Georgia had obviously told her family that we would visit and despite the language barrier the family made us most welcome.

Another memory of that adventure even before we had left home was that I had noticed a copy of the book: 'The Colonel's Greece,' criticising the political situation in Greece, lying in Gill's open suitcase. I was able to advise her to take the book out of her suitcase, for concerns, that if found, it may present us with a formal investigation. The military junta were in evidence everywhere and there were many buildings with barbed wire encircling them. A more relaxed view of the police came, when in Athens we were stopped by a traffic policeman on Easter Sunday at a crossroads and I was afeard that I had committed an offence. The policeman however, strode up to my window and produced two Easter eggs from his greatcoat pocket, which he handed through the window for our two young boys!

We were to stay several nights in Athens and visited the Parthenon and later from Porto Rafina, we visited the temple of Poseidon, the God of the Sea at Sounion. Then we proceeded further south over the Corinth Canal to stay at a campsite in Tolo on the Peloponnese. From Tolo we visited the theatre at Epidavros. Homeward bound our intention was to cross the Adriatic by ferry from Patras to Ancona in Italy before driving north to Milan for the return overnight train journey to Paris.

Since I had left Booker Line and passed my nautical examinations at Byrom Street navigation school, I had not had any necessity to find a use for my discharge book. A seaman's discharge book is the log of all voyages made along with comments on competency written by the ship's master as well as the recording of all certificates gained in the periods of training. I mention these facts at this point in my Greek story, for I was to find another important use for my personal discharge book, which was to benefit the whole family whilst on holiday.

Whilst waiting on board a pilot boat one day, not long before we were to set off for Greece, I was reading, as I often did, the day's copy of the 'Journal of Commerce', which was at that time a comprehensive list of ship's movements and maritime news. There in the adverts, I spotted one for a Greek ferry company, which ran from Patras in Greece to Ancona in Italy. This would be ideal for the family's return from Greece to catch the train back to Paris from Milan. Best of all with regards to cost, there was an attraction for seafarers who could produce their discharge books being given a huge discount.

We parked the car outside the shipping office in Patras and although there was some consternation when a British and not a Greek seafarer produced his discharge book, as I had taken the 'Journal of Commerce' advert with me as proof, the company honoured their offer. We were able to book the overnight crossing for next to nothing and had a smooth and uneventful crossing, which enabled us to make the car train from Milan in good time.

The only moment of concern, which I was to have on board the ferry, a converted Greek cargo ship, was simply that, whilst having dinner in the saloon with the family, I noticed that the captain and all three navigation officers were on the dance floor with other of our fellow passengers dancing the syrtaki[43]! Who was on the bridge?

I mentioned travelling through Yugoslavia shortly before Easter. On our long journeys along the country's 'two lane highways,' we were to observe many wreaths hanging in trees, on fences, by the roadside, in fact we were to comment, they were anywhere the 'unfortunate' had landed. The driving was intense and when

---

43 Syrtaki: Greek dance with the dancers, quite often all male, linking arms in a line. Not many realise that this 'traditional dance' was only created in the 1960's for the film: 'Zorba the Greek'.

I closed my eyes before going off to sleep each night on that journey, I could see the road stretching out before me.

On one leg of that journey, we were to be waved off the road by army motorcycle outriders along with all the other traffic. We sat there wondering what the problem was when a huge motorcade swept past. We had witnessed President Tito travelling south. Rear guard outriders waved us on our way when the motorcade was all past and clear.

Back home in Liverpool as a young pilot along with the 'flash' 'Flying Finns' and the 'Stroom boats' mentioned in an earlier chapter, there were four Yugoslav ships, also pretty 'flash' running between Yugoslavia and Liverpool on a regular run.

Their agency was Sievewright Bacon and it was always a pleasure to pilot these ships. They were fairly large for 'coasters' and in bad weather conditions could require tugs. I also placed them third in line for the best providers of first class cuisine. I always placed the French as first in line, closely followed by the Spanish. Possibly because their meals, like the other two, were normally enhanced with a glass of wine! I remember well the names of these ships: *Korcula, Krushevo, Cavtat* and the *Titov Veles* (we filled the car up with petrol in the town of Titov Veles). The crews were always so friendly and efficient.

Later in my career I was to pilot the Yugoslavian, (Croatian) crewed RoRo vessel, the *City of Dublin* several times and I got to know the captain quite well. I was to pilot the vessel inbound for the last time in the November of 1991, some months after the Balkan's War in Yugoslavia was already in progress. Following the death of Tito in 1980, the numerous countries, which made up the former Yugoslavia, were descending into the conflicts and ethnic cleansing, which became a blood bath. Years later, after some intervention from the United Nations, which was not at all straightforward, the war was to end in 1995.

On the day I last saw the Croatian captain after docking the ship in Liverpool, he shook me solemnly by the hand, bidding me 'farewell,' for the whole crew were returning home, presumably to join in the bloody conflict. I do not know whether he was to survive. I have my doubts.

Soon after the Warsaw Pact, tanks of the Soviet Union rolled into Prague on the 20th August 1968, just after I had been licensed as a pilot of the third class, I found myself inward bound from Point Lynas to Liverpool on board a Dutch coaster, the *Tridale*. Thinking of the people of Czechoslovakia in the night hours as we were proceeding up to Langton Lock, I wrote a poem, which was originally accompanied by guitar. Here are the words as an unaccompanied poem:

Freedom Whisper.

Night stealing softly and moonlight
The breeze whispers freedom
The world over the breeze whispers
Freedom, svoboda[44].

Birds on the wing, homing to roost
Feel the breeze ruffle their feathers
Hear the whisper and are free.

Fishes below in night's darkened waters
See the surface rippled by the breeze
Communicating the whisper,
They hear and are free.

Nocturnal creatures emerging for forage
From dark burrow or tree-stump's hollow,

---

44 'Svoboda:' Czechoslovakian for freedom.

Sniff the air with wrinkled noses,
Feel the breeze, hear the whisper
And know they are free.

Wisps of cloud in clear skies above,
Beyond above,
Man-made storm clouds gather,
Hang in oppression and depress.
Over suppression they loom and man...

Nature's creatures feel the breeze,
Freedom, svoboda.
Man too is nature's creature,
But Iron man with iron soul
Sits within his iron tank.
He does not feel the breeze,
Nor hear the whisper.

Outside the iron walls men sit within,
Others stand in the shadows
Of this moonlight night.
They feel the breeze,
Hear the whisper:
Freedom, svoboda
And long to be free

The invasion was to have serious consequences for the Soviet Union for although the invasion halted the pace of reform in Czechoslovakia, there is no doubt that it had long term consequences for the overall unity of the communist bloc. There was the bloodless, so called, 'Velvet Revolution' of 1989, which led to the end of communist rule in the country and in 1991, the Czech Republic split from Slovakia. All these changes were taking place in the Eastern Bloc and indeed this break up was running almost in parallel with the more violent breakup of Yugoslavia described above.

In my early years as a pilot, I was to pilot many Soviet Russian ships. They were registered in different ports all around the soviet coastline from the Black Sea to the White Sea. In fact there was, as I remember, a Black Sea fleet and a White Sea fleet .

I have told the story of inviting Boris Revunenkof, Captain of the *Kolymales* 'home for tea' earlier and in "East a Half South" more fully. In that volume I also mentioned the humour of me commenting how cold it was on the bridge of a large Russian bulker in Seaforth waiting for our tugs to make fast in winter and the very large, bear of a captain, wearing his Cossack hat, looking disdainfully down on me and telling me (truthfully) that I did not know what cold was. He came from Murnansk!

The soviet ships were of different calibre and age, the Ukrainian ships being amongst the finest, the country being known at one time as: 'The bread basket of Russia.' We know that since the 'wall came down' and with the end of Soviet Russia, the various separate countries have all fared differently, but for the purpose of this chapter and indeed the book, it is not my intention to delve too deeply into present day politics.

There were, not counting the 'War of Attrition' 1967-1970, two mayor Israeli/Egyptian conflicts in my time in the Liverpool Pilot Service. The first was the 'Six Day War' in 1967 and the second the 'Yom Kippur War' in 1973.

On the day that the 'Six Day War' broke out, I was leadsman on a Harrison boat returning to the pilot boat down at Point Lynas and the ship had just passed the Bar Light when the news came on the radio that the Israelis had launched their attack. For the 'Yom Kippur War,' I was at home between inward ships on sea turns. I was to pilot many Israeli and Egyptian ships during my career, but decided not to knowingly discuss the conflicts with either of the nationalities.

Later on the United Kingdom was to be involved with the 'weapons of mass destruction' conflict in March 2003, with Saddam Hussein in Iraq. I was returning home from shifting a small coastal tank, the *Stolt Petrel* from Gladstone to Eastham when the news broke that we were involved with the Americans in the bombing of Iraq. I remember telling Gill the news when I was climbing into bed in the early hours.

Throughout my career there seems to have been numerous conflicts in the Middle East including the Gulf War, also known as the Iran-Iraq War or First Persian Gulf War, which took place from 1980-1988. There was yet another Persian Gulf War, the Iraq-Kuwait conflict. I piloted ships from most, if not all of these countries both before and after the conflicts. I was once communication's assistant on a large tanker bound for Tranmere Oil Stages, which was one of the tankers struck by not one, but two missiles whilst traversing the Gulf of Hormuz during the first Persian Gulf War. The missiles both struck the forepart of the forward accommodation, but fortunately with little damage.

At the turn of the century I was almost involved in a private Israeli conflict when I was piloting an Israeli Zim Line ship of around 15,000 tons gross from Point Lynas to the Seaforth container terminal. We were to dock on the flood of a spring tide, but the ship was running late and it was touch and go if we were going to make the flood tide docking. The flood tide was generally considered easier than the ebb tide, for after swinging a vessel in the river north, the pilot is able to 'slide sideways' across the tide and enter the lock head or bow first. On the ebb tide the vessel must be backed into the lock and close to the entrance as the ebb tide is carrying her both across and away from the lock with a westerly set.

The old pilot's adage was that: if you are that close to a high water docking, the answer was to play safe and 'lift the handle' (reduce speed) and make it an ebb tide docking. After I had made my decision, I remembered that a younger pilot about to move up a class, Chris Booker (he who was to mastermind the visit of Cunard's 'Three Queens' in 2015) had asked me that if ever I was knowing in advance that I was to make an ebb tide docking with a fairly large ship, would I let him know so that if possible he could come with me as a leadsman.

As it was in the days of mobile phones, I rang Chris and he was able to make it down to the landing site at Woodside Landing Stage in time for a pilot launch to bring him up river north for him to board my ship and make the ebb tide docking. When the Israeli captain realised that Chris was to board, he firmly believed that I had deliberately slowed the ship, not for her safety, (which was the case) but rather that I might give a colleague the experience of witnessing a ship backing in on the ebb tide. Although this was not the case, it took until we were safely on the berth in Seaforth, before he relaxed and stopped being angry with me.

The conflict, which was to carry on for longest, indeed for thirty years of my career was close to home and was the Northern Irish conflict. The hostilities which first broke out in 1968, which was also the year I first became a pilot, was to last until 1998, when the 'Good Friday' agreement was signed in Tony Blair's tenure as prime minister.

During these long years I was to pilot Irish ships, particularly the green hulled coasters of Arklow Shipping, which were registered in Arklow and the Kelly boats, which were registered in Belfast.

The Northern Irish Conflict was more usually referred to as 'The Troubles' and was the cause of many deaths, which included members of both para-military units on both sides, civilians and members of the British armed forces.

The latter were ferried over to Belfast mainly from Liverpool on board vessels of the R.F.A. (Royal Fleet Auxiliary) The R.F.A. had a number of troop carriers, which were equipped with bow doors and could possibly be used as large landing craft by being beached to discharge their cargo of troops and vehicles. Mostly the ships were used as ferries as in the 'Troubles', travelling from one dockside ramp to another dockside ramp to both load and discharge their cargoes.

The class of vessel, which were operational during this period, were the 'Round Table' class, which had names of the knights of King Arthur's round table. *Sir Lancelot* was the lead ship of the class and the others all had names of King Arthur's knights from the Arthurian Legends. I was to pilot all of them, which ran the 'ferry service', at times more frequently than the passenger ferries ran in a twenty four hour period.

One of them was the *Sir Galahad*, which was to end her days in another war zone many miles away from Liverpool when she was sunk by bombs dropped by an Argentinian Skyhawk fighter plane in Bluff Cove during the Falkland's Conflict in 1982. In the same attack another Round Table class ship, which I had piloted, the *Sir Tristram* was badly damaged.

The year before the Falkland's War, I was to pilot the nuclear powered submarine H.M.S. *Superb* outward bound from the Royal Seaforth Dock to the Bar Light Vessel. Twelve months later she was reported to be in the vicinity of the Falklands by the press shortly after the Argentinian landing in the 'Malvenas'. This was untrue, as although correct information had her leaving Gibraltar at the time and the British press had 'presumed' that she was bound for the Falklands, she did not in fact proceed to the conflict. In truth it was H.M.S. *Spartan*, the 'Swiftsure' class submarine, which was eventually declared by the government to be the first of the British warships to be cruising off the islands, initially, to enforce the two hundred mile exclusion zone declared by the United Kingdom.

Another series of wars, which began in 1958 before I became a pilot, but continued until June 1976 were the Icelandic Cod Wars. There was a humorous boarding for me on a small Icelandic

coaster, which I believe was called the *Klajafoss*. I was boarded at
the Bar station and as I arrived on the bridge the captain ordered
'hard a port' and gave the helmsman a northerly course to steer.
We were bound for the Manchester Ship Canal and the course
should have been to the south east.

The captain was smiling and was obviously in a good mood.
Before shaking his hand I asked what exactly was 'going on?' He
explained that because of the latest developments in the 'Cod War'
he had been sent to capture a 'naval expert' and return with him to
Iceland. "You'll do" he said giggling before he gave the ship over to
my command to head back for our docking at Eastham.

All the way inbound, he argued the case for Iceland and by the time
I left the ship I was convinced of the Icelandic rights to the cod in
their own waters. In the Eastham Channel, the captain went below
and came back up with a frozen cod weighing about five pounds,
which he gave me as a present for being 'so understanding',
claiming that the fish was one of the last cod to have been left in
the seas around Iceland.

There is a sequel to this story, for I had reason to go over to
Liverpool that afternoon after docking the ship. By the time I was
back in the lift at James Street, a station of Mersey Rail, to return
back to the Birkenhead side of the river on my way home, the cod
had melted from its frozen state. As it was overhanging my brief
case at either end, it was obvious to the other passengers in the lift
as to where the 'fishy' smell was coming from and they all gave me
a 'wide berth!'

Another 'brush' with the Icelandic Cod Wars was when in 1993,
during the 50th anniversary of the Battle of the Atlantic, one of
the ships that I was to pilot was the Icelandic gunboat *Týr*. The
commander was very proud of the fact that he was the commander
on board the *Týr* who had outmanoeuvred the British navy during
the final stages of the Cod Wars. He was naturally very proud of

both representing Iceland in these, the last Battle of the Atlantic celebrations and of the fact that he had played a major part in Iceland 'winning' the third and last Cod War.

I had my own personal battle with him in convincing him that I had to navigate the vessel into the lock as we were fourth naval ship booked into the Langton Lock. Langton Lock has its own difficulties on the ebb tide, (not anywhere near the same as on the ebb at Gladstone Lock) but to have three frigates already in the lock, each with two tug boats left only 'our ship space' for us to fit in to. Although he had out manoeuvred the British Navy some years before, I was not prepared to let him risk causing damage with a difficult locking in with both no space and with tidal conditions, of which he was totally unaware. So many would have witnessed the damage if he had caused it and I was not going to allow that to happen. This was his final trip in command, for he was to retire after a long and illustrious career upon his return to Iceland.

I believe that I have now covered most of the country's ships, which I piloted from countries, which were involved with war zones during my career as a pilot, but maybe not all. I think back, for another example, to my first two trips to sea with the Clan Line and the oil bunkering visits to the Port of Aden, since 2015 now the temporary capital of the present war-torn country of the Yemen. There always seems to be, sadly, conflict somewhere in the World.

The Biafran War, or the Nigerian Civil War, raged between 1967-1970. As I was licensed as a pilot in 1968, I was only a pilot of the third class even when it ended, so I would not have piloted any of the Nigerian Nationalist Line Ships at that time. Later, when the war was over and I was a pilot of the first class, I did pilot a number of these vessels.

Strangely, it seemed that there was nearly always a gale blowing when I was manned on one of this company's ships, as I have recorded in the pages of "East a Half South" with the stories of the *River Jimini* and the *River Rima*, which were both docked into Liverpool in extreme gale to storm-force, wind conditions. Also in those pages is the reference to 'standing by' another of the companies ships, the *King Jaja*, which I attended over numerous tides in the north-west corner of Sandon Dock during a prolonged period of storms. Eventually I was to go on leave and another colleague was to take the ship outward bound.

This colleague was blighted by numerous engine breakdowns and other faults and also experienced another strengthening in the westerly wind, which came round to the north. I believe that it was this ship that on the outward bound passage, off Seaforth, with the old ship's slow speed, wind and tide pushed the vessel onto the first red boat-beacon, which then marked the beginning of the outward Crosby Channel.

The pilot reported the fact that his ship had made contact with the C22 Buoy to the V.T.S. Control at 'Mersey Radio.' A short time later, the controller at the V.T.S. called the ship back on the V.H.F. radio to ask the pilot if the red light on the C22 boat-beacon was still flashing. The pilot was obviously struggling with his charge, but was a man with a great sense of humour and came back with the simple reply: "Not unless it's waterproof." The ship had in fact sunk the buoy!

Over the several tides, which I was to attend the *King JaJa* in the December of 1974, I had numerous telephone calls from the Nigerian Superintendent of the Nigerian National Line in Liverpool, Captain Jonas. (The captain of the ship was white, British as was so often the case with what were considered to be 'Third World' countries at that time). Gill answered a phone call from a voice, which she believed to be that of Captain Jonas. As it turned out it was not the voice of Captain Jonas, but rather the voice of Hernan Rozenkranz-Shiklar, a Chilean refugee.

So we return to the beginning of this chapter and the reference to the query about piloting Chilean ships after the Allende coup in Chile in 1973. Gill and myself, had offered the University of Liverpool assistance to find Chilean refugees accommodation. There were quite a number of Chilean refugees who found their way to Liverpool.

Hernan, had been a lawyer in Santiago when the coup took place. His story of escape, which I always believed should have formed the basis of a book, began with a client who had booked an appointment with him in his office very soon after the coup had taken place. The client simply stated that he knew that Hernan supported Allende and that as he also admired him as a man, he was there to offer him a lifeline before he was to be arrested. 'If Hernan and his young wife Vivienna were to be at the crossroads at midnight...'

Hernan and Vivienna were at the crossroads and somehow were smuggled out of Chile and were then able to make their way to Liverpool. We found the pair a flat in Liverpool close to the University. Hernan was to be accepted to take a doctorate at the University by courtesy of one of Prime Minister Harold Wilson's education schemes for refugees.

When he had completed the doctorate at Liverpool, I was to 'move ' Hernan and Vivienna, with as many of their worldly goods as I could fit into my Volkswagen camping wagon, down south to Southampton, where Vivienna was to read a degree in Spanish. Vivienna, when we first met her, could not speak a word of English, but she was quick to learn and was very soon speaking the language fluently.

We had become firm friends, but the actual move was quite daunting. The night before the move, we had had the news that the marriage of close friends was breaking up. Also on that evening, before going up to the flat to see how many of their belongings

I could transport, Gill and myself went to see the Fred Zimmerman film: 'Julia,' starring Vanessa Redgrave in the title role. This Oscar -winning film's subject matter relates to two childhood, girl-friends and their successful attempt to transport funds to support an anti-Nazi movement in pre-Second World War Vienna. The plot is, however, in essence, a tragedy.

The film, combined with the news of our friend's marriage break up, put me in a sombre frame of mind and I was not to be cheered when later that evening I sighted the enormous amount of 'worldly goods' that Hernan and Vivienna hoped that I would be able to fit into the camping wagon. Physically it was not actually possible to take very much. The next morning I arrived back at the flat to find a great many of the couple's Chilean friends waiting both to help load the van and to see their friends off.

Very soon, very little was loaded into the space available, leaving room only for me to drive and my two friends to be seated. Even so the van was basically overloaded and I had to take great care to brake in good time whilst driving the whole distance from Liverpool to Southampton, slowly. This was a humbling experience.

Vivienna was to pass her degree with flying colours and became a social worker in London supporting displaced Spanish, speaking women. Hernan became a well-known and highly respected advocate for refugees in both Britain and Europe. He worked with the Refugee Education and Training Agency (Retas), part of the World University Service from 1987-2006. Hernan was to die shortly after an early retirement and I sadly had the honour of co-writing his obituary for the press along with a mutual Chilean friend.

I hope that the reader will have gathered from the stories, which I have recounted in this chapter, that the life of a pilot can take the fortunate man or woman into many distant, faraway places with a wealth of life experiences and all from the initial base of the navigation bridge of a foreign, registered ship. I was to pilot some six thousand ships during my career and the above stories were taken from relatively few of them.

"I MUST GO DOWN TO THE SEAS AGAIN..." JOHN MASEFIELD

Sun.

Elusive arcs of golden beauty
Dancing upon the waves
A Dazzling cavalcade of brilliants
With health and beauty for their slaves.

Moon.

Unending motion of darkened waters
Bathing in silver light,
Flowing, yet flowed over by a steady stream,
Bewitching mysteries of the night.

Two verses of poetry written on the 27th of November, 1963, one in the morning 'eight to twelve' watch and the second during the following night watch. On both occasions, I was 'stand-by a line man' waiting for the return of the punt to the embayment of the pilot boat and had been affected by the light on the rippled waves lapping against the ship's hull below me.

I wrote the lines down in a note book and thought: "That is poetry!" I painted oils whilst I was a pilot apprentice and read a lot of both art and poetry books (as well as Ian Fleming's James Bond books!) I visited the Earlston library in Wallasey every week in dock and made sure that I had a variety of reading material for the following cruise. One book I remember wading through was John Bunyan's "Pilgrims' Progress".

From the writing of the verse 'Sun,' I have continued to write poetry as is obvious through both this volume and the earlier "East a Half South." I have been published in numerous publications, books and leaflets. In 1969, the year after I qualified as a Third Class Pilot in the Port of Liverpool, a colleague, Henry Kernighan, contacted me to inform me that his wife Anne, along with Diana Hendry and Mary Raws had decided to start up a poetry group in the village of Burton on the Wirral going under the name of 'Jabberwocky', taken from the name of the poem by Lewis Carroll.

This slightly ridiculous named group ran for more than twenty years and I, thanks to Henry was to read at the very first evening. After only twelve months, Diana and the other two decided to hand the organisation of the group over to Peggy Poole, Chas Raws and myself. We ran a particularly successful group for over twenty years before 'giving it a break' with the advent of poetry workshops.

After a few years rest, we started up another group along with Alan Gaunt. Sadly both Chas and Peggy have both passed away. However, Alan and myself along with Kemal Houghton and now John Oldershaw are still running this successor to 'Jabberwocky' in Linghams Bookshop in Heswall. The 'new group' is called "First Thursday." Why? Because it is held on the first Thursday of every month except August.

'Jabberwocky' was held initially behind the art gallery of the artist Norman Cusden in Burton village before moving over the road to the delightful venue of Pear Tree Barn. (Now a private home). After many years we moved briefly to the Old School House in Parkgate before a longer residence in the centre at the Wirral Country Park at Thurstaston. The final venue was at the Friend's Meeting House in Heswall.

The basic format of the evenings involving poetry, music and art has evolved over the years but is basically still as the original concept envisaged by Diana Hendry. We decided quite early on that we would work with the Poetry Society of Great Britain and invite 'big name poets' to 'special' evenings from time to time.

In the early years we hosted local poets such as Adrian Henry and Roger McGough along with a host of poets from further afield. These included, Vernon Scammel, John Heath-Stubbs, Ursula Fanthorpe, Douglas Dunn, Thom Gunn, Ted Hughes, Seamus Heaney and Sir Stephen Spender.

Ursula Fanthorpe stayed with Peggy, but all the rest stayed with Gill and myself in West Kirby, save for Sir Stephen, whom we considered too venerable a figure to stay in our spare bedroom. The first time we were to put him up in Burton Manor where the evening was held.

The second time we put him up in the Adelphi Hotel, which was close to Lime Street Station as he came by train. He travelled in my Renault 4 car and it was a tight squeeze to fit his tall frame into the passenger seat. That evening was held at the Williamson Art Gallery in Birkenhead, but Chas, Peggy and myself had a meal with him in the Adelphi Hotel before I ferried him over to Birkenhead. I always have considered it a great privilege to have met these poets and to have listened to them reading their own poetry.

Anne Kernighan, Diana Hendry, Chas Raws, Peggy Poole, John Curry and Mary Raws with Sir Stephen Spender at Burton Manor College.

There are stories connected to all of these poets. Such as my children's amazement that Thom Gunn, when he had eaten his breakfast the following morning, was to swing is long legs with their leather cowboy boots up onto the table. The blind John Heath-Stubbs when asked if he would like a second croissant, hesitated, whilst he pondered the offer over before saying yes please to the one, which was supposed to be mine! (More amazement for my four children!)

Seamus Heaney was on his way down south to stay with Ted Hughes when they were to choose the poetry for the anthology 'Rattle Bag.' I was to drive him over to Lime Street Station giving him a letter from me to Ted, asking him to: "look after this poet!"

Seamus had brought over a litre bottle of "Paddy," Old Irish Whiskey, which was drunk at the soirée following the event, which was held at the Williamson Art Gallery. A number of friends used to come back to our home for these gatherings and on this occasion the litre of Paddy was emptied. Seamus signed the bottle before he left and we still have it in our kitchen.

Seamus was later to be awarded the Nobel Prize for Literature and Ted Hughes was to become Poet Laureate. I have left Ted to the last in the list as, for me, his visit turned out to be the most remarkable.

To coincide with the visits of most of the 'big names,' we liaised with the head of English at West Kirby Grammar School for girls, Jenny James. Jenny would organise a reading for all sixth formers taking English at A level in schools across Wirral and we from 'Jabberwocky' organised the venue, usually at the Concourse in West Kirby.

When Ted Hughes came for the first of his two visits, we could not make contact with him before the day of the readings. He was to read for the schools in the afternoon before the evening reading at the Friend's Meeting House in Heswall for 'Jabberwocky.'

I was given the task of welcoming him officially at the Concourse and so I was there early. It transpired that he had arrived in West Kirby the night before and had stayed in the Dee Hotel. In those days, in 1979, the Dee Hotel was a genuine hotel with guest rooms and was situated across the road from the West Kirby Concourse.

The imposing figure of Ted Hughes arrived, dressed in his famed black leather jacket and for me was, as he always seemed to me, a brooding, dark presence. I introduced myself and we discussed the programme for the day. He accepted an offer to accompany me home between readings for afternoon tea with a selected group, which included Jenny James. He then accepted an offer for dinner in Hoylake with Chas, Peggy, Jenny and myself at a Greek restaurant. But that was going to 'be it' for he 'had to leave' after the evening's reading in Heswall.

However, in his own words, Ted 'was drawn in' and returned with us to my home in West Kirby after the reading along with a group of the 'Jabberwocky' faithful. Suffice to say that he did not travel on that night and at four o'clock the following morning, the two of us were still sitting in my lounge discussing poetry and fishing, the latter, also being a passion shared by both of us.

When he left the next morning, he insisted that I must go fishing with him on the Taw or the Torridge the following season. We corresponded several times over the winter and when the season came, as the summer turned out to be a particularly dry one, both the Taw and the Torridge were at very low levels. As a result, Ted suggested that I join him to share a boat for the day, fly fishing for trout on a newly-flooded reservoir south-east of Exmoor which bore the unlikely name of Wimbleball.

I set off in my Volkswagen camping wagon and spent the day before Wimbleball fishing the Bristol Reservoir of Blagdon with the success of only one smallish trout for my efforts. I travelled on to Wimbleball and spent the night close by. I was there early and

I remember vividly Ted's 'dark presence' when he arrived and met me at the fishing lodge.

It still seems amazing to me to think that I spent the whole day in a rowing boat with Ted Hughes fishing for trout. To begin with, I had no success, whereas Ted had several good fish in the boat. We took it in turns to take the oars and our conversation ranged far and wide. I was studying the Open University's poetry course that year and apart from discussing his own poetry we also discussed that of Sylvia Plath.

As for the fishing, with my early lack of success, Ted insisted that I tried a fly specially tied for him by a friend, which was called a 'muddler minnow.' I tied the fly on and I just could not go wrong. It became almost embarrassing. Final count for the amazing day, Ted: five trout, John: twelve trout, a 'double bag limit!'

'THE' muddler minnow fly.

On one occasion when I was rowing, heading up an arm of the lake for shelter, my rod was pointing astern and the fly was, reeled in, just dipping/dapping in the water. (I was not intentionally fishing). The wind was quite strong and as the freeboard of the boat was low, the waves were splashing into her and we had to bail from time to time. As I rowed, my reel suddenly started to scream out. I believed that the fly had caught in the weed, for the arm of the lake was quite shallow. I did not want to lose the fly that Ted Hughes had given me, so I back paddled to stop the boat and lifted the rod to find, yet another trout had taken the 'magic' fly and Ted netted it for me when I had played it out.

It was dark when we made our farewells. Ted's last words were that I must go with him to Alaska to fish for salmon. Sadly that was not to be, but we did correspond on numerous occasions before his death and when referring to the fishing, Ted would always add: "But nothing like that day at Wimbleball."

"Each gleaming with its own magic."

When Ted became Poet Laureate, telegrams were still available and I sent him one with the words: "Tight Lines," which I believed had the double meaning both for his poetry and for the fisherman's wish, one to the other, for success with the rod.

Sir Stephen Spender has a rider to his visits too. Gill had spoken with him about our visits to Maussane les Alpilles in Provence where we had camped many times near to where Spender had an old farmhouse where he stayed with his wife, the concert pianist Natasha Spender.

One day, my son Nathan answered the phone and dashed upstairs to Gill whispering excitedly that Sir Stephen Spender was on the phone. Gill describes the very slow, positive voice of Spender calling her Mrs Curry and asking if both she and myself could 'house sit' the property in the Alpilles for him for three months later in the year. The property housed amongst other treasures, a Steinway piano, a valuable piece, which needed guarding. Sadly, Gill was a full time art teacher and I was a full time pilot, so we had to decline this fantastic offer from Sir Stephen.

We sometimes cycle from Maussane if we stay there nowadays and always refer to our ride up into the hills as the one to 'Stephen's place!'

Since 'First Thursday' has been flourishing, we have had, during the past twenty and more years some more 'big named poets.' Recently in consecutive years before 'Lockdown,' we hosted the then Poet Laureate: Carol Ann Duffy and the following year the newly appointed Poet Laureate Simon Armitage. Both read at the Williamson Art Gallery and we have hopes of more big names when the Covid crisis has passed. Neither Laureate was to stay with us as both are based fairly locally.

Those crude, early lines of poetry written on the pilot boat lead to some remarkable life experiences, which have left me with some wonderful memories.

Omphalos.

The day ended,
Cradled between darkness and the water.
A plash of oars
In the waves buffeting from wind-wards.
We sculled, you and I,
Homewards in the fading light
As clouds scurried towards the west.

The wind sang a chorale,
Earth whispered verses to the trees
And silver trout
Lay heaped on the bottom boards,
Each gleaming with its own magic.

Dawn had been damp
With both dew and raindrops
Falling from a broken sky.
Black feathered, ragged rooks
Littered the air
That grey morning,
Blown above green fields
In which plaintive, bleating
White flocks grazed.

You pulled away from the jetty
And the sun
Paled to golden through a rift
To light your dark presence
And the twinkle of your eyes
Smiling towards
Deeps and shallows of the hours.

We dined afloat, internationally
With crisp, Cloberg Laski,
Octopus from Spain,
Salata from Hungary,
Herrings from Norway
And Halva from Israel.

Below, small black flies
Searched the thermo-clime
As our offerings to Poseidon
In that quiet bay.

Later, we moored our black ship
In a long, wild arm
Where finned flanks
Rolled in the turbulence of spray
And Aeolian music
Sighed through the reeds.

Oracle of Delphi prophesy,
Centre of the Earth
Hold me fast.
Umbilicus sustain me,
Odysseus guide me,
Lull me
In this creel-cradled night.

With Ted Hughes at Wimbleball. 20:05:1980

LIVERPOOL'S "CLASS OF 1960"

The title for this chapter comes from a short article, which I wrote in 2009 for the July issue of 'The Pilot,' 'The official organ of the United Kingdom Maritime Pilot's Association.' The article was to commemorate the retirement, at the age of 65 years, the last three of six applicants who had been accepted into the service at the age of sixteen years in the autumn of 1960.

Before re-writing that article, there are a few other comments, which I wish to make regarding both broadcasts and publications, which I was to be involved in during my career. The earliest, which I remember, was an interview for BBC local radio made with an older colleague, John Tebay. We were involved with an informal chat show about the life of a marine pilot.

In 1985, shortly before I was to go abroad in the course of my studies for a joint honours degree in French and German, I was asked by the BBC to read some of my sea poems to be recorded on board a ship. I managed to arrange with a colleague who was taking a fairly large vessel outward bound from Gladstone dock for both myself and a BBC recording team to join him on the bridge from the berth to Gladstone lock. We were able to record a selection of my sea poems, which were broadcast later in the year.

Towards the end of my career, the younger pilots would often ask me to be the link with the service and interested parties who wished to have the service featured in books about Liverpool and there was also a notable contact with 'Bright Moon' films who were making a film about Liverpool in Liverpool's Year of Culture in 2008 by Roger Appleton and Dave Cotterill.

The two were given myself as a contact and asked for suggestions for filming. I suggested that I contacted them on a fine day when I was docking an A.C.L. vessel on the day tide. If they went over to New Brighton at the appointed hour, they would be able to film the vessel close to and film her as she was swung on the port helm through 180 degrees prior to docking in Gladstone lock across the river.

Then I suggested that they made their way over to Seaforth, where I would meet them at the Seaforth gate to accompany them back on board the ship to film me on the bridge. The filming was arranged and all went according to plan except that when I met them at the gate they were both wildly excited and said that although they would come with me back on board the ship there would be no further filming that day for they intended 'to come with me' on a future occasion.

The two contacted A.C L. management and arranged that they would drive to Antwerp where they would board my next inward bound A.C.L. so that they might film me boarding at Point Lynas and then film the whole passage from that point to the berth.

This worked remarkably well although on the day the ship was running late and missed the day tide, which she was booked for. Incredibly the docking in the dark made the footage even more exciting. They were to return in the dark on a further occasion to film another A.C.L. with me on board docking from the shore point of view. (The five G3 A.C.L.s all looked basically the same).

The film "Passport to Liverpool," featured all aspects of Liverpool life and was a great success having its premier at the Liverpool Philharmonic Hall. BBC showed the film numerous times, both later in that year and in subsequent years. For me, I was delighted that Roger and Dave chose not to place all the footage of the A.C.L. in one block, but rather ran the theme of both the passage and the docking throughout the film. For the success of the film this was to work extraordinarily well.

On another occasion in 2008, I was passing through Woodside pilotage rooms on a Monday on my way to Liverpool to take a ship outward bound. The Monday was the first in the month and thus the monthly pilot's meeting day. The time was shortly before ten o'clock in the morning when the meeting was due to start and so there were a great many of my colleagues present.

One of the then representatives, Gary Woodall was there talking to a stranger, who turned out to be Dan Kenyon, a photographer who was engaged in producing the book: 'Liverpool Sung and Unsung[45]. The highly successful work was a collection of superb photographs of people connected with the city who together, all helped to make Liverpool the great city, which it is. There are photographs of many well-known people, such as the playwrights Willy Russell and Alan Bleasedale and Dame Lorna Muirhead, then Lord Lieutenant of Liverpool. There are also photographs of others who, together, all contribute to the greatness of the city.

Dan asked for suggestions for a photograph of the Liverpool pilots who guide the ships safely both to and from the port. I thought for a moment and gave him a choice. We could keep in touch by mobile phone and he could come down to Woodside landing stage and photograph me landing from a pilot launch after I had piloted my ship safely out to sea, or…, I came up with what was a far better offer for my second choice.

I have written about the operation of the large pilot cutters earlier and that they could be operated by just seven pilot apprentice, 'boathands' in days gone past: "Two three handed watches and a float." I had noted some months before, that, although we had our full complement of working pilots, the service only had seven working pilots who had actually manned the pilot boats together. I suggested that, if I could get all seven to meet with him on the *Edmund Gardner* in Canning dry dock, we could take a photograph, not 'down aft' in the boathand's accommodation, but in the pilot's saloon. We would sit in 'order of seniority' as we would have sat in days gone by and he would be able to add 'our

---

45 Liverpool Sung and Unsung. Kenyon Dan. Smiling Wolf Press. 2008.

positions' in relation to each other in the caption if we were to 'man the boat' again on the day.

Dan was delighted with the idea. All seven of us managed to find a mutually acceptable time and Dan took a superb photograph, which I have had his permission to reproduce here below, a coloured version of the, perhaps more dignified, sepia version, which features in the book. A book, which I strongly recommend.

'Two Three handed watches and a float.' Photo: Dan Kenyon.

Both "Passport to Liverpool" and "Liverpool Sung and Unsung" were to be released in 2008, which was the same year I had my operation to replace both my hips. (Body damage brought about by continual and foolish 'diving' on squash courts in order to play the 'impossible to hit otherwise' squash ball!) After three months recovery time, I was to return to the river to pilot until my 65th birthday the following year.

I was to retire south-west of Ireland on board the *Atlantic Compass*, my last piloted ship, as related earlier. I wrote the following article for "The Pilot," which bears the same title as does this chapter.

May and June of this year, (2009) saw the retirement of the last three serving pilots of the 1960 Liverpool intake of apprentices or 'boathands,' which was the legal, 'Bye-Law' term for trainee pilots.

The three retired on their sixty fifth birthdays with John Curry retiring on the 26th May, Stuart Wood on the 20th June and Geoff Rafferty on the 27th June.

There were six successful candidates from that 1960 Autumn interview and of the other three, David Temple died at an early age in 1991, Simon Fearnett transferred to the Humber in 1988 and Alan Green retired from Liverpool in 2005.

The interviews were held at the purpose-built pilot office on Canning pier head to the south of the Liverpool landing stage and the famous waterfront. The interview panel consisted of master mariners, pilots, the Superintendent of Pilotage, not to mention the 'Marine Surveyor and Water-Bailiff' of the Port of Liverpool! How daunting would that illustrious gathering have been to a sixteen year old!

A White Star line, M.V. *Britannic* was making a flood way approach to the Prince's landing stage when an excited John Curry rang his parents from a phone box on the Pier Head to inform them that he had been accepted into the service.

After medicals, sight-tests, enrolments and other interviews, which I seem to remember we attended as a group, we were placed as cadet officers with shipping companies to gain deep-sea time prior to being called in to the service. John sailed with Clan Line to India and Australia. Stuart sailed with Brocklebanks to India and Geoff with Eder Dempters to the west coast of Africa.

The following year we were called to commence training as apprentice pilots who then crewed the four pilot vessels, which ran an efficient but costly pilot service for the Port of Liverpool. The apprentices were 'cheap labour' on the very low wages, which they were paid. Eventually this four vessel system became too expensive, being less efficient than a fast launch service, which was to replace it. (See the chapter on Pilotage Reorganisation).

The 'Class of 1960' worked their way through the system to all become pilots of the 'Third Class,' licensed between 1968 and 1969. All six progressed to become pilots of the First Class five years later. These six licences provided 'extras' to cope with the busy trade and brought the numbers of Liverpool Pilots up to 185. Sadly, the 'trade bubble' burst in the 1970s with the advent of the ever increasing size of tankers, along with the advent of containerisation, the latter, for which Liverpool was ill-prepared.

The six quitted themselves manfully through both good times and extremely bad ones. During the 'over-manned' years of the late seventies and early eighties, four went off to "pilot in the sand" as we used to call piloting out in Saudi and other foreign parts, thus proving to many, that piloting is first and foremost having the ability, skills and knowledge required to be a 'ship-handler.' Geoff and John stayed on in Liverpool.

With the 1988 Pilotage Act, we faced another new era. An era of 'employment,' a state, which Liverpool Pilots resented from day one and vowed to fight their way out of. This was eventually achieved with a return to self-employment in the summer of 1997.

This period also involved the necessity for "appropriation," (choice pilots) for the depleted numbers in the service since an ever increasing number of companies wished to avail themselves of this facility. The 'big one' of a number of appropriations, which Stuart was to hold was Shell and for Geoff and John, the 'big one' being Atlantic Container Line.

We also involved ourselves in the politics of pilotage, Stuart becoming a representative during the 'Battle Years' when

Liverpool fought its way back to self-employment and John served as Chairman of the pilot's committee for twelve years, which included the "Battle Years," of the troubled years of employment.

All three involved themselves in many activities outside pilotage. Stuart, amongst other activities, has involved himself with both sailing and sail training. He also gained a pilot's flying licence for light aircraft and became involved with local radio. Geoff amongst his other activities was to become a fount of knowledge on animal husbandry and is also a very competent furniture restorer. Geoff has been involved with the Mersey Mission to Seafarers, (and still is involved in retirement) over a very long period of time. John has a Joint-honours degree in French and German and has taught at the University of Liverpool. At present, he is the Lifeboat Operation's manager at the Hoylake All-Weather Lifeboat Station. (As I write, I am now the Chairman of the Hoylake and West Kirby Lifeboat Stations).

The last of the Class of 1960, mourn the loss of their dear friend and colleague David Temple, however, they themselves hope to enjoy long and happy retirements, enjoying life after serving in a profession, which brought each of them a whole lot of heartache, a whole lot of fun, but above all, a great sense of job satisfaction for a job well done.

We wish all our serving colleagues, quite simply: "Good Ships and Many of Them!"

For the final piece for this chapter, I have chosen to reproduce the speech, which I made at the 'Hotpot Dinner' held for the three of us in the November of 2009. This occasion was in effect our 'dining out' from the service. Geoff spoke on my behalf and I spoke on his. Stuart was not present having chosen to be away celebrating his retirement. Below is my reply to Geoff's speech on that November evening:

Mr. Chairman, Ladies and Gentlemen,

Having been a Peter Pan Pilot, never allowed to grow old, and a 'Junior Lad' for the majority of my career, I find it somewhat incredible to stand here before you, having completed a full serving career, having piloted some six thousand ships safely in or out of the Port of Liverpool, now as a retired pilot realising that: that's it! It's all over!

But of course Gentlemen, that is not the case. It is not all over. I move to another stage of my life with a great wealth of life experience, some amazing memories, not all pleasant, and the knowledge that I have had the good fortune to have had a profession, whose calling I would not have missed for anything.

I know that I owe so much, to so many within that calling, but perhaps, my greatest debt is to my father, the late Walter "Curly" Curry. This debt probably goes back to when I was only five years old when it would appear now, that my father had decided that the only job for his youngest son was that of a Liverpool Pilot.

He would take me with him on such illustrious craft as the *Hemsley I*, on shifting jobs in the dock or on lightning jobs in the river during the school holidays. We would walk back from Herculaneum Dock (he never took a bus) through an already aging South dock system to the Pilot Office on Canning Pier Head. He would talk with such enthusiasm, telling me of the Port's History and of different acts of pilotage undertaken by either himself or colleagues, out on the river. I find it a little uncanny that as the Liverpool Pilot's Hotpot is usually on the third Friday of November that for this, my retirement, that it has been altered to the first Friday, the sixth of November, my father's birthday!

It was he who taught me that you cannot do this job by yourself and of the importance of colleagues, agents, lockmasters, tugs and boatmen. To this list I would add, two more that were not in existence in my father's day: the V.T.S and the launch crews. I know that I found myself personally, apart from the many that fit into the calm seas and prosperous voyages category, in some frightening and certainly dangerous situations out there, and I know that without this comprehensive team, the pilot, despite the famed "Bridge Team" of the modern approach, is in fact figuratively, often alone on the bridge, and is liable to be nothing.

I am delighted that there are members of most, if not all of this illustrious team with us tonight. It would be impossible to name every man or woman by name who shaped the course of my career, but I will mention the following agents: Clive Schofield of Gracechurch as was, (now Borchard Line), Derek Gooding of E.M.R., Peter Rolands of I.C.L, Elliot Fish of Backhouse Blore, Paul Musgrave of North-West Trading, these are not in any particular order and so last, but certainly not least Chris Greenbank of A.C.L.

The team could not be complete without the launch crews who ferried me safely to and from the ships, the staff of the V.T.S., lockmasters, gatemen, boatmen and again, certainly not least, the tugs. I have been through so much with or without the tug's assistance, but when the chips were down it was always a comfort to have a couple of boats in there with you.

Both Tug Companies provided superb coverage for me during my career and my thanks tonight goes to each of them. I know that we have both Brad Cummins and Larry Larkin, skippers from the "*Donnau*" with us this evening. Both said they wouldn't miss tonight for anything, so I am not certain that it is appropriate to announce that in their absence the "*Donnau*" was last seen drifting upriver underneath Runcorn Bridge on the flood of this afternoon's tide! Great to have you both here and my regards to all who serve with you, Dave, Marty, Peter, Alf and the rest.

With regards to my colleagues and friends the Liverpool Pilots I can only thank you for having me along with you. That goes for both the serving pilots and the retired section.

In particular I wish to mention Dave Devey, who once brought me back from the pale, as it were. More recently, I wish to mention someone who has become an excellent serving pilot, the then Senior Representative, Gary Woodall, who had the faith in me that I would return to full duties after having experienced a double hip operation in the early part of last year. I am pleased that his faith in me was justified.

I can honestly say that in retrospect I believe that I enjoyed it all. The early years on Dutch barges drinking lukewarm coffee and eating cocoa-paste and cheese sandwiches for breakfast! The "Battle Years" as Chairman against the Dock Company and saving the best 'til the last, fighting an inward bound A.C.L. round the bend in a northerly gale inward bound at midnight.

Overall Gentlemen it really was a profession with so much job satisfaction for me that I would often look up at the vessel safely moored on the quay, or at her stern disappearing safely over the horizon to the West, and question myself, did I really do that?

I join my father who, in a reply to Stuart Wood, when being asked how he felt now that he had retired, he replied "Strange Stuart, for I realise that as from today I stop learning how to be a pilot!"

Gentlemen I thank whoever or whatever was responsible for the honour bestowed upon me in that I served as a Liverpool Pilot and I would request my fellow guests to rise and drink another toast to the future of the present and future Liverpool Pilots and indeed to the future of the Liverpool Pilot Service.

Gentlemen, "The Guardian's of the Dawn, The Liverpool Pilots. Good Ships and Many of Them."

Thank you.

John Curry. Liverpool Pilot. Rtd.

"HELM AMIDSHIPS, FINISHED WITH ENGINES"

Celebration.

At midnight,
'Era' Slipped silently
Over the stern
Into the Atlantic swell,
Returning to Poseidon's deeps
From whence she came,
A personal, mortal-lifetime ago.

'Era' left the storyteller
With a great gift,
A wealth
Of stored, word memories,
Yet to be written.

Stories
To be fashioned from sailor's yarn,
Watery, gale-blown seas
Spliced with
Hemp, tar and oakum.
Stories
To be read
In the comfort of armchairs
Before
Blazing, Viking hearth-fires
Burning.

Crackling echoes in the flames
Of rattling,
Creaking, wooden planks,

Of oars working in a swell
Beyond the reader's known horizons

Storms tearing at chimney pots,
Rain, dancing hornpipes
On rooftops above.
Words ferrying the reader
Far, far out into oceans of the mind.

The 'celebration' of the title of the poem was the celebration at the end of my personal 'Era' as a marine pilot in the Port of Liverpool. The poem was written in mid-Atlantic on my 'retirement voyage.' Many stories from that wealth: "Of stored, word memories" have now been written down on the page both in this volume and in "East a Half South." Some, I know I have repeated in the interest of relating sailor's yarns, which appertained, the one to the other in the context of a new angle taken on the original telling. Some, I know will never be written.

At this point on the page, we are homeward bound and another literary voyage is coming to an end. The flow of both 'words and tides' have taken us round the globe, as well as more locally within the waters of the Liverpool Pilotage District in the Liverpool Bay and the River Mersey. We have been on the bridges of the ships of memory and entertained on watch, held by yarns, which make up all our histories.

With all those ships piloted there will always be another 'forgotten story' coming to light as a memory lying dormant in the depths of the mind is brought to the surface by some external factor jogging my thoughts. My intention for the content of this 'homeward bound' chapter is to draw together some loose ends as the 'log book' of my life's seagoing experiences are to be bound up in this second volume.

I think, for example, of the captain of the Cuban vessel, the

XIII Congresso, which I piloted inbound from the Bar Station on the 10th/11th May 1979 to Birkenhead is immediately one of the stories, which could have appeared in a number of chapters. The 'Cuban Captain' as we called him, came home for Sunday lunch and afterwards we took him to Chester to a vintage car rally. The captain thought the world of our youngest son Nathan, whom he referred to as his 'Little Man.'

The vessel was to sail on the evening tide of the 10th May. I had promised that, if necessary, I would try and 'swap' turns so that I could pilot him outward-bound, but on that tide, I was manned on a large container ship of the day. She was the Hapag-Lloyd vessel the *Caraïbe* and that manning, for the prestige, won the day for me. I sent both my apologies and my regards with the outward pilot of the Cuban ship.

In addition to the Cuban captain, the Chinese captain Ho, the Russian captain Boris and two A.C.L. Captains came home for meals. Michael Lundquist came twice, once for a barbeque in the summer and once for Christmas dinner. Jonas Rahmerg, I have already written about coming for a meal on the day we docked with the then coxswain of the Hoylake Lifeboat, David Whiteley, who accompanied us on board the *Atlantic Cartier* as a 'passenger' on an inward voyage.

Captain Ho was the Captain of the large 'Red' Chinese ship *Jianse Hai*, which I shifted twice in the December of 1982. (We referred to mainland Chinese ships as 'Red,' as opposed to 'Hong Kong' Chinese registered ships). The agents were selling her full cargo of grain off in 'parcels' and she had to keep vacating the discharging berth of S2 to allow other vessels to discharge their cargoes. My second shift was from the layby berth on S10 back to S2 was just before Christmas day. I had spent quite some time with Ho on the two moves and we had become friends so I invited him to my home to join my family for Christmas dinner.

My son came with me to collect Ho from the ship. He could not come alone, so we also picked up another officer to join us for dinner. Whilst waiting, I took Nathan up onto the bridge. We were both horrified to sight a very large rat running across the bridge deck! A humorous memory of the dinner was that we started the meal with soup. Ho looked at the bowl, picked it up and started drinking from it. My children looked at me for guidance. I saw no option but to follow suit. The children were delighted and soon we were all slurping our soup from the bowls!

Gill, Ho, a ship's officer and myself. Christmas day 1989.

There was a chapter on my involvement with the R.N.L.I. in "East a Half South," 'Pull for the Shore Boys.' To follow on from that chapter, I continued as Lifeboat Operation's Manager well into retirement, being granted an extra two years, retiring at the age of 72, rather than at 70 years of age. Sadly my deputy's health had deteriorated and the station came to an agreement with Michael Vlasto the then Operation's Director of the R.N.L.I. at Poole for a smooth handover of positions at a particularly important watershed in the Hoylake station's history.

If I were happy to stay on as Operation's Manager for a further two years, (which I was) the then Coxswain, David Whitely, would 'receive' the new Shannon Class Lifeboat, 1306, in the December of 2014. He would be coxswain for just over twelve months when he would then retire as coxswain and become a Deputy Launching Authority with me with the view to take my position as Lifeboat Operation's Manager on my 72nd birthday in the May of that year, 2016. Andy Dodd, then Lifeboat Station Mechanic would and did become coxswain following in the footsteps of both his father, David Dodd and his grandfather Thomas Dodd. The icing on the cake for me was that James Lodder, then Chairman of the Hoylake and West Kirby Lifeboat Station's Management Group, saw the change-over as an opportunity for him to stand-down and I became Chairman. A position I hold as I write this book.

We all saw it loosely as a 'house of cards,' for the one 'changing position' affected the rest and ensured the continued smooth running of the two stations.

This extra time saw the arrival of the Shannon class lifeboat at Hoylake. The 16/17 knot Mersey class lifeboat 'Lady of Hilbre' was much loved and had saved many lives, but the new Shannon class lifeboat, driven by water jets and officially classed as a lifeboat with a full service speed of 25 knots (I have known her travel at somewhat faster speeds, but officially the speed is 25 knots to match the rest of the R.N.L.I. fleet) is an extremely versatile and manoeuvrable craft and has been well received at the Hoylake station.

During the summer of 2014 we were to have two Shannon class lifeboats at Hoylake for training purposes and the 'off the drawing board 'Supercat' tractor and carriage,' which were to replace the Tallis tractor and trailer which transported the Mersey class lifeboat across the beach. As Lifeboat Operation's Manager, I insisted that I made several trips across the beach as a passenger on board the 'Supercat' and that I also made a trip out on board the Shannon. I believed that as Operation's Manager I should know what the 'kit' I was to launch to save lives was actually capable of.

I was to take the helm of a Shannon in the River Dee and in the Hilbre Swash during these exercises and I was to be amazed at how well the boat handled. Basically this lifeboat can go in any direction at speed and from full speed ahead she can stop in her own length. It was an honour to take the helm.

I was to take the helm of Shannon 1306 on two further outings. The first of these was following an invitation from Andy Dodd, then coxswain, when we launched to escort the 'Three Queens,' on the 25th May 2015, (which was mentioned in relation to Chris Booker in an earlier chapter). The second was on the occasion of my retirement as Lifeboat Operation's Manager when I accompanied the crew on the exercise held immediately before my birthday in the May of 2016.

On the day of the 'Three Queens,' we had just beached the lifeboat when the coastguard called and requested the launch of the boat to a casualty out on Hilbre Island. This was an occasion to illustrate how efficient the Shannon's 'outfit' is. The boat was actually beached, but was 'recovered' onto the carriage, turned and relaunched, arriving at the casualty on Hilbre Island over a mile away in twelve minutes from the launch request! I had time to disembark by ladder and be taken back to the boathouse by the agricultural tractor to take up my duties as Launching Authority for the rescue operation.

On that rescue, a young man who had had the misfortune to fall from a high point on the island onto the rocks below was rescued by the lifeboat and transferred to a helicopter to be transported to hospital. Although badly injured, the young man was to make a sound recovery and came to visit us some months later. What you see on these amazing R.N.L.I., B.B.C. T.V. "Saving Lives at Sea" programmes is all so accurate.

Since I retired as Lifeboat Operation's Manager, that year in fact, Hoylake was to have a hovercraft stationed at the boathouse. This added rescue facility has launched many times from Hoylake and saved lives, including that of a porpoise, which was featured on the "Saving Lives at Sea" programme. An earlier programme featured the rescue of a horse in which the hovercraft was involved. The horse had become bogged down in mud on a rising tide. This rescue was a 'close run' thing, but was, thankfully, successful.

Shannon class lifeboat Edmund Hawthorn Mickelwood
on her naming day.

Sailing…

In another age,
Ropes,
Ties with the past
Are 'Gone and clear,'
Fore and aft
Finally…

Main engine,
'Full away,'
I sail to the west
To a New World
Of the future,
Ahead.

Another lifetime,
Falling astern.

Another of the poems from the: 'Poems From Mid-Atlantic' sequence, written outward bound into retirement on board my last piloted ship the *Atlantic Compass* with Gill on board accompanying me.

With my fountain pen and white cartridge paper, I settled down to write the chapter: 'A Near Death Experience' of "East a Half South" to see if my best critic, Gill, would pass favourable comments on the value of continuing writing. The comments were favourable and the book was completed to sell over 1500 copies as I write. I have mentioned this earlier but with another volume about to leave the 'stocks' and slide down the slipway into the reader's world, I find it comforting to remember how well the first book was received.

Some aspects of the 'retirement voyage' have been covered, but I have to say that the voyage was a wonderful way to literally 'sail into retirement' from a very active, exciting and satisfying life as a 'true bag carrying pilot' in the demanding approaches to the Port of Liverpool.

Gill and myself landed for a few hours ashore when the ship put into Halifax before 'signing off' the *Atlantic Compass* (as passengers!) in New York. I have related how A.C.L. management 'wined and dined us' at the Boathouse in Central Park. An event much appreciated by both of us.

We spent a most enjoyable week in New York staying in a hotel in Soho. From here we made sorties to various places of interest including the MOMA art gallery. Amazingly, having 'retired from a life on the sea' the day before, the first work I saw was Tacita Dean's seascape: 'The Roaring Forties, Seven Boards in Seven Days.' The fourteen pieces, which were not all on display, are boards treated with blackboard paint with white chalk drawings on them. The work includes scenes of a storm, a ship under full sail heeling with the wind and a series of muscled figures engaged in such activities as rowing a skiff or climbing in the rigging.

Tacita Dean's works on the wall in the MOMA Gallery

I found the work moving and overall an epic sea narrative, which reflected for me my own experiences afloat. As I complete this sequel to "East a Half South," these years of retirement from the sea to date, with all my interests, have been simply a long extension of 'time off' in line with that old, archaic, pilotage rule of: 'The Clearing Tide.'

"If by Conway, a heron you have espied…"
(Can you espy the heron?)

GLOSSARY

The following glossary is by no means intended to be comprehensive, but it is intended to assist those not familiar with nautical terminology to understand some of the terms, which have been used in the text.

A

Abeam. At right angles to the position, at which the navigator is standing when looking forward towards the bow of the ship. Aboard. On board or physically present on a ship.

Adrift. A vessel not made fast and drifting at the mercy of wind and tide.

Aft. Referring to the stern or back of a ship.

Aground. When a vessel has run out of water to float in, and is ashore on the seabed.

"All Hands." An expression, which encompasses every person present on board a ship.

Ahead. In front of a ship, or with reference to engines meaning that they are turning forward.

Aloft. Above or overhead.

Amidships. In the middle of a ship.

Anchorage. An area where it is considered safe for a vessel to anchor.

Ashore. Aground on land.

Astern. Behind a ship or with reference to engines meaning that they are turning in reverse.

Authorisation. That, which is bestowed upon an individual who has been examined by the Competent Harbour Authority to pilot ships in a port in the United Kingdom.

Awash. Almost submerged.

B

Back. Word used in the expression: "to back," relating to the direction of the wind altering in an anti-clockwise direction.

Barge. A small craft for transporting small parcels of cargo, sometimes a dummy barge without engines needing to be towed by a tug. Also, a slightly derogatory pilotage term for a small ship, which requires a pilot.

Batten Down. The securing of hatches, vents and other openings to prevent the ingress of water.

Ballast. Additional weight carried for stability. Water ballast is taken on board vessels to trim them particularly when they are sailing light or empty of cargo.

Beam. Referring to the width of a vessel.

Beaufort Scale. Scale depicting wind strength from zero to hurricane force.

Belay. To make fast a rope.

Berth. Safe place to moor or tie up a ship.

Bight. Loop in a coiled rope.

Bitts. Iron bollards usually in pairs on a ship, which are used to make fast, that is secure, the mooring ropes run to tie the ship alongside a berth or quay.

Boathand. The legal term for a Liverpool Pilot Apprentice.

Bollard. Squat iron post on the quayside used to moor a ship.

Bow. The front end of a ship.

Bring up. To stop a vessel dead in the water.

Buoy. A floating marker to indicate a safe channel or an obstruction. Literally: signposts of the sea.

By the head. A ship is said to be so when she is trimmed with a deeper draft forward than aft.

By the stern. As above, but trimmed with a deeper draft aft than forward.

C

Cable, 1. A very large diameter rope.

Cable, 2. A measurement of distance at sea. 100 fathoms, or 200 yards, or 183 metres.

Call sign. Every registered ship is allocated a group of letters, or letters and numbers to identify her.

Cant. The term given to a ship when turning to port or starboard, particularly when the engines are going astern or in reverse. Used by ship handlers to control a vessel.

Capsize. The term used for a vessel, which for whatever reason overturns.

Cargo ship. Vessel for carrying dry cargoes.

Cast off. The act of letting go mooring ropes holding a ship to the quay.

Chart. Map of an area of sea and the adjacent coastline.

Clear and away. The state when a vessel has cleared all hazards and is in the open sea.

Compass. The instrument used to ascertain true north on the Earth's surface from which a ship may then be steered on a course from one point to another.

Competent Harbour Authority. A port authority to which the government has given the powers to manage a port of the United Kingdom.

Course. The direction, in which a ship is to be steered.

Current. The directional flow of water.

D

Davit. The small crane, usually employed in pairs, used to both lower and lift small craft, particularly lifeboats, on board a larger, mother craft.

Deadline. Last possible moment possible for docking or sailing.

Derrick. Shipboard lifting device, now in the main replaced by cranes.

Deviation. An effect on the magnetic compass due to the magnetism of the individual ship, which alters with every new direction of the ship's head. Magnetic compasses are adjusted, and a table is made to allow for the necessary compensation to be made to the course or bearing.

Dock. Enclosed area in a port in which a ship berths. Liverpool, with the Georges Dock, was the first port to have an enclosed tidal dock where ships would float at low water of the tide.

Dog Watch. The half watch used to divide the working time fairly between the crew of a ship, usually during the hours of six to eight in the evening.

Dredger. A vessel used to deepen channels or enclosed docks with the use of grabs or suction pipes.

Drift. The distance and direction a ship moves as a result of the effect the wind has on the vessel.

Dry-dock. A dock, in which a ship may be dried out for repairs or maintenance.

E

Ebb. The outward going tide.

Echo Sounder. An instrument used to bounce sonar pulses off the seabed to determine the depth of water, in which a ship is floating.

Even Keel. This term describes a vessel, which has been loaded to an even trim.

F

Fairway. The navigable channel leading to or from a harbour.

Fathom. Unit of measurement, approximately six feet, used to mark depths of water. Now obsolete with the adaptation of metricification. A fathom is equal to 1.83 metres.

Fix. The process of obtaining a ship's position at sea by taking bearings of landmarks or by taking celestial sights.

Flood. The incoming tide.

Flow. Referring to the direction and strength of a tidal current.

Force. Referring to wind strength.

Freeboard. The distance measured between the main deck of a ship and her waterline.

G

Graving Dock. Similar to, and now better known as a dry dock.

H

Hand. Referring to a crewman or crew-woman.

Hatch. Opening in a ship's deck, into or from which cargo may be passed. A hatch cover is the wooden or metal cover, which closes the hatch opening in the ship's deck.

Hawse pipe. The pipe through which the anchor cable passes.

Head. The middle point of the bow, thus the ship's head indicates, in which direction the ship is "heading".

Heave-to. To ease off speed and stem the seas in heavy weather in order to ride out a storm.

Heaving Line. A light line thrown by a member of the crew for it to be the means, or link, in the passing of a heavier line to a tug or to a boatman.

Helm. A ship's wheel or tiller. Hence helmsman: one who is steering the ship.

Hold. The compartment below decks for storing cargo.

I

Inward bounder. A vessel proceeding inwards, or towards the port.

J

Jack Staff. A short mast mounted at the forepart of a ship to carry a small flag, such as the companies house flag. In the merchant navy, flag etiquette insists that only when a ship is moored in harbour can this flag be flown, it being lowered upon departure from the quay.

Jacob's Ladder. A rope ladder usually with round steps, used to climb up or down the side of a ship. Not to be confused with a pilot ladder, which has flat rungs and international safety specifications.

K

Kedge. A method of manoeuvring a vessel by using an anchor, hence the term to "kedge anchor."

Keel. The strake running along the bottom of a ship. Also bilge keels may be fitted for stabilisation on the hull.

L

Lead. The 7lbs. weight on the end of a lead line, used to take soundings.

Leadsman. Term used for a trainee on a training trip, taken from the time when one hand would "swing the lead" to ascertain the depth of water under a ship.

Leeway. The speed and distance, which a ship experiences in being taken off her desired course as a result of the effect that the wind has on the vessel.

List. The amount a ship heels over due to an imbalance in cargo loading or discharging or indeed through a cargo, which has shifted.

Log. An old method of determining distance covered by streaming an impeller over the stern, the other end of the rope streamed being connected to a log clock, which the impeller then turns recording distance covered.

Long shore. Term used for the period when pilots were working taking ships outward bound from the port.

Lynas Point. Point of land on the north coast of the island of Anglesey, off and in the shelter, of which is the western station of the Liverpool Pilots.

M

Merchant Navy. Commercial vessels of a country carrying cargo.

Minesweeper. A naval vessel designed to sweep and explode mines out at sea.

Moor. To make a ship safe and fast, either with anchors in a seaway, or with ropes in a harbour.

Muster. To assemble the crew of a ship.

N

Navigation. The art of conducting a ship safely from one point on the Earth's surface to another.

Neaped. A vessel, which is unable to dock because of insufficient water for her to float in through the approach channels on a given tide, is described as being neaped.

Neap tide. A tide with a low range of tidal difference between low and high water, which in Liverpool Bay can be around seven metres.

O

Offing. The safe distance a ship may be from the dangers of the shore.
Outward bounder. A vessel proceeding outwards, or away from the port.
Overhaul. To overtake, pass or indeed even to start to catch up with a vessel ahead.

P

Pilot. One authorised to pilot ships.
Port 1. Harbour where ships load and discharge cargo. A safe haven.
Port. 2. Referring to the left hand side of a ship.
Poseidon. Greek God of the sea.
Punt. The name given to the pilot's boarding boats, slung from davits on the mother ship. In these craft the Liverpool pilot, as a boathand, first came to learn about ship handling.

Q

Quarterdeck. The deck at the after end on a ship. Hence: Starboard quarter or port quarter indicating the side of the after end of the ship being referred to. On warships, often the point where a pilot will board.

R

Radar. Electronic instrument used to detect targets around a vessel at sea. A "picture" composed of returned electronic waves, which have been sent out from a radar scanner, and have struck obstructions, such as another ship, or landmasses, is shown on a radar screen. This can be interpreted by the trained navigator and is particularly useful in conditions of reduced visibility, such as dense fog. Not so efficient, any more than the eyes are, in heavy snow.
Reefer ship. Refrigerated ship.
Ro-Ro. Roll on roll off.
Royal Navy. Vessels of Her Majesty used to defend the realm.
Rudder. The moving "flap" at the stern of a ship operated by means, which allow it to pivot from the centre point to the left or to the right, thus enabling the vessel to alter course.
Rules of the Road. The set of rules, which constitute the "International Highway Code of the Sea."

S

Salvage. The name given to a reward for a person or persons who save a ship and her cargo from loss.
Scuppers. Draining holes or ports cut into the sides of a ship on decks to allow seawater to flow safely away over the ship's side.
Sea turns. Term used when the pilot was bringing ships into the port. (Usually considered the more difficult of the two directions. Presumably because the ship was running ever nearer to the dangers not encountered in the "open" sea.)
Sextant. Instrument used in celestial navigation to take sights of heavenly bodies.

Shackle. A u-shaped iron closed with a screwed pin used to secure the looped ends of ropes, or the ends of a chain, to other fittings such as anchors.

Sheer. An unexpected alteration, usually a drastic one, which a ship takes away from her intended course.

Signal Letters. The four numbers or letters, or combination of the two, used to identify any particular ship.

Sill. The "step" at the ends of a lock on which the lock gates sit.

Slack water. The period, either at high or low tide, when little or no stream runs.

Slings. Equipment in the form of a net used for handling cargo.

Snotter. Equipment in the form of a rope loop used for handling cargo.

Soundings. The depth of water recorded from instruments recording depths.

Splice. Method of joining ropes or forming loops in the ends of them by using the ropes themselves.

Spring. A rope employed to assist in the manoeuvring of a ship in leaving a quay. Also the name of a rope leading from forward or aft, away from the extremity of a vessel, which help to hold her securely to the quayside when she is moored.

Spring tide. A tide with a high range of tidal difference between low and high water, which in Liverpool Bay can be in excess of ten metres.

Spurling Pipe. Pipe leading the anchor chain down to the anchor locker on the inboard side of the windless.

Starboard. Referring to the right hand side of a ship.

Steer. To guide a ship in the required direction.

Steerage way. The lowest speed required for a vessel to answer her rudder.

Stem. The foremost part of a ship's bow.

Stern. The after, or back end of a ship.

T

Tank or tanker. Vessel for carrying liquids.

Tide. The ingress and egress of water into a port dependent on the attraction of the sun and the moon on the earth's surface. In Liverpool tides are semi-diurnal, that is; they occur twice in a twenty-four hour period.

Tide tables. The pilot's bible! Published lists of tides for each day of the year. With knowledge of the time of the tide, which the pilot is working on, I have always maintained that an experienced pilot could go out to sea stark naked, with no need for anything save his body, brain and his knowledge to be present on the bridge of a ship.

Tideway. Out in the tidal flow of the approaches to a port.

Tow. The operation of one vessel pulling another by means of a rope.

Trim. The way in which a ship floats in the water.

Tug. Small but powerful craft used in the towage of a vessel.

U

U boat. German submarine.

Underway. A vessel, which is moving through the water.

V

Variation. The angle contained between the true and magnetic meridians is the variation of any specific place on the Earth's surface. It is caused by the geographical and magnetic poles not coinciding. This varies over the years.
Veer. Word used in the expression, "to veer" relating to the direction of the wind altering in a clockwise fashion.

W

Warp. A rope used in moving, or "warping" a vessel along the quay.
Warship. A vessel used in warfare in the defence of a realm. In the United Kingdom one of the Royal Navy, belonging to her Majesty the Queen.
Watch. The twenty-four hour period at sea is divided between the crew into watches.
Well found. A vessel, which in a good seaworthy condition.
Windless. Winch mechanism for heaving anchors.

X

X-Boat. Inflatable carried by the R.N.L.I's All Weather Lifeboat Fleet.

Y

Yardarm. The outer extremities of the spars or yards, from which sails were hung on board a square-rigged sailing ship.
Yokahama Fender. Large form of a floating fender intended to keep ships off the quay. Also to be placed between two ships moored alongside each other to reduce the risk of damage between them.

Z

Zenith. Important in celestial navigation when the heavenly body, the sun for example, is at its 'zenith', a sight may be taken with a sextant to help fix the ship's position on the Earth's surface.

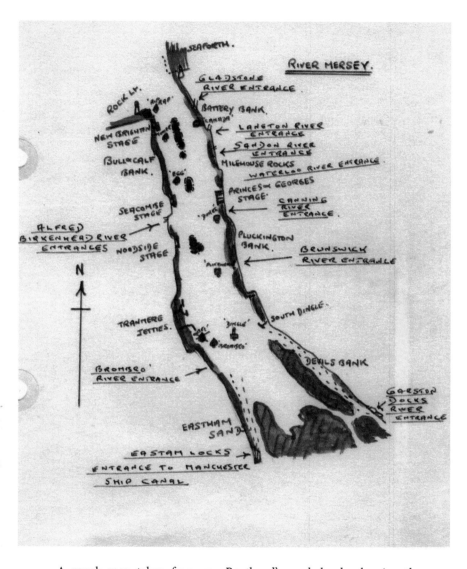

A rough map taken from my Boathand's mark book, showing the River Mersey with some geographical features, and indicating the river entrance locks referred to in the text.

BIBLIOGRAPHY

Suggestions for further associated reading:

East a Half South. Curry. John. 2015.

Beyond the Bar. A light History of the Liverpool Pilot Service. Youde. B. Laver. Liverpool. 1994.

Heart of Darkness. Conrad. J. Bantam. 1969.

History of the Liverpool Pilotage Service. Rees. J.S. Southport Guardian. 1949.

Life on the Mississippi. Mark Twain. Harper. 1896.

Marine Pilot. Foot. J. Henry. 2004.

The Ellan Vannin Story. Stafford. R. Mannin Media. 1999.

Unplanned Passage. Russell J.D. Pen Press. 2011.

Liverpool Sung and Unsung. Kenyon. Dan. Smiling Wolf Press 2008.

Mersey. The River that changed the World. Edited Wray. Ian. Photography McPherson. Colin. Bluecoat. 2007.